The Nibelungenlied

Translated by

Daniel B. Shumway

The Nibelungenlied

Copyright © 2022 Indo-European Publishing

The present edition is a reproduction of previous publication of this classic work. Minor typographical errors may have been corrected without note; however, for an authentic reading experience the spelling, punctuation, and capitalization have been retained from the original text.

ISBN: 978-1-64439-949-1

Contents

PREFACE

This work has been undertaken in the belief that a literal translation of as famous an epic as the "Nibelungenlied" would be acceptable to the general reading public whose interest in the story of Siegfried has been stimulated by Wagner's operas and by the reading of such poems as William Morris' "Sigurd the Volsung". Prose has been selected as the medium of translation, since it is hardly possible to give an accurate rendering and at the same time to meet the demands imposed by rhyme and metre; at least, none of the verse translations made thus far have succeeded in doing this. The prose translations, on the other hand, mostly err in being too continuous and in condensing too much, so that they retell the story instead of translating it. The present translator has tried to avoid these two extremes. He has endeavored to translate literally and accurately, and to reproduce the spirit of the original, as far as a prose translation will permit. To this end the language has been made as simple and as Saxon in character as possible. An exception has been made, however, in the case of such Romance words as were in use in England during the age of the romances of chivalry, and which would help to land a Romance coloring; these have been frequently employed. Very few obsolete words have been used, and these are explained in the notes, but the language has been made to some extent archaic, especially in dialogue, in order to give the impression of age. At the request of the publishers the Introduction Sketch has been shorn of the apparatus of scholarship and made as popular as a study of the poem and its sources would allow. The advanced student who may be interested in consulting authorities will find them given in the introduction to the parallel edition in the Riverside Literature Series. A short list of English works on the subject had, however, been added.

In conclusion the translator would like to thank his colleagues, C.G. Child and Cornelius Weygandt, for their helpful suggestions in starting the work, and also to acknowledge his indebtedness to the German edition of Paul Piper, especially in preparing the notes. —DANIEL BUSSIER SHUMWAY,

Philadelphia, February 15, 1909.

There is probably no poem of German literature that has excited such universal interest, or that has been so much studied and discussed, as the "Nibelungenlied". In its present form it is a product of the age of chivalry, but it reaches back to the earliest epochs of German antiquity, and embraces not only the pageantry of courtly chivalry, but also traits of ancient Germanic folklore and probably of Teutonic mythology. One of its earliest critics fitly called it a German "Iliad", for, like this great Greek epic, it goes back to the remotest times and unites the monumental fragments of half-forgotten myths and historical personages into a poem that is essentially national in character, and the embodiment of all that is great in the antiquity of the race. Though lacking to some extent the dignity of the "Iliad", the "Nibelungenlied" surpasses the former in the deep tragedy which pervades it, the tragedy of fate, the inevitable retribution for crime, the never-dying struggle between the powers of good and evil, between light and darkness.

That the poem must have been exceedingly popular during the Middle Ages is evinced by the great number of Manuscripts that have come down to us. We possess in all twenty-eight more or less complete MSS., preserved in thirty-one fragments, fifteen of which date from the thirteenth and fourteenth centuries. Of all these MSS., but nine are so well preserved that, in spite of some minor breaks, they can be considered complete. Of this number three, designated respectively as A, B, C, are looked upon as the most important for purposes of textual criticism, and around them a fierce battle has been waged, which is not even yet settled. (1) It is now generally conceded that the longest MS., C, is a later redaction with many additional strophes, but opinions are divided as to whether the priority should be given to A or B, the probabilities being that B is the more original, A merely a careless copy of B.

In spite of the great popularity of the "Nibelungenlied", the poem was soon forgotten by the mass of the people. With the decay of courtly chivalry and the rise of the prosperous citizen class, whose ideals and testes lay in a different direction, this epic shared the fate of many others of its kind, and was relegated to the dusty shelves of monastery or ducal libraries, there to wait till a more cultured age, curious as to the literature of its ancestors, should bring it forth from its hiding places. However, the figures of the old legend were not forgotten, but lived on among the people, and were finally embodied in a popular ballad, "Das Lied vom Hurnen Segfrid", which has been preserved in a print of the sixteenth century, although the poem itself is thought to go back at least to the thirteenth. The legend was also dramatized by Hans Sachs, the shoemaker poet of Nuremberg, and related in prose form in a chap book which still exists in prints of the eighteenth century. The story and the characters gradually became so vague and distorted, that only a trained eye could detect in the burlesque figures of the popular account the heroes of the ancient Germanic Legend.

The honor of rediscovering the "Nibelungenlied" and of restoring it to the world of literature belongs to a young physician by the name of J.H. Obereit, who found the manuscript C at the castle of Hohenems in the Tirol on June 29, 1755; but the scientific study of the poem begins with Karl Lachmann, one of the keenest philological critics that Germany has ever produced. In 1816 he read before the University of Berlin his epoch-making essay upon the original form of the "Nibelungenlied". Believing that the poem was made up of a number of distinct ballads or lays, he sought by means of certain criteria to eliminate all parts which were, as he thought, later interpolations or emendations. As a result of this sifting and discarding process, he reduced the poem to what he considered to have been its original form, namely, twenty separate lays, which he thought had come down to us in practically the same form in which they had been sung by various minstrels.

This view is no longer held in its original form. Though we have every reason to believe that ballads of Siegfried the dragon killer, of Siegfried and Kriemhild, and of the destruction of the Nibelungs existed in Germany, yet these ballads are no longer to be seen in our poem. They formed merely the basis or source for some poet who thought to revive the old heroic legends of the German past which were familiar to his hearers and to adapt them to the tastes of his time. In all probability we must assume two, three, or even more steps in the genesis of the poem. There appear to have been two different sources, one a Low German account, quite simple and brief, the other a tradition of the Lower Rhine. The legend was perhaps developed by minstrels along the Rhine, until it was taken and worked up into its present form by some Austrian poet. Who this poet was we do not know, but we do know that he was perfectly familiar with all the details of courtly etiquette. He seems also to have been acquainted with the courtly epics of Heinrich von Veldeke and Hartman von Ouwe, but his poem is free from the tedious and often exaggerated descriptions of pomp, dress, and court ceremonies, that mar the beauty of even the best of the courtly epics. Many painstaking attempts have been made to discover the identity of the writer of our poem, but even the most plausible of all these theories which considers Kurenberg, one of the earliest of the "Minnesingers", to be the author, because of the similarity of the strophic form of our poem to that used by him, is not capable of absolute proof, and recent investigations go to show that Kurenberg was indebted to the "Nibelungen" strophe for the form of his lyric, and not the "Nibelungenlied" to him. The "Nibelungen" strophe is presumably much older, and, having become popular in Austria through the poem, was adopted by Kurenberg for his purposes. As to the date of the poem, in its present form it cannot go back further than about 1190, because of the exactness of the rhymes, nor could it have been written later than 1204, because of certain allusions to it in the sixth book of "Parzival", which we know to have been written at this date. The two Low German poems which probably form the basis of our epic may have been united about 1150. It was revised and translated into High German and circulated at South German courts about 1170, and then received its present courtly form about 1190, this last version being the immediate source of our manuscripts.

The story of Siegfried, his tragic death, and the dire vengeance visited upon his slayers, which lies at the basis of our poem, antedates the latter by many centuries, and was known to all nations whose languages prove by their resemblance to the German tongue their original identity with the German people. Not only along the banks of the Rhine and the Danube and upon the upland plains of Southern Germany, but also along the rocky fjords of Norway, among the Angles and Saxons in their new home across the channel, even in the distant Shetland Islands and on the snow-covered wastes of Iceland, this story was told around the fires at night and sung to the harp in the banqueting halls of kings and nobles, each people and each generation telling it in its own fashion and adding new elements of its own invention. This great geographical distribution of the legend, and the variety of forms in which it appears, make it difficult to know where we must seek its origin. The northern version is in many respects older and simpler in form than the German, but still it is probable that Norway was not the home of the saga, but that it took its rise in Germany along the banks of the Rhine among the ancient tribe of the Franks, as is shown by the many geographical names that are reminiscent of the characters of the story, such as a Siegfried "spring" in the Odenwald, a Hagen "well" at Lorsch, a Brunhild "bed" near Frankfort, and the well-known "Drachenfels", or Dragon's Rock, on the Rhine. It is to Norway, however, that we must go for our knowledge of the story, for, singularly enough, with the exception of the "Nibelungenlied" and the popular ballad, German literature has preserved almost no trace of the legend, and such as exist are too late and too corrupt to be of much use in determining the original features of the story.

Just when the legend emigrated to Skandinavia we do not know, but certainly at an early date, perhaps during the opening years of the sixth century. It may have been introduced by German traders, by slaves captured by the Northmen on their frequent marauding expeditions, or, as Mogk believes, may have been taken by the Heruli on their return to Norway after their defeat by the Langobardi. By whatever channel, however, the story reached the North, it became part and parcel of Skandinavian folklore, only certain names still pointing to the original home of the legend. In the ninth century, when Harald Harfagr changed the ancient free constitution of the land, many Norwegians emigrated to Iceland, taking with them these acquired legends, which were better preserved in this remote island because of the peaceful introduction of Christianity, than on the Continent, where the Church was more antagonistic to the customs and legends of the heathen period.

The Skandinavian version of the Siegfried legend has been handed down to us in five different forms. The first of these is the poetic or older "Edda", also called Saemund's "Edda", as it was assigned to the celebrated Icelandic scholar Saemundr Sigfusson. The "Codex Regius", in which it is preserved, dates from the middle of the thirteenth century, but is probably a copy of an older manuscript. The songs it contains were written at various times, the oldest probably in the first half of the ninth century, the latest not much before the date of the earliest manuscript. Most of them, however, belong to the Viking period, when Christianity was already beginning to influence the Norwegians, that is, between the years 800 and 1000. They are partly heroic, partly mythological in character, and are written in alliterative strophes interspersed with prose, and have the form of dialogues. Though the legends on which these songs are based were brought from Norway, most of them were probably composed in Iceland. Among these songs, now, we find a number which deal with the adventures of Siegfried and his tragic end.

The second source of the Siegfried story is the so-called "Volsungasaga", a prose paraphrase of the "Edda" songs. The MS. dates from the beginning of the thirteenth century, but the account was probably written a century earlier. The adventures of Siegfried and his ancestors are here related in great detail and his ancestry traced back to Wodan. Although a secondary source, as it is based on the "Edda", the "Volsungasaga" is nevertheless of great importance, since it supplies a portion of the "Codex Regius" which has been lost, and thus furnishes us with the contents of the missing songs.

The third source is the prose "Edda", sometimes called the "Snorra Edda", after the famous Icelander Snorri Sturluson (1178-1241),to whom it was ascribed. The author was acquainted with both the poetic "Edda" and the "Volsungasaga", and follows these accounts closely. The younger "Edda" is not really a tale, but a book of poetics; it relates, however, the Siegfried saga briefly. It is considered an original source, since it evidently made use of songs that have not come down to us, especially in the account of the origin of the treasure, which is here told more in detail and with considerable differences. The "Nornagestsaga" or "Nornageststhattr", the story of "Nornagest", forms the fourth source of the Siegfried story. It is really a part of the Olaf saga, but contains the story of Sigurd and Gunnar (the Norse forms of Siegfried and Gunther), which an old man Nornagest relates to King Olaf Tryggvason, who converted the Norwegians to Christianity. The story was written about 1250 to illustrate the transition from heathendom to the Christian faith. It is based on the "Edda" and the "Volsungasaga", and is therefore of minor importance as a source.

These four sources represent the early introduction of the Siegfried legend into Skandinavia. A second introduction took place about the middle of the thirteenth century, at the time of the flourishing of the Hanseatic League, when the story was introduced together with other popular German epics. These poems are products of the age of chivalry, and are characterized by the romantic and courtly features of this movement. The one which concerns us here, as the fifth source of the Siegfried story, is the so-called "Thidreksaga", which celebrates the adventures of the famous legendary hero, Dietrich of Berne, the historical Theodorich of Ravenna. In as far as it contains the adventures of the Nibelungs, it is also called the "Niflungasaga". The "Thidreksaga" was written about 1250 by a Norwegian who, as he himself tells us, heard the story from Germans in the neighborhood of Bremen and Munster. Since it is thus based on Saxon traditions, it can be considered an independent source of the legend, and, in fact, differs from the earlier Norse versions in many important details. The author was acquainted, however, with the older versions, and sought to compromise between them, but mostly followed his German authorities.

The story, as given in the older Norse versions, is in most respects more original than in the "Nibelungenlied". It relates the history of the treasure of the Nibelungs, tracing it back to a giant by the name of "Hreithmar", who received it from the god "Loki" as a compensation for the killing of the former's son "Otur", whom Loki had slain in the form of an otter. Loki obtained the ransom from a dwarf named "Andwari", who in turn had stolen it from the river gods of the Rhine. Andwari pronounces a terrible curse upon the treasure and its possessors, and this curse passes from Loki to the Giant Hreithmar, who is murdered when asleep by his two sons "Fafnir" and "Regin". The latter, however, is cheated out of the coveted prize by Fafnir, who carries it away to the "Gnita" heath, where he guards it in the form of a dragon.

This treasure, with its accompanying curse, next passes into the hands of a human being named Sigurd (the Norse form of Siegfried, as we have seen), a descendant of the race of the Volsungs, who trace their history back to Wodan and are especially favored by him. The full story of Siegfried's ancestry is far too long to relate here, and does not especially concern us, as it has little or no influence on the later development of the story. It is sufficient for our purpose to know that Siegfried was the son of Siegmund, who was slain in battle before the birth of his son. Sigurd was carefully reared by his mother "Hjordis" and the wise dwarf Regin, who taught him the knowledge of runes and of many languages. (2) At the suggestion of Regin, Sigurd asks for and receives the steed "Grani" from the king, and is then urged by his tutor to help him obtain the treasure guarded by the latter's brother Fafnir. Sigurd promises, but first demands a sword. Two, that arc given him by Regin, prove worthless, and he forges a new one from the pieces of his father's sword, which his mother had preserved. With this he easily splits the anvil and cuts in two a flake of wool, floating down the Rhine. He first avenges the death of his father, and then sets off with Regin to attack the dragon Fafnir. At the advice of the former Sigurd digs a ditch across the dragon's peth and pierces him from below with his sword, as the latter comes down to drink. In dying the dragon warns Sigurd against the treasure and its curse, and against Regin, who, he says, is planning Sigurd's death, intending to obtain the treasure for himself.

When Regin sees the dragon safely dead, he creeps from his place of concealment, drinks of the blood, and, cutting out the heart, begs Sigurd to roast it for him. While doing so, Sigurd burns his fingers, and, putting them in his mouth, understands at once the language of the birds and hears them say that Sigurd himself should eat the heart and then he would be wiser than all other men. They also betray Regin's evil designs, and counsel the lad to kill his tutor. This Sigurd then does, cutting off Regin's head, drinking the blood of both brothers, and eating Fafnir's heart. (3) On the further advice of the birds Sigurd first fetches the treasure from the cave, and then journeys to the mountain "Hindarfjall", where he rescues the sleeping Valkyrie, "Sigrdrifu" ("Brynhild", "Brunhild"), who, stung by the sleep thorn of Wodan, and clad in full armor, lies asleep within a castle that is surrounded by a wall of flame. With the help of his steed Grani, Sigurd succeeds in penetrating through the fire to the castle. The sleeping maiden awakes when he cuts the armor from her with his sword, for it was as tight as if grown fast to the flesh. She hails her deliverer with great joy, for she had vowed never to marry a man who knew fear. At Sigurd's request she teaches him many wise precepts, and finally pledges her troth to him. He then departs, after promising to be faithful to her and to remember her teachings.

On his journeyings Sigurd soon arrives at the court of "Giuki" (the Norse form of the German "Gibicho", "Gibich"), a king whose court lay on the lower Rhine. Giuki has three sons, "Gunnar", "Hogni", and "Guthorm", and a daughter "Gudrun", endowed with great beauty. The queen bears the name of Grimhild, and is versed in magic, but possessed of an evil heart. (4) Sigurd is received with great honor, for his coming had been announced to Gudrun in dreams, which had in part been interpreted to her by Brynhild. The mother, knowing of Sigurd's relations to the latter, gives him a potion which produces forgetfulness, so that he no longer remembers his betrothed, and accepts the hand of Gudrun, which the king offers him at the queen's request. The marriage is celebrated with great pomp, and Sigurd remains permanently attached to Giuki's court, performing with the others many deeds of valor.

Meanwhile Grimhild urges her son Gunnar to sue for the hand of Brynhild. Taking with him Sigurd and a few others, Gunnar visits first Brynhild's father "Budli", and then her brother-in-law "Heimir", from both of whom he learns that she is free to choose whom she will, but that she will marry no one who has not ridden through the wall of flame. With this answer they proceed to Brynhild's castle, where Gunnar is unable to pierce the flames, even when seated on Sigurd's steed. Finally Sigurd and Gunnar change forms, and Sigurd, disguised as Gunnar, rides through the wall of fire, announces himself to Brynhild as Gunnar, the son of Giuki, and reminds her of her promise to marry the one who penetrated the fire. Brynhild consents with great reluctance, for she is busy carrying on a war with a neighboring king. Sigurd then passes three nights at her side, placing, however, his sword Gram between them, as a bar of separation. At parting he draws from her finger the ring, with which he had originally pledged his troth to her, and replaces it with another, taken from Fafnir's hoard. Soon after this the marriage of Gunnar and Brynhild is celebrated with great splendor, and all return to Giuki's court, where they live happily for some time.

One day, however, when the ladies go down to the river to take a bath, Brynhild will not bathe further down stream than Gudrun, that is, in the water which flows from Gudrun to her, (5) giving as the reason, that her father was mightier and her husband braver, since he had ridden through the fire, while Sigurd had been a menial. Stung at this, Gudrun retorts that not Gunnar but Sigurd had penetrated the flames and had taken from her the fateful ring "Andvaranaut", which she then shows to her rival in proof of her assertion. Brynhild turns deathly pale, but answers not a word. After a second conversation on the subject had increased the hatred of the queens, Brynhild plans vengeance. Pretending to be ill, she takes to her bed, and when Gunnar inquires what ails her, she asks him if he remembers the circumstances of the wooing and that not he but Sigurd had penetrated the flames. She attempts to take Gunnar's life, as she had pledged her troth to Sigurd, and is thereupon placed in chains by Hogni. Seven days she sleeps, and no one dares to wake her. Finally Sigurd succeeds in making her talk, and she tells him how cruelly she has been deceived, that the better man had been destined for her, but that she had received the poorer one. This Sigurd denies, for Giuki's son had killed the king of the Danes and also Budli's brother, a great warrior. Moreover, although he, Sigurd, had ridden through the flames, he had not become her husband. He begs her therefore not to harbor a grudge against Gunnar.

Brynhild remains unconvinced, and plans Sigurd's death, and threatens Gunnar with the loss of dominion and life, if he will not kill Sigurd. After some hesitation, Gunnar consents, and, calling Hogni, informs him that he must kill Sigurd, in order to obtain the treasure of the Rhinegold. Hogni warns him against breaking his oath to Sigurd, when it occurs to Gunnar, that his brother Gutthorm had sworn no oath and might do the deed. Both now proceed to excite the latter's greed, and give him wolf's and snake meat to eat to make him savage. Twice Gutthorm makes the attempt, as Sigurd lies in bed, but is deterred by the latter's penetrating glance. The third time he finds Sigurd asleep, and pierces him with his sword. Sigurd, awakening at the pain, hurls his own sword after his murderer, fairly cutting him in two. He then dies, protesting his innocence and designating Brynhild as the instigator of his murder. Brynhild at first laughs aloud at Gudrun's frantic grief, but later her joy turns into sorrow, and she determines to share Sigurd's death. In vain they try to dissuade her; donning her gold corselet, she pierces herself with a sword and begs to be burned on Sigurd's funeral pyre. In dying she prophesies the future, telling of Gudrun's marriage to "Atli" and of the death of the many men which will be caused thereby.

After Brynhild's death Gudrun in her sorrow flees to the court of King "Half" of Denmark, where she remains seven years. Finally Grimhild learns of the place of her daughter's concealment, and tries to bring about a reconciliation with Gunnar and Hogni. They offer her much treasure, if she will marry Atli. At first she refuses and thinks only of revenge, but finally she consents and the marriage is celebrated in Atli's land. After a time Atli, who is envious of Gunnar's riches, for the latter had taken possession of Sigurd's hoard, invites him to his court. A man named "Vingi", who was sent with the invitation, changes the runes of warning, which Gudrun had given him, so that they, too, read as an invitation. The brothers determine to accept the invitation, and, though warned by many dreams, they set out for Atli's court, which they reach in due time. Vingi now breaks forth into exultations, that he has lured them into a snare, and is slain by Hogni with a battle axe.

As they ride to the king's hall, Atli and his sons arm themselves for battle, and demand Sigurd's treasure, which belongs by right to Gudrun. Gunnar refuses to surrender it, and the fight begins, after some exchange of taunting words. Gudrun tries at first to reconcile the combatants, but, failing, arms herself and fights on the side of her brothers. The battle rages furiously with great loss on both sides, until nearly all of the Nibelungs are killed, when Gunnar and Hogni are forced to yield to the power of numbers and are captured and bound. Gunnar is asked, if he will purchase his life with the treasure. He replies that he first wishes to see Hogni's bleeding heart. At first the heart of a slave is cut out and brought to him, but Gunnar recognizes it at once as that of a coward. Then they cut out Hogni's heart, who laughs at the pain. This Gunnar sees is the right one, and is jubilant, for now Atli shall never obtain the treasure, as Gunnar alone knows where it is hid. In a rage Atli orders Gunnar to be thrown to the snakes. Though his hands are bound, Gunnar plays so sweetly with his toes on the harp, which Gudrun has sent him, that all the snakes are lulled to sleep, with the exception of an adder, which stings him to the heart, so that he dies.

Atli now walks triumphantly over the dead bodies, and remarks to Gudrun that she alone is to blame for what has happened. She refuses his offers of peace and reconciliation, and towards evening kills her two sons "Erp" and "Eitil", and serves them at the banquet, which the king gives for his retainers. When Atli asks for his sons, he is told that he had drunk their blood mixed with wine and had eaten their hearts. That night when Atli is asleep, Gudrun takes Hogni's son "Hniflung", who desires to avenge his father, and together they enter Atli's room and thrust a sword through his breast. Atli awakes from the pain, only to be told by Gudrun that she is his murderess. When he reproaches her with thus killing her husband, she answers that she cared only for Sigurd. Atli now asks for a fitting burial, and on receiving the promise of this, expires. Gudrun carries out her promise, and burns the castle with Atli and all his dead retainers. Other Edda songs relate the further adventures of Gudrun, but they do not concern us here, as the "Nibelungenlied" stops with the death of the Nibelungs.

This in brief is the story of Siegfried, as it has been handed down to us in the Skandinavian sources. It is universally acknowledged that this version, though more original than the Gorman tradition, does not represent the simplest and most original form of the tale; but what the original form was, has long been and still is a matter of dispute. Two distinctly opposite views are held, the one seeing in the story the personification of the forces of nature, the other, scouting the possibility of a mythological interpretation, seeks a purely human origin for the tale, namely, a quarrel among relatives for the possession of treasure. The former view is the older, and obtained almost exclusively at one time. The latter has been gaining ground of recent years, and is held by many of the younger students of the legend. According to the mythological view, the maiden slumbering upon the lonely heights is the sun, the wall of flames surrounding her the morning red ("Morgenrote"). Siegfried is the youthful day who is destined to rouse the sun from her slumber. At the appointed time he ascends, and before his splendor the morning red disappears. He awakens the maiden; radiantly the sun rises from its couch and joyously greets the world of nature. But light and shade are indissolubly connected; day changes of itself into night. When at evening the sun sinks to rest and surrounds herself once more with a wall of flames, the day again approaches, but no longer in the youthful form of the morning to arouse her from her slumber, but in the sombre shape of Gunther, to rest at her side. Day has turned into night; this is the meaning of the change of forms. The wall of flame vanishes, day and sun descend into the realm of darkness. Under this aspect the Siegfried story is a day myth; but under another it is a myth of the year. The dragon is the symbol of winter, the dwarfs of darkness. Siegfried denotes the bright summer, his sword the sunbeams. The youthful year grows up in the dark days of winder. When its time has come, it goes forth triumphantly and destroys the darkness and the cold of winter. Through the symbolization the abstractions gain form and become persons; the saga is thus not a mere allegory, but a personification of nature's forces. The treasure may have entered the saga through the widespread idea of the dragon as the guardian of treasure, or it may represent the beauty of nature which unfolds when the season has conquered. In the last act of the saga, Siegfried's death, Wilmanns, the best exponent of this view, sees again a symbolic representation of a process of nature. According to him it signifies the death of the god of the year in winter. In the spring he kills the dragon, in the winter he goes weary to his rest and is foully slain by the hostile powers of darkness. Later, when this act was connected with the story of Gunther's wooing Brunhild, the real meaning was forgotten, and Siegfried's death was attributed to the grief and jealousy of the insulted queen.

Opposed now to the mythological interpretation is the other view already spoken of, which denies the possibility of mythological features, and does not seek to trace the legend beyond the heroic stage. The best exponent of this view is R. C. Boer, who has made a remarkable attempt to resolve the story into its simplest constituents. According to him the nucleus of the legend is an old story of the murder of relatives ("Verwandienmord"), the original form being perhaps as follows. Attila (i.e., the enemy of Hagen under any name) is married to Hagen's sister Grimhild or Gudrun. He invites his brother-in-law to his house, attacks him in the hope of obtaining his treasure, and kills him. According to this view Hagen was originally the king, but later sinks to a subordinate position through the subsequent connection of the story with the Burgundians. It is of course useless to hunt for the date of such an episode in history. Such a murder could have frequently occurred, and can be localized anywhere. Very early we find this Hagen story united with the Siegfried legend. If the latter is mythological, then we have a heterogeneous combination, a mythical legend grafted on a purely human one. This Boer thinks unlikely, and presents a number of arguments to disprove the mythical character of the Siegfried story, into which we cannot enter here. He comes, however, to the conclusion, that the Siegfried tale is likewise purely human, and consisted originally of the murder of relatives, that is, a repetition of the Hagen title. Siegfried is married to Hagen's sister, and is killed by his brother-in-law because of his treasure. The kernel of the legend is, therefore, the enmity between relatives, which exists in two forms, the one in which the son-in-law kills his father-in-law, as in the "Helgi" saga, the other in which Hagen kills his son-in-law and is killed by him, too, as in the "Hilde" saga. The German tradition tries to combine the two by introducing the new feature, that Kriemhild causes the death of her relatives, in order to avenge her first husband. Boer is of the opinion that both the Norse and the German versions have forgotten the original connection between the two stories, and that this connection was nothing more nor less than the common motive of the treasure. The same treasure, which causes Hagen to murder Siegfried, causes his own death in turn through the greed of Attila. There was originally, according to Boer, no question of revenge, except the revenge of fate, the retribution which overtakes the criminal. This feeling for the irony of fate was lost when the motive, that Hagen kills Siegfried because of his treasure, was replaced by the one that he does it at the request of Brunhild. This leads Boer to the conclusion, that Brunhild did not originally belong to the Siegfried story, but to the well-known fairy tale of Sleeping Beauty ("Erlosungsmurchen"), which occurs in a variety of forms. The type is that of a hero who rescues a maiden from a magic charm, which may take the form of a deep sleep, as in the case of Sleeping Beauty, or of being sewed into a garment, as in No. 111 of Grimm's fairy tales. By the union of the two stories, i.e., the Hagen-Siegfried saga with the Sleeping Beauty tale, Siegfried stands in relation to two women; on the one hand his relation to Sigrdrifa-Brynhild, the maiden whom he rescues on the rock, on the other his marriage with Grimhild-Gudrun and his consequent death. This twofold relation had to be disposed of, and since his connection with Grimhild was decisive for his fate, his relation to Brunhild had to be changed. It could not be entirely ignored, for it was too well known, therefore it was given a different interpretation. Siegfried still rescues a maiden from the rock, not for himself, however, but for another. The exchange of forms on the part of Siegfried and Gunther is a reminiscence of the older form. It gives the impression, that Siegfried, and yet not Siegfried, won the bride. This alteration probably took place when the Burgundians were introduced into the legend. With this introduction an unlocalized saga of unknown heroes of ancient times became one of events of world-wide importance; the fall of a mighty race was depicted as the result of Siegfried's death. To render this plausible, it was necessary on the one hand to idealize the hero, so that his death should appear as a deed of horror demanding fearful vengeance, and on the other, to make the king of the Burgundians an active participator in Siegfried's death, for otherwise it would not seem natural, that the whole race should be exterminated for a crime committed by the king's brother or vassal. As the role of Brunhild's husband had become vacant, and as Gunther had no special role, it was natural that it should be given to him. Boer traces very ingeniously the gradual development of this exchange of roles through the various sources.

Another method of explaining away Siegfried's relation to two women is to identify them, and this has been done by the Seyfrid ballad. Here the hero rescues Kriemhild from the power of the dragon, marries her, and then is later killed by her brothers through envy and hatred. As Brunhild and Kriemhild are here united in one person, there is no need of a wooing for the king, nor of vengeance on the part of Brunhild, accordingly the old motive of greed (here envy) reappears.

As to the fight with the dragon, Boer believes that it did not originally belong to the saga, for in none of the sources except the popular ballad is the fight with the dragon connected with the release of Brunhild. If the Siegfried-Hagen story is purely human, then the dragon cannot have originally belonged to it, but was later introduced, because of the widespread belief in the dragon as the guardian of treasure, and in order to answer the question as to the provenience of the hoard. This is, however, only one answer to the question. Another, widespread in German legends, is that the treasure comes from the Nibelungs, that is, from the dwarfs. Many identify the dwarfs and the dragon, but this finds no support in the sources, for here the dwarfs and Fafnir are never confused. The "Nibelungenlied" describes an adventure with each, but the treasure is only connected with the dwarfs. The "Thidreksaga" knows only the dragon fight but not the dwarfs, as is likewise the case with the Seyfrid ballad. Only in the Norse sources do we find a contamination. The story of Hreithmar and his sons, who quarrel about the treasure, resembles that of Schilbung and Nibelung in the "Nibelungenlied", and probably has the same source. One of the sons, because of his guarding the treasure, is identified with the dragon, and so we read that Fafnir becomes a dragon, after gaining the treasure. Originally, however, he was not a dragon, but a dwarf. These two independent forms can be geographically localized. The dwarf legend is the more southern; it is told in detail in the "Nibelungenlied". The dragon legend probably originated in the Cimbrian peninsula, where the "Beowulf" saga, in which the dragon fight plays such an important part, likewise arose.

There thus stand sharply opposed to each other two theories, one seeing in the Siegfried saga a personification of natural forces, the other tracing it back to a purely human story of murder through greed. It may be, that the true form of the original saga lies half way between these two views. The story of the fall of the Nibelungs, that is, their killing at Etzel's court, may go back to the tale of the murder of relatives for money. On the other hand it is hard to believe that the Siegfried saga is nothing but a repetition of the Attila motive, for this is too brief a formula to which to reduce the long legend of Siegfried, with its many deeds. Even if we discard the mythological interpretation, it is the tale of a daring hero, who is brought up in the woods by a cunning dwarf. He kills a dragon and takes possession of his hoard, then rescues a maiden, imprisoned upon a mountain, as in the older Norse version and the popular ballad, or in a tower, as in the "Thidreksaga", and surrounded either by a wall of fire, as in the Norse, or by a large body of water, as in the "Nibelungenlied". After betrothing himself to the maiden, he sets forth in search of further adventures, and falls into the power of an evil race, who by their magic arts lure him to them, cause his destruction, and then obtain his treasure and the maiden for themselves. By her very name Sigrdrifa belongs to Siegfried, just as Gunther and Gudrun-Grimhild belong together, and it seems hardly possible that she should have entered the story later, as Boer would have us believe. After all, it is largely a matter of belief, for it is impossible to prove positively that mythical elements did or did not exist in the original.

To the combined Siegfried-Nibelung story various historical elements were added during the fifth century. At the beginning of this period the Franks were located on the left bank of the Rhine from Coblenz downward. Further up the river, that is, to the south, the Burgundians had established a kingdom in what is now the Rhenish Palatinate, their capital being Worms and their king "Gundahar", or "Gundicarius", as the Romans called him. For twenty years the Burgundians lived on good terms with the surrounding nations. Then, growing bolder, they suddenly rose against the Romans in the year 436, but the rebellion was quietly suppressed by the Roman general Aetius. Though defeated, the Burgundians were not subdued, and the very next year they broke their oaths and again sought to throw off the Roman yoke. This time the Romans called to their aid the hordes of Huns, who had been growing rapidly in power and were already pressing hard upon the German nations from the east. Only too glad for an excuse, the Huns poured into the land in great numbers and practically swept the Burgundian people from the face of the earth. According to the Roman historians, twenty thousand Burgundians were slain in this great battle of the Catalaunian Fields. Naturally this catastrophe, in which a whole German nation fell before the hordes of invading barbarians, produced a profound impression upon the Teutonic world. The King Gundahar, the Gunther of the "Nibelungenlied", who also fell in the battle, became the central figure of a new legend, namely, the story of the fall of the Burgundians.

Attila is not thought to have taken part in the invasion, still, after his death in 454, his name gradually came to be associated with the slaughter of the Burgundians, for a legend operates mainly with types, and as Attila was a Hun and throughout the Middle Ages was looked upon as the type of a cruel tyrant, greedy for conquest, it was but natural for him to play the role assigned to him in the legend. Quite plausible is Boer's explanation of the entrance of Attila into the legend. The "Thidreksaga" locates him in Seest in Westphalia. Now this province once bore the haute of "Hunaland", and by a natural confusion, because of the similarity of the names, "Huna" and "Huns", Attila, who is the chief representative of Hunnish power, was connected with the legend and located at Seest. This would show that the original extension of the legend was slight, as Xanten, the home of Hagen, is but seventy miles from Seest. The original form would then be that Hagen was slain by a king of "Hunaland", then because history relates that the Burgundians were slain by the Huns, the similarity of the names led to the introduction of Attila and the identification of the Nibelungs with the Burgundians. The fact, too, that the Franks rapidly took possession of the district depopulated by the crushing defeat of the Burgundians likewise aided the confusion, and thus the Franks became the natural heirs of the legend concerning the death of Gunther, and so we read of the fall of the Nibelungs, a name that is wholly Frankish in character. This identification led also to Attila's being considered the avenger of Siegfried's death. Poetic justice, however, demands that the slaughter of the Burgundians at the hands of Attila be also avenged. The rumor, that Attila's death was not natural, but that he had been murdered by his wife Ildico ("Hildiko"), gave the necessary features to round out the story. As Kriemhild was the sister of the Burgundian kings, it was but natural to explain her killing of Attila, as described in the Norse versions, by her desire to avenge her brothers.

In our "Nibelungenlied", however, it is no longer Attila, but Kriemhild, who is the central figure of the tragedy. Etzel, as he is called here, has sunk to the insignificant role of a stage king, a perfectly passive observer of the fight raging around him. This change was brought about perhaps by the introduction of Dietrich of Berne, the most imposing figure of all Germanic heroic lore. The necessity of providing him with a role corresponding to his importance, coupled with a growing repugnance on the part of the proud Franks to acknowledge defeat at the hands of the Huns, caused the person of Attila to dwindle in importance. Gradually, too, the role played by Kriemhild was totally changed. Instead of being the avenger of her brothers, as depicted in the Norse versions, she herself becomes the cause of their destruction. Etzel is not only innocent of any desire to harm the Nibelungs, but is even ignorant of the revenge planned by his wife. This change in her role was probably due to the feeling that it was incumbent upon her to avenge the murder of Siegfried.

Our "Nibelungenlied" knows but little of the adventures of Siegfried's youth as depicted in the Norse versions. The theme of the poem is no longer the love of Sigurd, the homeless wanderer, for the majestic Valkyrie Brunhild, but the love idyll of Siegfried, the son of the king of the Netherlands, and the dainty Burgundian princess Kriemhild. The poem has forgotten Siegfried's connection with Brunhild; it knows nothing of his penetrating the wall of flames to awake and rescue her, nothing of the betrothal of the two. In our poem Siegfried is carefully reared at his father's court in the Netherlands, and sets out with great pomp for the court of the Burgundians. In the Norse version he naturally remains at Gunther's court after his marriage, but in our poem he returns to the Netherlands with his bride. This necessitates the introduction of several new scenes to depict his arrival home, the invitation to the feast at Worms, and the reception of the guests on the part of the Burgundians.

In the "Nibelungenlied" the athletic sports, as an obstacle to the winning of Brunhild, take the place of the wall of flames of the older Norse versions. Siegfried and Gunther no longer change forms, but Siegfried dons the "Tarnkappe", which renders him invisible, so that while Gunther makes the motions, Siegfried really does the work, a thing which is rather difficult to imagine. The quarrel of the two queens is likewise very differently depicted in the "Nibelungenlied" from what it is in the Norse version. In the latter it takes place while the ladies are bathing in the river, and is brought on by the arrogance of Brunhild, who refuses to stand lower down the stream and bathe in the water flowing from Gudrun to her. In the "Thidreksaga" it occurs in the seclusion of the ladies' apartments, but in our poem it culminates in front of the cathedral before the assembled court, and requires as its background all the pomp and splendor of medieval chivalry. With a master hand and a wonderful knowledge of female character, the author depicts the gradual progress of the quarrel until it terminates in a magnificent scene of wounded pride and malignant hatred. Kriemhild, as usual, plays the more important part, and, while standing up for her rights, tries in every way to conciliate Brunhild and not to hurt her feelings. At last, however, stung by the taunts of the latter, she in turn loses her patience, bursts out with the whole story of the twofold deception to which Brunhild has been subjected, and then triumphantly sweeps into the church, leaving her rival stunned and humiliated by the news she has heard. In the Norse tradition the scene serves merely to enlighten Brunhild as to the deception played upon her. In the "Nibelungenlied" it becomes the real cause of Siegfried's death, for Brunhild plans to kill Siegfried to avenge the public slight done to her. She has no other reason, as Siegfried swears that there had been no deception. Brunhild appeals to us much less in the "Nibelungenlied" than in the Norse version. In the latter she feels herself deeply wronged by Siegfried's faithlessness, and resolves on his death because she will not be the wife of two men. In our poem she has no reason for wishing his death except her wounded pride. In the "Nibelungenlied", too, she disappears from view after Siegfried's death, whereas in the Norse tradition she ascends his funeral pyre and dies at his side.

The circumstances of Siegfried's death are likewise totally different in the two versions. In the Norse, as we have seen, he is murdered while asleep in bed, by Gunnar's younger brother Gutthorm. In our poem he is killed by Hagen, while bending over a spring to drink. This is preceded by a scene in which Hagen treacherously induces Kriemhild to mark the one vulnerable spot on Siegfried's body, on the plea of protecting him. This deepens the tragedy, and renders Kriemhild's misery and self-reproaches the greater. After Siegfried's burial his father, who had also come to Worms with his son, vainly endeavors to persuade Kriemhild to return with him to the Netherlands. Her refusal is unnatural in the extreme, for she had reigned there ten years or more with Siegfried, and had left her little son behind, and yet she relinquishes all this and remains with her brothers, whom she knows to be the murderers of her husband. This is evidently a reminiscence of an earlier form in which Siegfried was a homeless adventurer, as in the "Thidreksaga".

The second half of the tale, the destruction of the Nibelungs, is treated of very briefly in the early Norse versions, but the "Nibelungenlied", which knows so little of Siegfried's youth, has developed and enlarged upon the story, until it overshadows the first part in length and importance and gives the name to the whole poem. The main difference between the two versions is that in the older Norse tradition it is Attila who invites the Nibelungs to his court and attacks them in order to gain possession of the treasure, while Gudrun (Kriemhild) first tries to reconcile the warring parties, and, not succeeding in this, snatches up a sword and fights on the side of her brothers and later kills her husband as an act of revenge. In the "Thidreksaga" and the "Nibelungenlied", however, she is the instigator of the fight and the cause of her brothers' death, and finally suffers death herself at the hands of Master Hildebrand, who is furious that such noble heroes should fall at a woman's hand. The second part of the poem is grewsome reading at best, with its weltering corpses and torrents of blood. The horror is relieved only by the grim humor of Hagen and by the charming scene at Rudeger's court, where the young prince Giselher is betrothed to Rudeger's daughter. Rudeger is without doubt the most tragic figure of this part. He is bound on the one hand by his oath of allegiance to Kriemhild and on the other by ties of friendship to the Burgundians. His agony of mind at the dilemma in which Kriemhild's command to attack the Burgundians places him is pitiful. Divided between love and duty, the conviction that he must fulfill his vow, cost what it may, gradually forces itself upon him and he rushes to his death in combat with his dearest friends.

Towering above all others in its gloomy grandeur stands the figure of Hagen, the real hero of the second half of the poem. Fully aware that he is going to his death, he nevertheless scorns to desert his companions-in-arms, and awaits the fate in store for him with a stoicism that would do honor to a Spartan. He calmly accepts the consequences of his crime, and to the last mocks and scoffs at Kriemhild, until her fury knows no bounds. No character shows so little the refining influences of Christianity as does his. In all essential respects he is still the same old gigantic Teuton, who meets us in the earliest forms of the legend.

As to the various minor characters, many of which appear only in the "Nibelungenlied", space will not permit of their discussion here, although they will be treated of briefly in the notes. Suffice it to say, that the "Nibelungenlied" has introduced a number of effective scenes for the purpose of bringing some of them, especially Folker and Dankwart, into prominence. Among the best of these are, first, the night watch, when Folker first plays the Burgundians to sleep with his violin, and then stands guard with Hagen, thus preventing the surprise planned by Kriemhild; further, the visit to the church on the following morning, when the men of both parties clash; and lastly the tournament between the Huns and the Burgundians, which gives the author an excellent chance to show the prowess of the various heroes.

Let us pass now to the consideration of the strophic form of the "Nibelungenlied". The two Danish ballads of "Grimhild's Revenge" ("Grimhild's Haevn"), which are based upon the first combination of the Low German, i.e., Saxon, and the Rhenish traditions, prove that the strophe is considerably older than the preserved redactions of our poem, and that it was probably of Saxon origin. The metrical form goes back most probably to the four-accented verse of the poet Otfrid of the ninth century, although some have thought that Latin hymns, others that the French epic verse, may have been of influence. The direct derivation from Otfrid seems, however, the most plausible, as it accounts for the importance of the caesura, which generally marks a pause in the sense, as well as in the verse, and also for its masculine ending. The "Nibelungen" strophe consists of four long lines separated by a caesura into two distinct halves. The first half of each line contains four accents, the fourth falling upon the last syllable. This last stress, however, is not, as a rule as strong as the others, the effect being somewhat like that of a feminine ending. On this account some speak of three accents in the first half line, with a feminine ending. The fourth stress is, however, too strong to be thus disregarded, but because of its lighter character is best marked with a grave accent. The second half of each line ends in a masculine rhyme. The first three lines have each three stresses in the second half, while the second half of the fourth line has four accents to mark the end of the strophe. This longer fourth line is one of the most marked characteristics of the "Nibelungen" strophe. The rhymes are arranged in the order of "a", "a", "b", "b", though in a few isolated cases near the end of the poem but one rhyme is used throughout the strophe.

The opening lines of the poem may serve to illustrate the strophic form and scansion, and at the same time will give the reader an idea of the Middle High German language in which the poem is written:

Uns ist in alten maeren   wunders vil geseit
von heleden lobebaeron,   von grozer arebeit,
von froude und hochgeziten,   von weinen und von klagen,
von kuener recken striten   muget ir nu wunder hoeren sagen.

Ez wuochs in Burgonden   ein edel magedin,
daz in allen landen   niht schoeners mohte sin,
Kriemhild geheizen;   si wart ein scoene wip,
darambe muosen degene   vil verliesen den lip.

Der minneclichen meide triuten wol gezam,
ir muotten kuene recken, niemen was ir gram,
ane ma zen schoene so was ir edel lip;
der iunevrouwen tugende zierten anderiu wip.

Ir pilagen drie kilnege edel unde rich,
Ganther ande Geruot, die recken lobelieh,
und Giselher der iunge, ein uz erwelter degen,
diu frouwe was ir swester, die fu'rsten hetens in ir pflegen.

Die herren waren milte, von arde hohe erborn,
mit kraft unmazen kuene, die recken uz erkorn,
dazen Burgonden so was ir lant genant,
si framden starkiu wunder sit in Etzelen lant.

Ze Wormze bidem Rine si wenden mit ir kraft,
in diende von ir landen stolziu ritterscaft
mit lobelichen eren unz an ir endes zit,
sit sturben si inemerliche von zweier edelen frouwen nit.

Some of the final rhymes with proper names, such as "Hagene": "degene" (str. 84) or "Hagene": "tragene" (str. 300) appear to be feminine, but it is really the final "e" that rhymes, and a scansion of the line in question shows that the three accents are not complete without this final "e". In this respect our poem differs from most of the Middle High German poems, as this practice of using the final "e" in rhyme began to die out in the twelfth century, though occasionally found throughout the period. The rhymes are, as a rule, quite exact, the few cases of impure rhymes being mainly those in which short and long vowels are rhymed together, e.g. "mich": "rich" or "man": "han". Caesural rhymes are frequently met with, and were considered by Lachmann to be the marks of interpolated strophes, a view no longer held. A further peculiarity of the "Nibelungen" strophe is the frequent omission of the unaccented syllable in the second half of the last line of the strophe between the second and third stresses. Examples of this will be found in the second, third, and fifth strophes of the passage given above.

The language of the "Nibelungenlied" is the so-called Middle High German, that is, the High German written and spoken in the period between 1100 and 1500, the language of the great romances of chivalry and of the "Minnesingers". More exactly, the poem is written in the Austrian dialect of the close of the twelfth century, but contains many archaisms, which point to the fact of its having undergone a number of revisions.

In closing this brief study of the "Nibelungenlied", just a word or two further with reference to the poem, its character, and its place in German literature. Its theme is the ancient Teutonic ideal of "Treue" (faithfulness or fidelity), which has found here its most magnificent portrayal; faithfulness unto death, the loyalty of the vassal for his lord, as depicted in Hagen, the fidelity of the wife for her husband, as shown by Kriemhild, carried out with unhesitating consistency to the bitter end. This is not the gallantry of medieval chivalry, which colors so largely the opening scenes of the poem, but the heroic valor, the death-despising stoicism of the ancient Germans, before which the masters of the world, the all-conquering Romans, were compelled to bow.

In so far as the "Nibelungenlied" has forgotten most of the history of the youthful Siegfried, and knows nothing of his love for Brunhild, it is a torso, but so grand withal, that one hardly regrets the loss of these integral elements of the old saga. As it is a working over of originally separate lays, it is not entirely homogeneous, and contains not a few contradictions. In spite of these faults, however, which a close study reveals, it is nevertheless the grandest product of Middle High German epic poetry, and deservedly the most popular poem of older German literature. It lacks, to be sure, the grace of diction found in Gottfried von Strassburg's "Tristan und Isolde", the detailed and often magnificent descriptions of armor and dress to be met with in the epics of Hartman von Ouwe; it is wanting in the lofty philosophy of Wolfram von Eschenbach's "Parzival", and does not, as this latter, lead the reader into the realms of religious doubts and struggles. It is imposing through its very simplicity, through the grandeur of the story, which it does not seek to adorn and decorate. It nowhere pauses to analyze motives nor to give us a picture of inner conflict as modern authors are fond of doing. Its characters are impulsive and prompt in action, and when they have once acted, waste no time in useless regret or remorse.

It resembles the older "Spielmannsdichtung", or minstrel poetry, in the terseness and vigor of its language and in the lack of poetic imagery, but it is free from the coarseness and vulgar and grotesque humor of the latter. It approaches the courtly epic in its introduction of the pomp of courtly ceremonial, but this veneer of chivalry is very thin, and beneath the outward polish of form the heart beats as passionately and wildly as in the days of Herman, the Cheruscan chief. There are perhaps greater poems in literature than the "Nibelungenlied", but few so majestic in conception, so sublime in their tragedy, so simple in their execution, and so national in their character, as this great popular epic of German literature.

ENDNOTES:
(1) A is a parchment MS. of the second half of the thirteenth century, now found in Munich. It forms the basis of Lachmann's edition. It is a parchment MS. of the middle of the thirteenth century, belonging to the monastery of St. Gall. It has been edited by Bartsch, "Deutsche Klassiker des Mittelalters", vol. 3, and by Piper, "Deutsche National-Literatur", vol. 6. C is a parchment MS., of the thirteenth century, now in the ducal library of Donauesehingen. It is

the best written of all the MSS., and has been edited by Zarncke.

(2) The "Thidreksaga" differs from the other Norse versions in having "Sigfrod", as he is called here, brought up in ignorance of his parents, a trait which was probably borrowed from the widespread "Genoveva" story, although thought by some to have been an original feature of our legend.

(3) The "Thidreksaga", which has forgotten the enmity of the brothers, and calls Sigurd's tutor "Mimr", tells the episode in somewhat different fashion. The brothers plan to kill Sigurd, and the latter is attacked by the dragon, while burning charcoal in the forest. After killing the monster with a firebrand, Sigurd bathes himself in the blood and thus become covered with a horny skin, which renders him invulnerable, save in one place between the shoulder blades, which he could not reach. This bathing in the blood is also related in the Seyfrid ballad and in the "Nibelungenlied", with the difference, that the vulnerable spot is caused by a linden leaf falling upon him.

(4) The fact that all but one of these names alliterate, shows that the Norse version is here more original. Gunnar is the same as Gunther (Gundaharius), Hogni as Hagen; Gutthorm (Godomar) appears in the German version as Gernot. In this latter the father is called Danerat, the mother Uote, and the name Grimhild is transferred from the mother to the daughter.

(5) In the prose "Edda", in the water which drips from Gudrun's hair.

THE NIBELUNGENLIED (1)

ADVENTURE I (2)

Full many a wonder is told us in stories old, of heroes worthy of praise, of hardships dire, of joy and feasting, of the fighting of bold warriors, of weeping and of wailing; now ye may hear wonders told.

In Burgundy there grew so noble a maid that in all the lands none fairer might there be. Kriemhild (3) was she called; a comely woman she became, for whose sake many a knight must needs lose his life. Well worth the loving was this winsome maid. Bold knights strove for her, none bare her hate. Her peerless body was beautiful beyond degree; the courtly virtues of this maid of noble birth would have adorned many another woman too.

Three kings, noble and puissant, did nurture her, Gunther (4) and Gernot, (5) warriors worthy of praise, and Giselher, (6) the youth, a chosen knight. This lady was their sister, the princes had her in their care. The lordings were free in giving, of race high-born, passing bold of strength were they, these chosen knights. Their realm hight Burgundy. Great marvels they wrought hereafter in Etzel's (7) land. At Worms (8) upon the Rhine they dwelt with all their power. Proud knights from out their lands served them with honor, until their end was come. Thereafter they died grievously, through the hate of two noble dames.

Their mother, a mighty queen, was called the Lady Uta, (9) their father, Dankrat, (10) who left them the heritage after his life was over; a mighty man of valor that he was, who won thereto in youth worship full great. These kings, as I have said, were of high prowess. To them owed allegiance the best of warriors, of whom tales were ever told, strong and brave, fearless in the sharp strife. Hagen (11) there was of Troneg, thereto his brother Dankwart, (12) the doughty; Ortwin of Metz (13); Gere (14) and Eckewart, (15) the margraves twain; Folker of Alzei, (16) endued with fullness of strength. Rumolt (17) was master of the kitchen, a chosen knight; the lords Sindolt and Hunolt, liegemen of these three kings, had rule of the court and of its honors. Thereto had they many a warrior whose name I cannot tell. Dankwart was marshal; his nephew, Ortwin, seneschal unto the king; Sindolt was cupbearer, a chosen knight; Hunolt served as chamberlain; well they wot how to fill these lofty stations. Of the forces of the court and its far-reaching might, of the high worship (18) and of the chivalry these lords did ply with joy throughout their life, of this forsooth none might relate to you the end.

In the midst of these high honors Kriemhild dreamed a dream, of how she trained a falcon, strong, fair, and wild, which, before her very eyes, two eagles rent to pieces. No greater sorrow might chance to her in all this world. This dream then she told to Uta her mother, who could not unfold it to the dutiful maid in better wise than this: "The falcon which thou trainest, that is a noble man, but thou must needs lose him soon, unless so be that God preserve him."

"Why speakest thou to me of men, dear brother mine? I would fain ever be without a warrior's love. So fair will I remain until my death, that I shall never gain woe from love of man."

"Now forswear this not too roundly," spake the mother in reply. "If ever thou shalt wax glad of heart in this world, that will chance through the love of man. Passing fair wilt thou become, if God grant thee a right worthy knight."

"I pray you leave this speech," spake she, "my lady. Full oft hath it been seen in many a wife, how joy may at last end in sorrow. I shall avoid them both, then can it ne'er go ill with me."

Thus in her heart Kriemhild forsware all love. Many a happy day thereafter the maiden lived without that she wist any whom she would care to love. In after days she became with worship a valiant here's bride. He was the selfsame falcon which she beheld in her dream that her mother unfolded to her. How sorely did she avenge this upon her nearest kin, who slew him after! Through his dying alone there fell full many a mother's son.

ENDNOTES:
(1) "Nibelungenlied", the lay of the Nibelungs. The ordinary
   etymology of this name is 'children of the mist'
   ("Nebelkinder", O.N. "Niflungar"), and it is thought to have
   belonged originally to the dwarfs. Piper, I, 50, interprets
   it as 'the sons of Nibul'; Boer, II, 198, considers
   "Hniflungar" to be the correct Norse form and interprets it
   as 'the descendants of Hnaef' (O.E. "Hnaef", O.H.G.
   "Hnabi"), whose death is related in the "Finnsaga".
(2) "Adventure" (M.H.G. "aventiure", from O.F. "aventure", Lat.
   "adventura"). The word meant originally a happening,
   especially some great event, then the report of such an
   event. Here it is used in the sense of the different cantos
   or "fitts" of the poem, as in the "Gudrun" and other M.H.G.
   epics. Among the courtly poets it also frequently denotes
   the source, or is the personification of the muse of poetry.
(3) "Kriemhild" is the Upper German form of the Frankish
   "Grimhild". In the MSS., the name generally appears with a
   further shifting as "Chriemhilt", as if the initial
   consonant were Germanic "k". On the various forms of the

2

name, which have never yet been satisfactorily explained, see Mullenhoff, ZsfdA. xii, 299, 413; xv, 313; and Bohnenberger, PB. Beit. xxiv, 221-231.

(4) "Gunther" is the historical "Gundahari", king of the Burgundians in the fifth century.

(5) "Gernot" was probably introduced by some minstrel in place of the historical "Godomar", who appears in the Norse version as "Gutthormr", though the names are not etymologically the same, as "Godomar" would be "Guthmarr" in Old Norse.

(6) "Giselher" is the historical "Gislaharius". Although mentioned by the "Lex Burgundionum" as one of the Burgundian kings, he does not appear in the early Norse version, or in other poems dealing with these persons, such as the "Waltharius", the "Rabenschlacht", the "Rosengarten", etc., and was probably introduced at a late date into the saga. Originally no role was ascribed to him, and not even his death is told. He probably came from some independent source.

(7) "Etzel" is the German form for the historical "Attila" (Norse "Atli"). A discussion of his connection with the saga will be found in the introduction.

(8) "Worms" is the ancient "Borbetomagus", which in the first century B.C. was the chief city of the German tribe of the "Vangioni". In the fifth century it was the capital of the Burgundian kingdom, but was destroyed by the Huns. The Merovingians rebuilt it, and in the seventh century it became a bishopric where Charlemagne at times held his court. It was later noted as the meeting-place of many imperial diets. It remained a free city till 1801. In the "Thidreksaga" the name is corrupted into "Wernize".

(9) "Uta" (M.H.G. "Uote"). The name means ancestress, and is frequently used for the mother of heroes. The modern German form is "Ute", but in order to insure its being pronounced with two syllables, the form "Uta" was chosen.

(10) "Dankrat" (M.H.G. "Dancrat") appears as the father only in the "Nibelungenlied" and poems dependent on it, e.g., the "Klage" and "Biterolf", elsewhere as "Gibiche" (Norse "Giuki").

(11) "Hagen of Troneg". Troneg is probably a corruption of the name of the Latin colony, "colonia Trajana", on the Lower Rhine, which as early as the fifth century was written as "Troja", giving rise to the legend that the Franks were descended from the ancient Trojans. "Troja" was then further corrupted to "Tronje" and "Tronege". Hagen was therefore originally a Frank and had no connection with the Burgundian kings, as the lack of alliteration also goes to

show. Boer thinks that not Siegfried but Hagen originally lived at Xanten (see note 3 to Adventure II), as this was often called Troja Francorum. When the Hagen story was connected with the Burgundians and Hagen became either their brother or their vassal, his home was transferred to Worms and Siegfried was located at Xanten, as he had no especial localization. Thus Siegfried is never called Siegfried of Troneg, as is Hagen. Other attempts to explain Troneg will be found in Piper, I, 48.

(12) "Dankwart" is not an historical character nor one that belonged to the early form of the legend. He may have come from another saga, where he played the principal role as Droege (ZsfdA. 48, 499) thinks. Boer considers him to be Hagen's double, invented to play a part that would naturally fall to Hagen's share, were he not otherwise engaged at the moment. In our poem he is called "Dancwart der snelle", a word that has proved a stumbling-block to translators, because in modern German it means 'speedy', 'swift'. Its original meaning was, however, 'brave', 'warlike', although the later meaning is already found in M.H.G. In all such doubtful cases the older meaning has been preferred, unless the context forbids, and the word 'doughty' has been chosen to translate it.

(13) "Ortwin of Metz" appears also in the "Eckenlied", "Waltharius", and in "Biterolf". He is most likely a late introduction (but see Piper, I, 44). Rieger thinks that he belonged to a wealthy family "De Metis". Though the "i" is long in the original, and Simrock uses the form "Ortewein" in his translation, the spelling with short "i" has been chosen, as the lack of accent tends to shorten the vowel in such names.

(14) "Gere" is likewise a late introduction. He is perhaps the historical Margrave Gere (965) of East Saxony, whom Otto the Great appointed as a leader against the Slavs. See O. von Heinemann, "Markgraf Gero", Braunschweig, 1860, and Piper, L 43.

(15) "Eckewart" is also a late accession. He is perhaps the historical margrave of Meissen (1002), the first of the name. He, too, won fame in battle against the Slavs.

(16) "Folker of Alzet" (M.H.G. "Volker von Alzeije"), the knightly minstrel, is hardly an historical personage, in spite of the fact that Alzey is a well-known town in Rhine Hesse on the Selz, eighteen miles southwest of Mainz. The town has, to be sure, a violin in its coat of arms, as also the noble family of the same name. It is most likely, however, that this fact caused Folker to be connected with Alzei. In the "Thidreksaga" Folker did not play the role of

4

minstrel, and it is probable that some minstrel reviser of our poem developed the character and made it the personification of himself.

(17) "Rumolt", "Bindolt", and "Hunolt" have no historical basis and merely help to swell the retinue of the Burgundians.

(18) "Worship". This word has been frequently used here in its older meaning of 'worth', 'reverence', 'respect', to translate the M.H.G. "eren", 'honors'.

ADVENTURE II
Of Siegfried

In the Netherlands there grew the child of a noble king (his father had for name Siegemund, (1) his mother Siegelind), (2) in a mighty castle, known far and wide, in the lowlands of the Rhine: Xanten, (3) men called it. Of this hero I sing, how fair he grew. Free he was of every blemish. Strong and famous he later became, this valiant man. Ho! What great worship he won in this world! Siegfried hight this good and doughty knight. Full many kingdoms did he put to the test through his warlike mood. Through his strength of body he rode into many lands. Ho! What bold warriors he after found in the Burgundian land! Mickle wonders might one tell of Siegfried in his prime, in youthful days; what honors he received and how fair of body he. The most stately women held him in their love; with the zeal which was his due men trained him. But of himself what virtues he attained! Truly his father's lands were honored, that he was found in all things of such right lordly mind. Now was he become of the age that he might ride to court. Gladly the people saw him, many a maid wished that his desire might ever bear him hither. Enow gazed on him with favor; of this the prince was well aware. Full seldom was the youth allowed to ride without a guard of knights. Siegmund and Siegelind bade deck him out in brave attire. The older knights who were acquaint with courtly custom, had him in their care. Well therefore might he win both folk and land.

Now he was of the strength that he bare weapons well. Whatever he needed thereto, of this he had enow. With purpose he began to woo fair ladies; these bold Siegfried courted well in proper wise. Then bade Siegmund have cried to all his men, that he would hold a feasting with his loving kindred. The tidings thereof men brought into the lands of other kings. To the strangers and the home-folk he gave steeds and armor. Wheresoever any was found who, because of his birth, should become a knight, these noble youths were summoned to the land for the feasting. Here with the youthful prince they gained the knightly sword. Wonders might one tell of this great feast; Siegmund and Siegelind wist well how to gain great worship with their gifts, of which their hands dealt out great store. Wherefore one beheld many strangers riding to their realm. Four hundred sword-thanes (4) were to put on knightly garb with Siegfried. Many a fair maid was aught but idle with the work, for he was beloved of them all. Many precious stones the ladies inlaid on the gold, which together with the edging they would work upon the dress of the proud young warriors, for this must needs be done.

6

The host bade make benches for the many valiant men, for the midsummer festival, (5) at which Siegfried should gain the name of knight. Then full many a noble knight and many a high-born squire did hie them to the minster. Right were the elders in that they served the young, as had been done to them afore. Pastimes they had and hope of much good cheer. To the honor of God a mass was sung; then there rose from the people full great a press, as the youths were made knights in courtly wise, with such great honors as might not ever lightly be again. Then they ran to where they found saddled many a steed. In Siegmund's court the hurtling (6) waxed so fierce that both palace (7) and hall were heard to ring; the high-mettled warriors clashed with mighty sound. From young and old one heard many a shock, so that the splintering of the shafts reechoed to the clouds. Truncheons (8) were seen flying out before the palace from the hand of many a knight. This was done with zeal. At length the host bade cease the tourney and the steeds were led away. Upon the turf one saw all to-shivered (9) many a mighty buckler and great store of precious stones from the bright spangles (10) of the shields. Through the hurtling this did hap.

Then the guests of the host betook them to where men bade them sit. With good cheer they refreshed them and with the very best of wine, of which one bare frill plenty. To the strangers and the home-folk was shown worship enow. Though much pastime they had throughout the day, many of the strolling folk forsware all rest. They served for the largess, which men found there richly, whereby Siegmund's whole land was decked with praise. Then bade the king enfeoff Siegfried, the youth, with land and castles, as he himself had done. Much his hand bestowed upon the sword-companions. The journey liked them well, that to this land they were come. The feasting lasted until the seventh day. Siegelind, the noble queen, for the love of her son, dealt out ruddy gold in time-honored wise. Full well she wot how to make him beloved of the folk. Scarce could a poor man be found among the strolling mimes. Steeds and raiment were scattered by their hand, as if they were to live not one more day. I trow that never did serving folk use such great bounty. With worshipful honors the company departed hence. Of the mighty barons the tale doth tell that they desired the youth unto their lord, but of this the stately knight, Sir Siegfried, listed naught. Forasmuch as both Siegmund and Siegelind were still alive, the dear child of them twain wished not to wear a crown, but fain would he become a lord against all the deeds of force within his lands, whereof the bold and daring knight was sore adread.

ENDNOTES:
(1) "Siegmund" (M.H.G. "Sigemunt") was originally the hero of an independent saga. See "Volsungasaga", chaps. 3-8.
(2) "Siegelind" (M.H.G. "Sigelint") is the correct name of Siegfried's mother, as the alliteration shows. The Early Norse version has "Hjordis", which has come from the "Helgi saga".
(3) "Xanten" (M.H.G. "Santen" from the Latin "ad sanctos") is at

present a town in the Rhenish Prussian district of Dusseldorf. It does not now lie on the Rhine, but did in the Middle Ages.

(4) "Sword-thanes" (M.H.G. "swertdegene") were the young squires who were to be made knights. It was the custom for a youthful prince to receive the accolade with a number of others.

(5) "Midsummer festival". The M.H.G. "sunewende" means literally the 'sun's turning', i.e., the summer solstice. This was one of the great Germanic festivals, which the church later turned into St. John's Eve. The bonfires still burnt in Germany on this day are survivals of the old heathen custom.

(6) "Hurtling" translates here M.H.G. "buhurt", a word borrowed from the French to denote a knightly sport in which many knights clashed together. Hurtling was used in older English in the same significance.

(7) "Palace" (M.H.G. "palas", Lat. "palatium") is a large building standing alone and largely used as a reception hall.

(8) "Truncheons" (M.H.G. "trunzune", O.F. "troncon", 'lance splinters', 'fragments of spears'.

(9) "To-shivered", 'broken to pieces', in imitation of the older English to-beat, to-break, etc.

(10) "Spangles" (M.H.G. "spangen"), strips of metal radiating from the raised centre of the shield and often set, as here, with precious stones.

8

ADVENTURE III

How Siegfried Came to Worms

It was seldom that sorrow of heart perturbed the prince. He heard tales told of how there lived in Burgundy a comely maid, fashioned wondrous fair, from whom he thereafter gained much of joy, but suffering, too. Her beauty out of measure was known far and wide. So many a here heard of her noble mind, that it alone brought many a guest (1) to Gunther's land. But however many were seen wooing for her love, Kriemhild never confessed within her heart that she listed any for a lover. He was still a stranger to her, whose rule she later owned. Then did the son of Siegelind aspire to lofty love; the wooing of all others was to his but as the wind, for well he wot how to gain a lady fair. In later days the noble Kriemhild became bold Siegfried's bride. Kinsmen and liegemen enow advised him, since he would have hope of constant love, that he woo one who was his peer. At this bold Siegfried spake: "Then will I choose Kriemhild, the fair maid of Burgundy, for her beauty beyond measure. This I know full well, never was emperor so mighty, and he would have a wife, that it would not beseem him to love this noble queen."

Tidings of this reached Siegmund's ear; through the talk of the courtiers he was made ware of the wish of his son. Full loth it was to the king, that his child would woo the glorious maid. Siegelind heard it too, the wife of the noble king. Greatly she feared for her child, for full well she knew Gunther and his men. Therefore they sought to turn the hero from this venture. Up spake then the daring Siegfried: "Dear father mine, I would fain ever be without the love of noble dames, if I may not woo her in whom my heart hath great delight; whatsoever any may aver, it will avail but naught."

"And thou wilt not turn back," spake the king, "then am I in sooth glad of thy will and will help thee bring it to pass, as best I may. Yet hath this King Gunther full many a haughty man. If there were none else but Hagen, the doughty knight, he can use such arrogance that I fear me it will repent us sore, if we woo this high-born maid."

Then Siegfried made reply: "Wherefore need that hinder us? What I may not obtain from them in friendly wise, that my hand and its strength can gain. I trow that 1 can wrest from him both folk and land."

To this Prince Siegmund replied: "Thy speech liketh me not, for if this tale were told upon the Rhine, then durst thou never ride unto that land. Long time have Gunther and Gernot been known to me. By force may none win the maid, of this have I been well assured; but wilt thou ride with warriors unto this land, and we still have aught of friends, they shall be summoned soon."

"It is not to my mind," spake again Siegfried, "that warriors should follow me to the Rhine, as if for battle, that I constrain thereby the noble maid. My single hand can win her well—with eleven (2) comrades I will fare to Gunther's land; thereto shalt thou help me, Father Siegmund." Then to his knights they gave for garments furs both gray and vair. (3)

Now his mother Siegelind also heard the tale. She began to make dole for her loved child, whom she feared to lose through Gunther's men. Sorely the noble queen gan weep. Lord Siegfried hied him straightway to where he saw her; to his mother he spake in gentle wise: "Lady, ye must not weep for me; naught have I to fear from all his fighting men. I pray you, speed me on my journey to the Burgundian land, that I and my warriors may have array such as proud heroes can wear with honor; for this I will say you gramercy i' faith."

"Since naught will turn thee," spake then the Lady Siegelind, "so will I speed thee on thy journey, mine only child, with the best of weeds that ever knight did wear, thee and thy comrades. Ye shall have enow."

Siegfried, the youth, then made low obeisance to the queen. He spake: "None but twelve warriors will I have upon the way. Let raiment be made ready for them, I pray, for I would fain see how it standeth with Kriemhild."

Then sate fair ladies night and day. Few enow of them, I trow, did ease them, till Siegfried's weeds had all been wrought. Nor would he desist from faring forth. His father bade adorn the knightly garb in which his son should ride forth from Siegmund's land. The shining breastplates, too, were put in trim, also the stanch helmets and their shields both fair and broad. Now their journey to the Burgundian land drew near; man and wife began to fear lest they never should come home again. The heroes bade lade their sumpters with weapons and with harness. Their steeds were fair and their trappings red with gold. No need were there to live more proudly than Siegfried and his men. Then he asked for leave to journey to the land of Burgundy; this the king and queen sorrowfully vouchsafed. Lovingly he comforted them twain. "For my sake," spake he, "must ye not weep, nor have fear for me or for my life."

The warriors, too, were sad and many a maiden wept; I ween, their hearts did tell them rightly that many of their kinsmen would come to death because of this. Just cause had they for wailing; need enow they had in sooth.

Upon the seventh morning, forth upon the river sand at Worms the brave warriors pricked. Their armor was of ruddy gold and their trappings fashioned fair. Smoothly trotted the steeds of bold Siegfried's men. Their shields were new; gleaming and broad and fair their helmets, as Siegfried, the bold, rode to court in Gunther's land. Never had such princely attire been seen on heroes; their sword-points hung down to their spurs. Sharp javelins were borne by these chosen knights. Siegfried wielded one full two spans broad, which upon its edges cut most dangerously. In their hands they held gold-colored bridles; their martingales were silken: so they came into the land. Everywhere the folk began to gape amazed and many of Gunther's men fared forth to meet them. High-mettled warriors, both knight and squire, betook them to the lords (as was but right), and received into the land of their lords these guests and took from their hands the black sumpters which bore the shields. The steeds, too, they wished to lead away for easement. How boldly then brave Siegfried spake: "Let stand the mounts of me and of my men. We will soon hence again, of this have I great desire. Whosoever knoweth rightly where I can find the king, Gunther, the mighty, of Burgundian land, let him not keep his peace but tell me."

Then up spake one to whom it was rightly known: "Would ye find the king, that can hap full well. In yon broad hall with his heroes did I but see him. Ye must hither hie you; there ye may find with him many a lordly man."

To the king now the word was brought, that full lusty knights were come, who wore white breastplates and princely garb. None knew them in the Burgundian land. Much it wondered the king whence came these lordly warriors in such shining array, with such good shields, both new and broad. Loth was it to Gunther, that none could tell him this. Then Ortwin of Metz (a bold and mighty man was he) made answer to the king: "Since we know them not, ye should send for mine uncle Hagen, and let him see them. To him are known (4) all kingdoms and foreign lands. If so be he knoweth these lords, he will tell us straightway."

Then bade the king that Hagen and his men be brought. One saw him with his warriors striding in lordly wise unto the court.

"What would the king of me?" asked Hagen.

"There be come to my house strange warriors, whelm here none knoweth. If ye have ever seen them, I pray you, Hagen, tell me now the truth."

"That will I," spake then Hagen. He hied him to a window and over the guests he let his glances roam. Well liked him their trappings and their array, but full strange were they to him in the Burgundian land. He spake: "From wheresoever these warriors be come unto the Rhine, they may well be princes or envoys of kings, for their steeds are fair and their garments passing good. Whencesoever they bear these, forsooth high-mettled warriors be they."

"I dare well say," so spake Hagen, "though I never have seen Siegfried, yet can I well believe, however this may be, that he is the warrior that strideth yonder in such lordly wise. He bringeth new tidings hither to this land. By this here's hand were slain the bold Nibelungs, Schilbung and Nibelung, (5) sons of a mighty king. Since then he hath wrought great marvels with his huge strength. Once as the hero rode alone without all aid, he found before a mountain, as I have in sooth been told, by Nibelung's hoard full many a daring man. Strangers they were to him, till he gained knowledge of them there.

"The hoard of Nibelung was borne entire from out a hollow hill. Now hear a wondrous tale, of how the liegemen of Nibelung wished to divide it there. This the hero Siegfried saw and much it gan wonder him. So near was he now come to them, that he beheld the heroes, and the knights espied him, too. One among them spake: 'Here cometh the mighty Siegfried, the hero of Netherland.' Passing strange were the tidings that, he found among the Nibelungs. Schilbung and Nibelung greeted well the knight; with one accord these young and noble lordings bade the stately man divide the hoard. Eagerly they asked it, and the lord in turn gan vow it to them.

"He beheld such store of gems, as we have heard said, that a hundred wains might not bear the lead; still more was there of ruddy gold from the Nibelung land. All this the hand of the daring Siegfried should divide. As a guerdon they gave him the sword of Nibelung, but they were served full ill by the service which the good knight Siegfried should render them. Nor could he end it for them; angry of mood (6) they grew. Twelve bold men of their kith were there, mighty giants these. What might that avail them! Siegfried's hand slew them soon in wrath, and seven hundred warriors from the Nibelung land he vanquished with the good sword Balmung. (7) Because of the great fear that, many a young warrior had of the sword and of the valiant man, they made the land and its castles subject to his hand. Likewise both the mighty kings he slew, but soon he himself was sorely pressed by Alberich. (8) The latter weened to venge straightway his masters, till he then discovered Siegfried's mighty strength; for no match for him was the sturdy dwarf. Like wild lions they ran to the hill, where from Alberich he won the Cloak of Darkness. (9) Thus did Siegfried, the terrible, become master of the hoard; those who had dared the combat, all lay there slain. Soon bade he cart and bear the treasure to the place from whence the men of Nibelung had borne it forth. He made Alberich, the strong, warden of the hoard and bade him swear an oath to serve him as his knave; and fit he was for work of every sort."

So spake Hagen of Troneg: "This he hath done. Nevermore did warrior win such mighty strength. I wot yet more of him: it is known to me that the hero slew a dragon and bathed him in the blood, so that his skin became like horn. Therefore no weapons will cut him, as hath full oft been seen. All the better must we greet this lord, that we may not earn the youthful warrior's hate. So bold is he that we should hold him as a friend, for he hath wrought full many a wonder by his strength."

Then spake the mighty king: "Thou mayst well have right. Behold how valiantly he with his knights doth stand in lust of battle, the daring man! Let us go down to meet the warrior."

"That ye may do with honor," spake then Hagen; "he is of noble race, son of a mighty king. God wot, methinks, he beareth him in such wise, that it can be no little matter for which he hath ridden hither."

"Now be he welcome to us," spake then the king of the land. "He is both noble and brave, as I have heard full well. This shall stand him in good stead in the Burgundian land." Then went Lord Gunther to where Siegfried stood.

The host and his warriors received the guest in such wise that full little was there lack of worship. Low bowed the stately man, that they had greeted him so fair. "It wondereth me," spake the king straightway, "whence ye, noble Siegfried, be come unto this land, or what ye seek at Worms upon the Rhine."

Then the stranger made answer to the king: "This will I not conceal from you. Tales were told me in my father's land, that here with you were the boldest warriors that ever king did gain. This I have often heard, and that I might know it of a truth, therefore am I come. Likewise do I hear boasting of your valor, that no bolder king hath ever been seen. This the folk relate much through all these lands. Therefore will I not turn back, till it be known to me. I also am a warrior and was to wear a crown. Fain would I bring it to pass that it may be said of me: Rightly doth he rule both folk and land. Of this shall my head and honor be a pledge. Now be ye so bold, as hath been told me, I reck not be it lief or loth to any man, I will gain from you whatso ye have—land and castles shall be subject to my hand."

The king had likewise his men had marvel at the tidings they here heard, that he was willed to take from them their land. The knights waxed wroth, as they heard this word. "How have I earned this," spake Gunther, the knight, "that we should lose by the force of any man that which my father hath rules so long with honor? We should let it ill appear that we, too, are used in knightly ways."

"In no wise will I desist," spake again the valiant man. "Unless it be that through thy strength thy land have peace, I will rule it all. And shouldst thou gain, by thy strength, my ancestral lands, they shall be subject to thy sway. Thy lands, and mine as well, shall lie alike; whether of us twain can triumph over the other, him shall both land and people serve."

Hagen and Gernot, too, straightway gainsaid this. "We have no wish," spake Gernot, "that we should conquer aught of lands, or that any man lie dead at hero's hands. We have rich lands, which serve us, as is meet, nor hath any a better claim to them than we."

There stood his kinsmen, grim of mood; among them, too, Ortwin of Metz. "It doth irk me much to hear these words of peace," spake he; "the mighty Siegfried hath defied you for no just cause. Had ye and your brothers no meet defense, and even if he led a kingly troop, I trow well so to fight that the daring man have good cause to leave this haughty mien."

At this the hero of Netherland grew wonderly wroth. He spake: "Thy hand shall not presume against me. I am a mighty king, a king's vassal thou. Twelve of thy ilk durst not match me in strife."

Then Ortwin of Metz called loudly for swords. Well was he fit to be Hagen of Troneg's sister's son. It rued the king that he had held his peace so long. Then Gernot, the bold and lusty knight, came in between. He spake to Ortwin: "Now give over thy anger. Lord Siegfried hath done us no such wrong, but that we may still part the strife in courteous wise. Be advised of me and hold him still as friend; far better will this beseem us."

Then spake the doughty Hagen: "It may well grieve us and all thy knights that he ever rode for battle to the Rhine. He should have given it over; my lordings never would have done such ill to him."

To this Siegfried, the mighty man, made answer: "Doth this irk you, Sir Hagen, which I spake, then will I let you see that my hands shall have dominion here in the Burgundian land."

"I alone will hinder this," answered Gernot, and he forbade his knights speak aught with haughtiness that might cause rue. Siegfried, too, then bethought him of the noble maid.

"How might it beseem us to fight with you?" spake Gernot anew. "However really heroes should lie dead because of this, we should have scant honor therefrom and ye but little gain."

To this Siegfried, the son of Siegmund, made reply: "Why waiteth Hagen, and Ortwin, too, that he hasteth not to fight with his kin, of whom he hath so many here in Burgundy?"

At this all held their peace; such was Gernot's counsel. Then spake Queen Uta's son: "Ye shall be welcome to us with all your war-mates, who are come with you. We shall gladly serve you, I and all my kin."

Then for the guests they bade pour out King Gunther's wine. The master of the land then spake: "All that we have, if ye desire it in honorable wise, shall owe fealty to you; with you shall both life and goods be shared."

14

At this Lord Siegfried grew of somewhat gentler mood. Then they bade that care be taken of the armor of the guests. The best of hostels that men might find were sought for Siegfried's squires; great easement they gave them. Thereafter they gladly saw the guest in Burgundy. Many a day they offered him great worship, a thousand fold more than I can tell you. This his prowess wrought; ye may well believe, full scant a one he saw who was his foe.

Whenever the lordings and their liegemen did play at knightly games, Siegfried was aye the best, whatever they began. Herein could no one match him, so mighty was his strength, whether they threw the stone or hurled the shaft. When through courtesie the full lusty knights made merry with the ladies, there were they glad to see the hero of Netherland, for upon high love his heart was bent. He was aye ready for whatso they undertook, but in his heart he bare a lovely maid, whom he had never seen. She too, who in secret spake full well of him, cherished him alone. Whenever the pages, squires, and knights would play their games within the court, Kriemhild, the noble queen, watched them from the windows, for no other pastime she needed on such days. Had he known that she gazed on him thus, whom he bare within his heart, then had he had pastime enough, I trow, for well I wot that no greater joy in all this world could chance to him.

Whenever he stood by the heroes in the court, as men still are wont to do, for pastime's sake, so winsome was the posture of Siegelind's son, that many a lady loved him for very joy of heart. But he bethought him many a day: "How shall that hap, that I with mine own eyes may see the noble maid, whom I do love with all my heart and so have done long time. Sadly must I stand, sith she be still a stranger to me."

Whenever the mighty kings fared forth into their land, the warriors all must needs accompany them at hand, and Siegfried, too. This the lady rued, and he, too, suffered many pangs for love of her. Thus he dwelt with the lordings, of a truth, full a year in Gunther's land, and in all this time he saw not once the lovely maid, from whom in later days there happed to him much joy and eke much woe.

ENDNOTES:
(1) "Guest" translates here the M.H.G. "gest", a word which may
    mean either 'guest' or 'stranger,' and it is often
    difficult, as here, to tell to which meaning the preference
    should be given.
(2) "Eleven" translates the M.H.G. "selbe zwelfte", which means
    one of twelve. The accounts are, however, contradictory, as
    a few lines below mention is made of twelve companions of
    Siegfried.
(3) "Vair" (O.F. "vair", Lat. "varius"), 'variegated', like the
    fur of the squirrel.

(4) "Known". It was a mark of the experienced warrior, that he was acquainted with the customs and dress of various countries and with the names and lineage of all important personages. Thus in the "Hildebrandslied" Hildebrand asks Hadubrand to tell him his father's name, and adds: "If thou tellest me the one, I shall know the other."

(5) "Schilbung" and "Nibelung", here spoken of as the sons of a mighty king, were originally dwarfs, and, according to some authorities, the original owners of the treasure. Boer, ix, 199, thinks, however, that the name Nibelungs was transferred from Hagen to these dwarfs at a late stage in the formation of the saga.

(6) "Angry of mood". The reason of this anger is apparent from the more detailed account in "Biterolf", 7801. The quarrel arose from the fact that, according to ancient law, Siegfried acquired with the sword the rights of the first born, which the brothers, however, refused to accord to him.

(7) "Balmung". In the older Norse version and in the "Thidreksaga" Siegfried's sword bore the name of Gram.

(8) "Alberich" is a dwarf king who appears in a number of legends, e.g., in the "Ortnit saga" and in "Biterolf". Under the Romance form of his name, "Oberon", he plays an important role in modern literature.

(9) "Cloak of Darkness". This translates the M.H.G. "tarnkappe", a word often retained by translators. It is formed from O.H.G. tarni, 'secret' (cf. O.E. "dyrne"), and "kappe" from late Latin "cappa", 'cloak'. It rendered the wearer invisible and gave him the strength of twelve men.

ADVENTURE IV

How He Fought with the Saxons (1)

Now there came strange tales to Gunther's land, though messengers sent them from afar—tales of unknown warriors, who bare them hate. When they heard this word, in sooth it pleased them not. These warriors will I name to you: there was Liudeger of Saxon land, a great and lordly prince, and then from Denmark Lindegast, the king. For their journey they had gathered many a lordly stranger.

To Gunther's land were come the messengers his foes had sent. Men asked the strangers for their tidings and bade them hie them soon to court unto King Gunther. The king gave them greeting fair; he spake: "Be ye welcome. I have not heard who sent you hither, but let that now be told." So spake the right good king. But they feared full sore King Gunther's warlike mood.

"Will ye, O King, permit that we tell the tales we bring, then we shall not hold our tongue, but name to you the lordings who have sent us hither: Liudegast and Liudeger; they would march upon this land. Ye have earned their wrath, indeed we heard that both lords bear you mortal hate. They would harry at Worms upon the Rhine and have the aid of many a knight; that may ye know upon our faith. Within twelve weeks the journey must befall. And ye have aught of good friends, who will help guard your castles and your lands, let this soon be seen. Here shall be carved by them many a helm and shield. Or would ye parley with them, let messengers be sent. Then the numerous bands of your mighty foes will not ride so near you, to give you pain of heart, from which full many a lusty knight and a good must die."

"Now bide a time," spake the good king, "till I bethink me better; then ye shall know my mind. Have I aught of trusty men, I will not withhold from them these startling tales, but will make complaint thereof unto my friends."

To Gunther, the mighty king, it was loth enow, but in his heart he bare the speech in secret wise. He bade Hagen be fetched and others of his men, and sent eftsoon to court for Gernot. Then came the very best of men that could be found. The king spake: "Men would seek us here in this our land with mighty armies, now make ye wail for that."

To this Gernot, a brave and lusty knight, made answer: "That will we fend

17

indeed with swords. Only the fey (2) will fall. So let them die; for their sake I will not forget my honor. Let these foes of ours be welcome to us."

Then spake Hagen of Troneg: "This thinketh me not good. Liudegast and Liudeger bear great arrogance; nor can we summon all our men in such short time. Why tell ye not Siegfried of the thing?" So spake the valiant knight.

To the messengers they bade give lodging in the town. Whatever hate they bore them, yet Gunther, the mighty, bade purvey them well, as was but right, till he discovered of his friends who there was who would lend him aid. Yet in his fears the king was ill at ease. Just then full blithe a knight, who wot not what had happed, saw him thus sad and prayed King Gunther to tell him of the matter. "Much it wondereth me," spake Siegfried, for he it was, "that ye thus have changed your merry wont, which ye have used thus far with us."

To this Gunther, the stately knight, replied: "It liketh me not to tell all folk the grievance which I must bear within my heart in secret wise. Only to trusty friends should one confide his woe of heart."

At this Siegfried's color waxed both pale and red. To the king he spake: "I have denied you naught and will gladly help you turn aside your woes. And ye seek friends, I will be one of them and trow well to deport myself with honor until mine end."

"Now God reward you, Sir Siegfried, your speech thinketh me good, and though your prowess help me not, yet do I rejoice to hear that ye are friend to me, and live I yet a while, I shall repay you well. I will let you hear why I stand thus sad; from the messengers of my foes I have heard that they would visit me with war, a thing which knights have never done to us in all these lands."

"Regard this lightly," spake then Siegfried, "and calm your mood. Do as I pray you. Let me gain for you both worship and advantage and do ye command your knights, that they gather to your aid. Should your mighty foes be helped by thirty thousand (3) men, yet could I withstand them, had I but a thousand; for that rely on me."

Then spake King Gunther: "For this I'll serve you ever."

"So bid me call a thousand of your men, since of mine own I have but twelve, and I will guard your land. Faithfully shall the hand of Siegfried serve you. Hagen shall help us and also Ortwin, Dankwart, and Sindolt, your trusty men. Folker, the valiant man, shall also ride along; he shall bear the banner, for to none would I liefer grant it. Let now the envoys ride home to their masters' lands. Give them to understand they soon shall see us, that our castles may rest in peace."

Then the king bade summon both his kinsmen and his men. The messengers of Liudeger betook them to the court. Fain they were that they should journey home again. Gunther, the good king, made offrance of rich gifts and gave them safe-convoy. At this their spirits mounted high. "Now say unto my foes," spake then Gunther, "that they may well give over their journey and stay at home; but if they will seek me here within my lands, hardships shall they know, and my friends play me not false."

Rich gifts men bare then for the envoys; enow of these had Gunther to bestow, nor durst the men of Liudeger refuse them. When at last they took their leave, they parted hence in merry mood.

Now when the messengers were come to Denmark and King Liudegast had heard how they parted from the Rhine, as was told him, much he rued, in sooth, their (4) proud defiance. The envoys said that Gunther had full many a valiant man-at-arms and among them they saw a warrior stand, whose name was Siegfried, a hero from Netherland. Little liked it Liudegast when he heard aright this tale. When the men of Denmark had heard these tidings told, they hasted all the more to call their friends; till Sir Liudegast had gathered for his journey full twenty thousand knights from among his valiant men. Then King Liudeger, also, of Saxon land, sent forth his summons, till they had forty thousand men and more, with whom they thought to ride to the Burgundian land.

Likewise at home King Gunther got him men-at-arms among his kin and the liegemen of his brothers, and among Hagen's men whom they wished to lead thence for battle. Much need of this the heroes had, but warriors soon must suffer death from this. Thus they made them ready for the journey. When they would hence, Folker, the daring, must bear the flag. In such wise they thought to ride from Worms across the Rhine. Hagen of Troneg was master of the troop; with them rode Sindolt and Hunolt, too, who wist well how to merit Gunther's gold. Dankwart, Hagen's brother, and Ortwin, too, well could they serve with honor in this war.

"Sir King," spake then Siegfried, "stay ye at home; since that your warriors are willed to follow me, remain ye with the ladies and keep your spirits high. I trow well to guard for you both honor and estate. Well will I bring it to pass that those who thought to seek you out at Worms upon the Rhine, had better far have stayed at home. We shall ride so nigh unto their land that their proud defiance shall be turned to fear."

From the Rhine they rode through Hesse with their warriors towards Saxon land, where they later fought. With fire and pillage, too, they harried all the countryside, so that the two kings did learn of it in dire distress. Then came they to the border; the warriors marched along. Siegfried, the strong, gan ask: "Who shall now guard here the troop?" Forsooth never did men ride more scathfully to the Saxons. They spake: "Let the valiant Dankwart guard the young upon the way, he is a doughty knight. Thus shall we lose the less through Liudeger's men. Let him and Ortwin guard the rear."

"Then I myself will ride," spake Siegfried, the knight, "and play the outlook toward the foe, until I discover aright where these warriors be." Quickly the son of fair Siegelind donned his harness. The troop he gave in charge to Hagen, when he would depart, and to Gernot, the valiant man. Thus he rode hence into the Saxon land alone and many a helmet band he cut to pieces on that day. Soon he spied the mighty host that lay encamped upon the plain and far outweighed the forces of his men. Forty thousand or better still there were. Full blithely Siegfried saw this in lofty mood. Meantime a warrior full well arrayed had mounted to the outlook 'gainst the foe. Him Sir Siegfried spied, and the bold man saw him, too. Each began to watch the other in hostile wise. Who it was, who stood on guard, I'll tell you now; a gleaming shield of gold lay by his hand. It was the good King Liudegast, who was guarding here his band. The noble stranger pricked along in lordly wise.

Now had Sir Liudegast espied him with hostile eye. Into the flanks of their horses they plunged the spurs; with all their might they couched the spears against the shields. At this great fear befell the mighty king. After the thrust the horses carried past each other the royal knights, as though borne upon the wind. With the bridles they wheeled in knightly wise and the two fierce champions encountered with their swords. Then smote Sir Siegfried, so that the whole field did ring. Through the hero's hand from out the helmets, as from firebrands, flew the bright red sparks. Each in the other found his match. Sir Liudegast, too, struck many a savage blow; the might of each broke full upon the shields. Thirty of Liudegast's men stood there on guard, but ere they could come to his aid, Siegfried had won the fight, with three groat wounds which he dealt the king through his gleaming breastplate, the which was passing good. The blood from the wounds gushed forth along the edges of the sword, whereat King Liudegast stood in sorry mood. He begged for life and made offrance of his lands and said that his name was Liudegast. Then came his warrior's, who had witnessed what there had happed upon the lookout. As Siegfried would lead his captive thence, he was set upon by thirty of these men. With mighty blows the hero's hand guarded his noble prize. The stately knight then wrought worse scathe. In self-defense he did thirty unto death; only one he left alive, who rode full fast to tell the tale of what here had chanced. By his reddened helmet one might see the truth. It sorely grieved the men of Denmark, when the tale was told them that their king was taken captive. Men told it to his brother, who at the news began to rage with monstrous wrath, for great woe it brought him.

Liudegast, the warrior, then was led away by Siegfried's might to Gunther's men and given to Hagen in charge. When that they heard it was the king, full moderate was their dole. The Burgundians now were bidden raise their banner. "Up, men," cried Siegfried, "here shall more be done, ere the day end, and I lose not my life. Full many a stately dame in Saxon land shall rue this fight. Ye heroes from the Rhine, give heed to me, for I can guide you well to Liudeger's band. So shall ye see helmets carved by the hands of goodly knights; ere we turn again, they shall become acquaint with fear."

To their horses Gernot and all his men now hasted, and soon the stalwart minstrel, Sir Folker, grasped the battle-flag and rode before the band. Then were all the comrades arrayed in lordly wise for strife; nor had they more than a thousand men, and thereto Siegfried's twelve men-at-arms. Now from the road gan rise the dust, as across the land they rode; many a lordly shield was seen to gleam from out their midst. There, too, were come the Saxons with their troops and well-sharpened swords, as I since have heard. Sore cut these weapons in the heroes' hands, for they would fain guard both their castles and their land against the strangers. The lordings' marshals led on the troop. Siegfried, too, was come with his men-at-arms, whom he had brought from Netherland. In the storm of battle many a hand this day grew red with blood. Sindolt and Hunolt and Gernot, too, slew many a knight in the strife, ere these rightly knew the boldness of their foes. This many a stately dame must needs bewail. Folker and Hagen and Ortwin, too, dimmed in the battle the gleam of many a helm with flowing blood, these storm-bold men. By Dankwart, too, great deeds were done.

The men of Denmark proved well their hands; one heard many a shield resounding from the hurtling and from the sharp swords as well, many of which were wielded there. The battle-bold Saxons did scathe enow, but when the men of Burgundy pressed to the fight, by them was really a wide wound carved. Then down across the saddles the blood was seen to flow. Thus they fought for honors, these knights both bold and good. Loud rang the sharp weapons in the heroes' hands, as those of Netherland followed their lording through the sturdy host. Valiantly they forced their way in Siegfried's wake, but not a knight from the Rhine was seen to follow. Through the shining helmets one could see flow the bloody stream, drawn forth by Siegfried's hand, till at last he found Liudeger before his men-at-arms. Thrice had he pierced the host from end to end. Now was Hagen come, who helped him achieve in the battle all his mind. Before them many a good knight must needs die this day.

When the mighty Liudeger espied Siegfried and saw that he bore high in hand the good sword Balmung and did slay so many a man, then waxed the lording wroth and fierce enow. A mighty surging and a mighty clang of swords arose, as their comrades pressed against each other. The two champions tried their prowess all the more. The troops began to yield; fierce grew the hate. To the ruler of the Saxons the tale was told that his brother had been captured; great dole this gave him. Well he knew it was the son of Siegelind who had done the deed. Men blamed Sir Gernot, but later he learned the truth.

So mighty were the blows of Liudeger that Siegfried's charger reeled beneath the saddle. When the steed recovered, bold Siegfried took on a frightful usance in the fray. In this Hagen helped him well, likewise Gernot, Dankwart, and Folker, too. Through them lay many dead. Likewise Sindolt and Hunolt and Ortwin, the knight, laid many low in strife; side by side in the fray the noble princes stood. One saw above the helmets many a spear, thrown by here's hand, hurtling through the gleaming shields. Blood-red was colored many a lordly buckler; many a man in the fierce conflict was unhorsed. At each other ran Siegfried, the brave, and Liudeger; shafts were seen to fly and many a keen-edged spear. Then off flew the shield-plates, struck by Siegfried's hand; the hero of Netherland thought to win the battle from the valiant Saxons, wondrous many of whom one saw. Ho! How many shining armor-rings the daring Dankwart broke!

Then Sir Liudegor espied a crown painted on the shield in Siegfried's hand. Well he knew that it was Siegfried, the mighty man. To his friends the hero loudly called: "Desist ye from the strife, my men, here I have seen the son of Siegmund, Siegfried, the strong, and recognized him well. The foul fiend himself hath sent him hither to the Saxon land." The banners bade he lower in the fight. Peace he craved, and this was later granted him, but he must needs go as hostage to Gunther's land. This was wrung from him by valiant Siegfried's hand. With one accord they then gave over the strife and laid aside the many riddled helmets and the broad, battered bucklers. Whatever of these was found, bore the hue of blood from the Burgundians' hand. They captured whom they would, for this lay in their power. Gernot and Hagen, the full bold warriors, bade bear away the wounded; five hundred stately men they led forth captive to the Rhine. The worsted knights rode back to Denmark, nor had the Saxons fought so well that one could give them aught of praise, and this the heroes rued full sore. The fallen, too, were greatly mourned by friends.

Then they bade place the weapons on sumpters for the Rhine. Siegfried, the warrior, and his heroes had wrought full well, as Gunther's men must needs confess. Sir Gernot now sent messengers homeward to Worms in his native land, and bade tell his kin what great success had happed to him and to his men, and how these daring knights had striven well for honor. The squirelings ran and told the tale. Then those who afore had sorrowed, were blithe for joy at the pleasing tidings that were come. Much questioning was heard from noble dames, how it had fared with the liegemen of the mighty king. One of the messengers they bade go to Kriemhild; this happed full secretly (openly she durst not), for she, too, had amongst them her own true love. When she saw the messenger coming to her bower, fair Kriemhild spake in kindly wise: "Now tell me glad news, I pray. And thou dost so without deceit, I will give thee of my gold and will ever be thy friend. How fared forth from the battle my brother Gernot and others of my kin? Are many of them dead perchance? Or who wrought there the best? This thou must tell me."

Quickly then the envoy spake: "Ne'er a coward did we have, but, to tell the truth, O noble queen, none rode so well to the strife and fray, as did the noble stranger from Netherland. Mickle wonders the hand of valiant Siegfried wrought. Whate'er the knights have done in strife, Dankwart and Hagen and other men of the king, however much they strove for honor, 'tis but as the wind compared with Siegfried, the son of Siegmund, the king. They slew full many a hero in the fray, but none might tell you of the wonders which Siegfried wrought, whenever he rode into the fight. Great woe he did the ladies through their kin; upon the field the love of many a dame lay dead. His blows were heard to ring so loud upon the helmets, that from the wounds they drew forth the blood in streams. In every knightly art he is a worthy knight and a brave. Whatever Ortwin of Metz achieved (and he whom he could reach with his good sword, fell sorely wounded, but mostly dead), yet your brother wrought the direst woe that could ever chance in battle. One must say of the chosen knights in truth, that these proud Burgundians acquitted them so well that they can well preserve their honor from every taint of shame. Through their hands we saw many a saddle bare, while the field resounded with the flashing swords. So well rode the warriors from the Rhine, that it were better for their foes had it been avoided. The valiant men of Troneg, also, wrought dire woe, when in great numbers the armies met. Bold Hagen's hand did many a one to death; of this full many stories might be told here in the Burgundian land. Sindolt and Hunolt, Gernot's men, Rumolt the brave, have done such deeds that it may well ever rue Liudeger that he made war upon thy kinsmen by the Rhine. The very best fight that happed from first to last, that one has ever seen, was made full lustily by Siegfried's hand. Rich hostages he bringeth to Gunther's land. He won them by his prowess, this stately man. Of this King Liudegast must bear the loss and eke his brother Liudeger of Saxon land. Now listen to my tale, most noble queen: by the hand of Siegfried the twain were caught. Never have men brought so many hostages to this land, as now are coming to the Rhine through him. Men are bringing to our land five hundred or more unharmed captives; and of the deadly wounded, my lady, know, not less than eighty blood-red biers. These men were mostly wounded by bold Siegfried's hand. Those who in haughty pride sent a challenge to the Rhine, must now needs be the captives of Gunther, the king, and men are bringing them with joy unto this land."

Still higher rose Kriemhild's color when she heard this tale. Her fair face blushed a rosy red, that Siegfried, the youth, the stately knight, had fared forth so joyfully from the dangerous strife. These tidings could not have pleased her better. For her kinsmen, too, she rejoiced in duty bound. Then spake the lovely maid: "A fair tale thou hast told me; therefore shalt thou have as guerdon rich attire. Likewise I'll have thee brought ten marks of gold." (5) Small wonder that such tales are gladly told to noble dames.

They gave him then his guerdon, the garments and the gold. Then many a fair maid hied her to the casement and gazed upon the street, where many high-mettled warriors were seen riding into the Burgundian land. There came the champions, the wounded and the sound. Without shame they heard the

23

greetings of their friends. Merrily the host rode forth to meet his guests, for his great sorrow had been turned to joy. Well greeted he his vassals and the strangers, too; for it was only meet that the mighty king in courtly wise should thank those who were come back to him, because in the storm of battle they had won the fight with honor. Gunther bade his kinsmen tell who had been slain upon the march; but sixty had been lost, whom one must mourn, as is the wont with heroes. Many a riven shield and battered helm the unharmed warriors brought to Gunther's land. The men alighted from their steeds before the palace of the king. Loud was heard the joyous sound of the merry welcome; then order was given to lodge the warriors in the town. The king bade minister well unto his guests, attend the wounded and give them good easement. His courtesie was cleverly seen upon his foes. He spake to Liudegast: "Now be ye welcome. Much damage have I ta'en because of you; for this I shall now be repaid, if fortune favor. God reward my kinsmen, for they have given me joy."

"Well may ye thank them," answered Liudeger; "such noble hostages hath king never gained afore. For fair treatment we offer great store of wealth, that ye may act with mercy towards your foes."

"I will let you both go free," spake Gunther, "but I must have surety that my foes remain here with me, that they do not leave the land against my will." To that Liudeger pledged his hand.

Men brought them to their lodgings and gave them easement. The wounded were bedded well, and for the sound were poured out good mead and wine. Never could the comrades have been more merry. Their battered shields were borne away for keeping, and enow there was of bloody saddles which one bade hide away, that the ladies might not weep. Many a good knight returned aweary from the fray. The king did make his guests great cheer. His lands were full of strangers and of home-folk. He bade ease the sorely wounded in kindly wise; their haughty pride was now laid low. Men offered to the leeches rich rewards, silver without weight and thereto shining gold, if they would heal the heroes from the stress of war. To his guests the king likewise gave great gifts. Those that were minded to set out for home, were asked to stay, as one doth to friends. The king bethought him how he might requite his men, for they had brought to pass his wish for fame and honor.

Then spake Lord Gernot: "Let them ride away, but be it made known to them that in six weeks they must come again for a mighty feast. By then will many a one be healed who now lieth sorely wounded."

Then Siegfried of Netherland also asked for leave, but when King Gunther learned his wish, lovingly he bade him stay erstwhile. Were it not for the king's sister, this were never done. He was too rich to take reward, though he well deserved it and the king liked him well, as also did the kinsmen, who had seen what happed in battle through his strength. For the sake of one fair lady he thought to stay, if perchance he might espy her. Later it was done, and according to his wish he met the maid. He rode thereafter joyfully to Siegmund's land.

At all times the host bade practice knighthood, and many a youthful knight did this right gladly. Meanwhile he ordered seats prepared upon the sand before the town of Worms for those who were to visit him in the Burgundian land. At the time when they should come, fair Kriemhild heard it said that the king would hold a feasting for the sake of his dear friends. Then comely women hasted apace with robes and headgear which they were to don. The noble Uta heard tales told of the proud warriors who were to come. Then many rich dresses were taken from the press. To please her children she bade make garments ready, that many ladies and many maids might therewith be decked and many youthful knights of the Burgundian land. Also for many of the strangers she bade fashion lordly robes.

ENDNOTES:
(1) "Saxons". This war with the Saxons does not appear in the poetic "Edda", but was probably introduced into the story later to provide the heroes with a suitable activity in the period elapsing between Siegfried's marriage and the journey to Brunhild's land. (In our poem it is placed before the marriage.) It reflects the ancient feuds between the Franks on the one hand and the Saxons and Danes on the other. Originally Siegfried probably did not take part in it, but was later introduced and made the leader of the expedition in place of the king, in accordance with the tendency to idealize him and to give him everywhere the most important role. The two opposing leaders are "Liudeger", lord of the Saxons, and "Liudegast", king of Denmark. In "Biterolf" Liudeger rules over both Saxons and Danes, and Liudegast is his brother.
(2) "Fey". This Scotch and older English word has been chosen to translate the M.H.G. "veige", 'fated', 'doomed', as it is etymologically the same word. The ancient Germans were fatalists and believed only those would die in battle whom fate had so predestined.
(3) "Thirty thousand". The M.H.G. epics are fond of round numbers and especially of thirty and its multiples. They will be found to occur very frequently in our poem. See Lachmann, "Anmerkungen zu den Nibelungen", 474 1.
(4) "Their". The original is obscure here; the meaning is, 'when he heard with what message they were come, he rued the haughtiness of the Burgundians'.
(5) "Marks of gold". A mark (Lat. "mares") was half a pound of gold or silver.

25

ADVENTURE V

How Siegfried First Saw Kriemhild

One saw daily riding to the Rhine those who would fain be at the feasting. Full many of these who for the king's sake were come into the land, were given steeds and lordly harness. Seats were prepared for all, for the highest and the best, as we are told, for two and thirty princes at the feast. For this, too, the fair ladies vied in their attire. Giselher, the youth, was aught but idle; he and Gernot and all their men received the friends and strangers. In truth, they gave the knights right courtly greetings. These brought into the land many a saddle of golden red, dainty shields and lordly armor to the feasting on the Rhine. Many a wounded man was seen full merry since. Even those who lay abed in stress of wounds, must needs forget the bitterness of death. Men ceased to mourn for the weak and sick and joyed in prospect of the festal day, and how well they would fare at the feasting of the king. Pleasure without stint and overabundance of joy pervaded all the folk which there were seen. Therefore great rejoicing arose throughout the whole of Gunther's land.

Upon a Whitsun morning five thousand or more brave men, clad in glad attire, were seen going forth to the high festal tide. On all sides they vied with each other in knightly sports. The host marked well, what he already wet, how from his very heart the hero of Netherland did love his sister, albeit he had never seen her, whose comeliness men praised above all maids. Then spake the knight Ortwin to the king: "Would ye have full honor at your feast, so should ye let be seen the charming maids, who live in such high honors here in Burgundy. What were the joy of man, what else could give him pleasure, but pretty maids and noble dames? Pray let your sister go forth before the guests." To the joy of many a hero was this counsel given.

"This will I gladly do," spake then the king, and all who heard it were merry at the thought. Then bade he say to the Lady Uta and her comely daughter, that with their maidens they should come to court. From the presses they took fair raiment and whatso of rich attire was laid away. Of rings and ribbons, too, enow they had. Thus each stately maiden decked herself with zeal. Full many a youthful knight upon that day was of the mind that he was so fair to look upon for ladies, that he would not exchange this chance for the lands of any mighty king. Gladly they gazed on those whom till now they had not known. Then bade the mighty king full a hundred of his men, who were his kin and hers, escort his sister and serve her thus. These were the court retainers of the Burgundian land and carried swords in hand. Soon one saw the noble Uta coming with her child. Full hundred or more fair ladies had she taken for her train, who wore rich robes. Likewise there followed her daughter many a stately maid. When from out a bower men saw them come, there rose a mighty press of knights who had the hope, if that might be, to gaze with joy upon the noble maid. Now came she forth, the lovely fair, as doth the red of dawn from out the lowering clouds. He then was reft of many woes who bore her in his heart so long a time, when he saw the lovely maid stand forth so glorious. How shone full many a precious stone upon her robes! In lovely wise her rose-red hue appeared. Whatever one might wish, he could not but confess that never in the world had he beheld a fairer maid. As the radiant moon, whose sheen is thrown so brightly on the clouds, doth stand before the stars, so stood she now before full many a stately dame. Therefore higher rose the spirits of the comely knights. Richly appareled chamberlains marched on in front, while the high-mettled warriors forsooth must press where they might see the lovely maid. At this Lord Siegfried felt both joy and dole. To himself he thought: "How could that chance, that I should love thee? That is a foolish dream. But if I now must lose thee, then were I better dead." At thought of this his color came and went. There stood the son of Siegmund in such dainty grace, as he were limned on parchment by skillful master's art. Indeed 'twas said of him that never had so fair a knight been seen. The escort of the ladies now bade everywhere give way and many a man obeyed. These high-born hearts rejoiced full many a wight, as thus so many a noble dame appeared in courtly bearing.

Then spake Lord Gernot of Burgundy: "Dear brother Gunther, him who offered service in such kindly wise, ye should in like manner requite before these knights; nor shall I ever rue this counsel. Bid Siegfried now approach my sister, that the maid may greet him; this will ever be our gain. She who never greeted warrior shall greet him fair, that by this means we now may win the stately knight."

Then went the kinsmen of the host to fetch the hero. To the champion from Netherland they spake: "You hath the king permitted to go to court; his sister is to greet you. This hath he decreed to do you honor."

At this the lord grew blithe of mood, for in his heart he bare joy without alloy, that he thus should see fair Uta's child. With lovely grace she greeted Siegfried then, but when she saw the haughty knight stand thus before her, her cheeks flamed bright. "Be welcome, Sir Siegfried, most good and noble knight," the fair maid spake, and at this greeting his spirits mounted high. Courteously he made obeisance; she took him by the hand. How gallantly he walked by the lady's side! Upon each other this lord and lady gazed with kindling eyes. Full secretly this happed. Was perchance a white hand there fervently pressed by heart-felt love? That know I not; yet I cannot believe that this was left undone, for soon had she betrayed to him her love. Nevermore in summertide nor in the days of May bare he within his heart such lofty joy as now he gained, when hand in hand he walked with her whom he fain would call his love.

Then thought full many a knight: "Had that but happed to me, to walk thus with her hand in hand, as now I see him do, or to lie beside her, I'd bear it willingly."

Never has warrior better served to gain a queen. From whatever land the guests were come, all gazed alike upon this pair alone. She then was bidden kiss the stately man, to whom no such delight had ever happened in this world.

Then spake the king of Denmark: "Because of this high greeting many a warrior lieth wounded (this wot I well), through Siegfried's hand. God grant that he may never come again to my kingly lands."

On all sides they bade make way for Kriemhild, as thus to church one saw her go with many a valiant knight in courtly wise. Then soon the stately knight was parted from her side. Thus went she to the minster, followed by many a dame. So full of graces was this queenly maid that many a daring wish must needs be lost. Born she was to be the eyes' delight of many a knight. Siegfried scarce could wait till mass was sung. Well might he think his fortune that she did favor him, whom thus he bare in heart. Cause enow he had to love the fair.

When she came forth from out the minster, they begged the gallant knight again to bear her company, as he had done afore. Then first the lovely maid began to thank him that he had fought so gloriously before so many knights. "Now God requite you, Sir Siegfried," spake the comely maid, "that ye have brought to pass with your service, that the warriors do love you with such fealty as I hear them say."

Then upon Dame Kriemhild he began to gaze in loving wise. "I will serve them ever," spake then the knight, "and while life shall last, never will I lay my head to rest till I have done their will; and this I do, my Lady Kriemhild, to win your love."

A twelfth-night long, on each and every day, one saw the winsome maid beside the knight, when she should go to court to meet her kin. This service was done from sheer delight. A great rout of joy and pleasure was daily seen in front of Gunther's hall, without and eke within, from many a daring man. Ortwin and Hagen began to do great marvels. Whatever any wished to play, these lusty knights were fully ready; thus they became well known to all the guests and so the whole of Gunther's land was decked with honor. Those who had lain wounded were now seen coming forth; they, too, would fain have pastime with the troop and guard themselves with bucklers and hurl the shaft. Enow there were to help them, for there was great store of men.

At the feasting the host bade purvey them with the best of cheer. He kept him free from every form of blame that might befall a king; men saw him move in friendly wise among his guests. He spake: "Ye worthy knights, ere ye go hence, pray take my gifts. I am minded to deserve it of you ever. Do not disdain my goods, the which I'll share with you, as I have great desire."

Then up spake they of Denmark: "Ere we ride homeward to our land, we crave a lasting peace; we knights have need thereof, for many a one of our kinsmen lieth dead at the hands of your men-at-arms."

Liudegast, the Saxon chief, was now cured of his wounds and had recovered from the fray, though many dead they left within this land. Then King Gunther went to find Sir Siegfried; to the knight he spake: "Now tell me what to do. Our foes would fain ride early and beg for lasting peace of me and of my men. Advise me now, Knight Siegfried, what thinketh thee good to do? What the lordings offer me will I tell thee; what of gold five hundred steeds can bear, that would they gladly give me, and I set them free again."

Then spake the mighty Siegfried: "That were done but ill. Let them ride hence unhindered, but make each of the lordings give surety with his hand, that their noble knights henceforth forbear all hostile riding hither to your land."

"This counsel will I follow." Herewith they parted, and to the king's foes was told that no one craved the gold they proffered. For their loved friends at home the battle-weary warriors longed. Many a shield full of treasure was then brought forth which the king dealt out unweighed to his many friends, to each five hundred marks of gold, and to a few, still more. Gernot, the brave, had counseled Gunther this. Then they all took leave, sith they would hence. One saw the guests draw nigh to Kriemhild and also to where Dame Uta sate. Never yet were knights dismissed in better wise. Lodgings grew empty as they rode away, but still there stayed at home the king and all his kin and many a noble liegeman. Daily they were seen as they went to Lady Kriemhild. The good knight Siegfried now would likewise take his leave; he weened not to win that on which his mind was set. The king heard said that he would hence, but Giselher, the youth, quite won him from the journey.

"Whither would ye ride now, noble Siegfried? Pray tarry with the knights, I beg you, with Gunther the king and with his men. Here, too, are many comely dames whom we shall gladly let you see."

Then spake the mighty Siegfried: "Let stand the steeds. I listed to ride hence, but now will I desist. The shields, too, bear away. To my land I craved to go, in truth, but Giselher with his great love hath turned me from it."

So the valiant knight stayed on to please his friends, nor could he have fared more gentilly in any land. This happed because he daily saw Kriemhild, the fair; for the sake of her unmeasured beauty the lording stayed. With many a pastime they whiled the hours away, but still her love constrained him and often gave him dole. Because of this same love in later days the valiant knight lay pitiful in death.

ADVENTURE VI

How Gunther Fared To Isenland (1) for Brunhild

New tidings came across the Rhine. 'Twas said that yonder many a fair maid dwelt. The good king Gunther thought to win him one of these; high therefore rose the warrior's spirits. There lived a queen beyond the sea, whose like men knew not anywhere. Peerless was her beauty and great her strength. With doughty knights she shot the shaft for love. The stone she hurled afar and sprang far after it. He who craved her love must win without fail three games from this high-born dame. When the noble maid had done this passing oft, a stately knight did hear it by the Rhine. He turned his thoughts upon this comely dame, and so heroes must needs later lose their lives.

One day when the king and his vassals sate and pondered to and fro in many a wise, whom their lord might take to wife, who would be fit to be their lady and beseem the land, up spake the lord of the Rhinelands: "I will go down to the sea and hence to Brunhlld, however it may go with me. For her love I'll risk my life. I will gladly lose it and she become not my wife."

"Against that do I counsel you," spake then Siegfried, "if, as ye say, the queen doth have so fierce a wont, he who wooeth for her love will pay full dear. Therefore should ye give over the journey."

Then spake King Gunther: "Never was woman born so strong and bold that I might not vanquish her with mine own hand."

"Be still," spake Siegfried, "ye little know her strength."

"So will I advise you," spake Hagen then, "that ye beg Siegfried to share with you this heavy task. This is my rede, sith he doth know so well how matters stand with Brunhild."

The king spake: "Wilt thou help me, noble Siegfried, to woo this lovely maid? And thou doest what I pray thee and this comely dame become my love, for thy sake will I risk both life and honor."

To this Siegfried, the son of Siegmund, answered: "I will do it, and thou give me thy sister Kriemhild, the noble queen. For my pains I ask no other meed."

"I'll pledge that, Siegfried, in thy hand," spake then Gunther, "and if fair

31

Brunhild come hither to this land, I'll give thee my sister unto wife. Then canst thou live ever merrily with the fair."

This the noble warriors swore oaths to do, and so the greater grew their hardships, till they brought the lady to the Rhine. On this account these brave men must later be in passing danger. Siegfried had to take with him hence the cloak which he, the bold hero, had won 'mid dangers from a dwarf, Alberich he hight. These bold and mighty knights now made them ready for the journey. When Siegfried wore the Cloak of Darkness he had strength enow: the force of full twelve men beside his own. With cunning arts he won the royal maid. This cloak was fashioned so, that whatsoever any wrought within it, none saw him. Thus he won Brunhild, which brought him dole.

"Now tell me, good Knight Siegfried, before our trip begin, shall we not take warriors with us into Brunhild's land, that we may come with passing honors to the sea? Thirty thousand men-at-arms can soon be called."

"However many men we take," quoth Siegfried, "the queen doth use so fierce a wont that they must perish through her haughty pride. I'll give thee better counsel, O brave and worthy king. Let us fare as wandering knights adown the Rhine, and I will tell thee those that shall be of the band. In all four knights, we'll journey to the sea and thus we'll woo the lady, whatever be our fate thereafter. I shall be one of the four comrades, the second thou shalt be. Let Hagen be the third (then have we hope of life), Dankwart then the fourth, the valiant man. A thousand others durst not match us in the fight."

"Gladly would I know," spake then the king, "ere we go hence ('t would please me much), what garments we should wear before Brunhild, which would beseem us there. Pray tell this now to Gunther."

"Weeds of the very best which can be found are worn all times in Brunhild's land. We must wear rich clothes before the lady, that we feel no shame when men shall hear the tidings told."

The good knight spake: "Then will I go myself to my dear mother, if perchance I can bring it to pass that her fair maids purvey us garments which we may wear with honor before the high-born maid."

Hagen of Troneg spake then in lordly wise: "Wherefore will ye pray your mother of such service? Let your sister hear what ye have in mind, and she'll purvey you well for your journey to Brunhild's court."

Then sent he word to his sister, that he would fain see her, and Knight Siegfried, too, sent word. Ere this happed the fair had clad her passing well. That these brave men were coming, gave her little grief. Now were her attendants, too, arrayed in seemly wise. The lordings came, and when she heard the tale, from her seat she rose and walked in courtly wise to greet the noble stranger and her brother, too.

"Welcome be my brother and his comrade. I'd gladly know," so spake the maid, "what ye lords desire, sith ye be thus come to court. Pray let me hear how it standeth with you noble knights."

Then spake king Gunther: "My lady, I'll tell you now. Maugre our lofty mood, yet have we mickle care. We would ride a-wooing far into foreign lands, and for this journey we have need of costly robes."

"Now sit you down, dear brother," spake the royal maid, "and let me hear aright who these ladies be whom ye fain would woo in the lands of other kings."

By the hand the lady took the chosen knights and with the twain she walked to where she sate afore upon a couch, worked, as well I wot, with dainty figures embossed in gold. There might they have fair pastime with the ladies. Friendly glances and kindly looks passed now full oft between the twain. In his heart he bare her, she was dear to him as life. In after days fair Kriemhild became strong Siegfried's wife.

Then spake the mighty king: "Dear sister mine, without thy help it may not be. We would go for knightly pastime to Brunhild's land, and have need of princely garb to wear before the dames."

Then the noble maiden answered: "Dear brother mine, I do you now to wit, that whatever need ye have of help of mine, that stand I ready to give. Should any deny you aught, 't would please Kriemhild but ill. Most noble knights, beseech me not with such concern, but order me with lordly air to do whatso ye list. I stand at your bidding and will do it with a will." So spake the winsome maid.

"We would fain, dear sister, wear good attire, and this your noble hand shall help to choose. Your maidens then must make it fit us, for there be no help against this journey." Then spake the princess: "Now mark ye what I say. Silks I have myself; see ye that men do bring us jewels upon the shields and thus we'll work the clothes. Gunther and Siegfried, too, gave glad assent.

"Who are the comrades," spake the queen, "who shall fare with you thus clad to court?"

He spake: "I shall be one of four. My liegemen twain, Dankwart and Hagen, shall go with me to court. Now mark ye well, my lady, what I say. Each of us

33

four must have to wear for four whole days three changes of apparel and such goodly trappings that without shame we may quit Brunhild's land."

In fitting wise the lords took leave and parted hence. Kriemhild, the queen, bade thirty of her maidens who were skillful in such work, come forth from out their bowers. Silks of Araby, white as snow, and the fair silk of Zazamanc, (2) green as is the clover, they overlaid with precious stones; that gave garments passing fair. Kriemhild herself, the high-born maiden, cut them out. Whatso they had at hand of well-wrought linings from the skin of foreign fish, but rarely seen of folk, they covered now with silk, as was the wont to wear. (3) Now hear great marvels of these shining weeds. From the kingdom of Morocco and from Libya, too, they had great store of the fairest silks which the kith of any king did ever win. Kriemhild made it well appear what love she bore the twain. Sith upon the proud journey they had set their minds, they deemed ermine to be well fit. (4) Upon this lay fine silk as black as coal. This would still beseem all doughty knights at high festal tides. From out a setting of Arabian gold there shone forth many a stone. The ladies' zeal, it was not small, forsooth; in seven weeks they wrought the robes. Ready, too, were the weapons for the right good knights.

When now they all stood dight, (5) there was built for them in haste upon the Rhine a sturdy little skiff, that should bear them downward to the sea. Weary were the noble maids from all their cares. Then the warriors were told that the brave vestures they should wear were now prepared; as they had craved it, so it now was done. Then no longer would they tarry on the Rhine; they sent a message to their war-companions, if perchance they should care to view their new attire, to see if it be too long or short. All was found in fitting measure, and for this they gave the ladies thanks. All who saw them could not but aver that never in the world had they seen attire more fair. Therefore they wore it gladly at the court. None wist how to tell of better knightly weeds. Nor did they fail to give great thanks. Then the lusty knights craved leave to go, and this the lordings did in courtly wise. Bright eyes grew dim and moist thereat from weeping.

Kriemhild spake: "Dear brother, ye might better tarry here a while and pay court to other dames, where ye would not so risk your life; then would I say well done. Ye might find nearer home a wife of as high a birth."

I ween their hearts did tell them what would hap. All wept alike, no matter what men said. The gold upon their breasts was tarnished by their tears, which thick and fast coursed downward from their eyes.

She spake: "Sir Siegfried, let this dear brother of mine be commended to your fealty and troth, that naught may harm him in Brunhild's land." This the full brave knight vowed in Lady Kriemhild's hand.

34

The mighty warrior spake: "If I lose not my life, ye may be free from every care, my lady. I'll bring him to you sound again hither to the Rhine; that know of a surety." The fair maid bowed her thanks.

Men bare their gold-hued shields out to them upon the sands and brought them all their harness. One bade lead up the steeds, for they would ride away. Much weeping then was done by comely dames. The winsome maids stood at the easements. A high wind stirred the ship and sails; the proud war fellowship embarked upon the Rhine.

Then spake King Gunther: "Who shall be the captain of the ship?"

"That will I," quoth Siegfried, "I wot well how to steer you on the flood. That know, good knights, the right water ways be well known to me."

So they parted merrily from out the Burgundian land. Siegfried quickly grasped an oar and from the shore the stalwart man gan push. Bold Gunther took the helm himself, and thus the worshipful and speedy knights set forth from land. With them they took rich food and eke good wine, the best that could be found along the Rhine. Their steeds stood fair; they had good easement. Their ship rode well; scant harm did hap them. Their stout sheet-rope was tightened by the breeze. Twenty leagues they sailed, or ever came the night, with a good wind, downward toward the sea. These hard toils later brought the high-mettled warriors pain.

Upon the twelfth-day morning, as we hear say, the winds had borne them far away to Isenstein in Brunhild's land. To none save Siegfried was this known; but when King Gunther spied so many castles and broad marches, too, how soon he spake: "Pray tell me, friend Siegfried, is it known to you whose are these castles and this lordly land?"

Siegfried answered: "I know it well. It is the land and folk of Brunhild and the fortress Isenstein, as ye heard me say. Fair ladies ye may still see there to-day. Methinketh good to advise you heroes that ye be of one single mind, and that ye tell the selfsame tale. For if we go to-day before Brunhild, in much jeopardy must we stand before the queen. When we behold the lovely maiden with her train, then, ye far-famed heroes, must ye tell but this single tale: that Gunther be my master and I his man; then what he craveth will come to pass." Full ready they were for whatever he bade them vow, nor because of pride did any one abstain. They promised what he would; wherefrom they all fared well, when King Gunther saw fair Brunhild. (6)

"Forsooth I vow it less for thy sake than for thy sister's, the comely maid, who is to me as mine own soul and body. Gladly will I bring it to pass, that she become my wife."

ENDNOTES:

(1) "Isenland" translates here M.H.G. "Islant", which has, however, no connection with Iceland in spite of the agreement of the names in German. "Isen lant", the reading of the MSS. BJh, has been chosen, partly to avoid confusion, and partly to indicate its probable derivation from "Isenstein", the name of Brunhild's castle. Boer's interpretation of "Isen" as 'ice' finds corroboration in Otfrid's form "isine steina" ('ice stones', i.e. crystals) I, 1. 70. Isenstein would then mean Ice Castle. In the "Thidreksaga" Brunhild's castle is called "Saegarthr" ('Sea Garden'), and in a fairy tale (No. 93 of Grimm) "Stromberg", referring to the fact that it was surrounded by the sea. Here, too, in our poem it stands directly on the shore.

(2) "Zazamanc", a fictitious kingdom mentioned only here and a few times in Parzival, Wolfram probably having obtained the name from this passage. (See Bartsch, "Germanistische Studien", ii, 129.)

(3) "Wont to wear". In the Middle Ages costly furs and fish-skins were used as linings and covered, as here described, with silk or cloth. By fish such amphibious animals as otter and beaver were often meant.

(4) "Well fit". In this passage "wert", the reading of A and D, has been followed, instead of unwert of B and C, as it seems more appropriate to the sense.

(5) "Dight", 'arrayed'; used by Milton.

(6) "Brunhild". The following words are evidently a late interpolation, and weaken the ending, but have been translated for the sake of completeness. They are spoken by Siegfried.

ADVENTURE VII

How Gunther Won Brunhild

Meanwhile their bark had come so near the castle that the king saw many a comely maiden standing at the casements. Much it irked King Gunther that he knew them not. He asked his comrade Siegfried: "Hast thou no knowledge of these maidens, who yonder are gazing downward towards us on the flood? Whoever be their lord, they are of lofty mood."

At this Sir Siegfried spake: "I pray you, spy secretly among the high-born maids and tell me then whom ye would choose, and ye had the power."

"That will I," spake Gunther, the bold and valiant knight. "In yonder window do I see one stand in snow-white weeds. She is fashioned so fair that mine eyes would choose her for her comeliness. Had I power, she should become my wife."

"Right well thine eyes have chosen for thee. It is the noble Brunhild, the comely maid, for whom thy heart doth strive and eke thy mind and mood." All her bearing seemed to Gunther good.

When bade the queen her high-born maids go from the windows, for it behooved them not to be the mark of strangers' eyes. Each one obeyed. What next the ladies did, hath been told us since. They decked their persons out to meet the unknown knights, a way fair maids have ever had. To the narrow casements they came again, where they had seen the knights. Through love of gazing this was done.

But four there were that were come to land. Through the windows the stately women saw how Siegfried led a horse out on the sand, whereby King Gunther felt himself much honored. By the bridle he held the steed, so stately, good and fair, and large and strong, until King Gunther had sat him in the saddle. Thus Siegfried served him, the which he later quite forgot. Such service he had seldom done afore, that he should stand at any here's stirrup. Then he led his own steed from the ship. All this the comely dames of noble birth saw through the casements. The steeds and garments, too, of the lusty knights, of snow-white hue, were right well matched and all alike; the bucklers, fashioned well, gleamed in the hands of the stately men. In lordly wise they rode to Brunhild's hall, their saddles set with precious stones, with narrow martingales, from which hung bells of bright and ruddy gold. So they came to the land, as well befit their prowess, with newly sharpened spears, with well-wrought swords, the which hung down to the spurs of these stately men. The swords the bold men bore were sharp and broad. All this Brunhild, the high-born maid, espied.

With the king came Dankwart and Hagen, too. We have heard tales told of how the knights wore costly raiment, raven black of hue. Fair were their bucklers, mickle, good and broad. Jewels they wore from the land of India, the which gleamed gloriously upon their weeds. By the flood they left their skiff without a guard. Thus the brave knights and good rode to the castle. Six and eighty towers they saw within, three broad palaces, (1) and one hall well wrought of costly marble, green as grass, wherein Brunhild herself sate with her courtiers. The castle was unlocked and the gates flung wide. Then ran Brunhild's men to meet them and welcomed the strangers into their mistress' land. One bade relieve them of their steeds and shields.

Then spake a chamberlain: "Pray give us now your swords and your shining breastplates, too."

"That we may not grant you," said Hagen of Troneg; "we ourselves will bear them."

Then gan Siegfried tell aright the tale. "The usage of the castle, let me say, is such that no guests may here bear arms. Let them now be taken hence, then will all be well."

Unwillingly Hagen, Gunther's man, obeyed. For the strangers men bade pour out wine and make their lodgings ready. Many doughty knights were seen walking everywhere at court in lordly weeds. Mickle and oft were these heroes gazed upon.

Then the tidings were told to Lady Brunhild, that unknown warriors were come in lordly raiment, sailing on the flood. The fair and worthy maid gan ask concerning this. "Pray let me hear," spake the queen, "who be these unknown knights, who stand so lordly in my castle, and for whose sake the heroes have journeyed hither?"

Then spake one of the courtiers: "My lady, I can well say that never have I set eyes on any of them, but one like Siegfried doth stand among them. Him ye should give fair greetings; that is my rede, in truth. The second of their fellowship is so worthy of praise that he were easily a mighty king over broad and princely lands, and he had the power and might possess them. One doth see him stand by the rest in such right lordly wise. The third of the fellowship is so fierce and yet withal so fair of body, most noble queen. By the fierce glances he so oft doth east, I ween he be grim of thought and mood. The youngest among them is worshipful indeed. I see the noble knight stand so charmingly, with courtly bearing, in almost maiden modesty. We might all have cause for fear, had any done him aught. However blithely he doth practice chivalry, and howso fair of body he be, yet might he well make many a comely woman weep, should he e'er grow angry. He is so fashioned that in all knightly virtues he must be a bold knight and a brave."

Then spake the queen: "Now bring me my attire. If the mighty Siegfried be come unto this land through love of mine, he doth risk his life. I fear him not so sore, that I should become his wife."

Brunhild, the fair, was soon well clad. Then went there with her many a comely maid, full hundred or more, decked out in gay attire. The stately dames would gaze upon the strangers. With them there walked good knights from Isenland, Brunhild's men-at-arms, five hundred or more, who bore swords in hand. This the strangers rued. From their seats then the brave and lusty heroes rose. When that the queen spied Siegfried, now hear what the maid did speak.

"Be ye welcome, Siegfried, here in this our land! What doth your journey mean? That I fain would know."

"Gramercy, my Lady Brunhild, that ye have deigned to greet me, most generous queen, in the presence of this noble knight who standeth here before me, for he is my liege lord. This honor I must needs forswear. By birth he's from the Rhine; what more need I to say? For thy sake are we come hither. Fain would he woo thee, however he fare. Methink thee now betimes, my lord will not let thee go. He is hight Gunther and is a lordly king. An' he win thy love, he doth crave naught more. Forsooth this knight, so well beseen, did bid me journey hither. I would fain have given it over, could I have said him nay."

She spake: "Is he thy liege and thou his man, dare he assay the games which I mete out and gain the mastery, then I'll become his wife; but should I win, 't will cost you all your lives."

Then up spake Hagen of Troneg: "My lady, let us see your mighty games. It must indeed go hard, or ever Gunther, my lord, give you the palm. He troweth well to win so fair a maid."

"He must hurl the stone and after spring and cast the spear with me. Be ye not too hasty. Ye are like to lose here your honor and your life as well. Bethink you therefore rightly," spake the lovely maid.

Siegfried, the bold, went to the king and bade him tell the queen all that he had in mind, he should have no fear. "I'll guard you well against her with my arts."

Then spake King Gunther: "Most noble queen, now mete out whatso ye list, and were it more, that would I all endure for your sweet sake. I'll gladly lose my head, and ye become not my wife."

When the queen heard this speech, she begged them hasten to the games, as was but meet. She bade purvey her with good armor for the strife: a breastplate of ruddy gold and a right good shield. A silken surcoat, (2) too, the maid put on, which sword had never cut in any fray, of silken cloth of Libya. Well was it wrought. Bright embroidered edging was seen to shine thereon.

Meanwhile the knights were threatened much with battle cries. Dankwart and Hagen stood ill at ease; their minds were troubled at the thought of how the king would speed. Thought they: "Our journey will not bring us warriors aught of good."

Meanwhile Siegfried, the stately man, or ever any marked it, had hied him to the ship, where he found his magic cloak concealed. Into it he quickly slipped and so was seen of none. He hurried back and there he found a great press of knights, where the queen dealt out her lofty games. Thither he went in secret wise (by his arts it happed), nor was he seen of any that were there. The ring had been marked out, where the games should be, afore many valiant warriors, who were to view them there. More than seven hundred were seen bearing arms, who were to say who won the game.

Then was come Brunhild, armed as though she would battle for all royal lands. Above her silken coat she wore many a bar of gold; gloriously her lovely color shone beneath the armor. Then came her courtiers, who bare along a shield of ruddy gold with large broad strips as hard as steel, beneath the which the lovely maid would fight. As shield-thong there served a costly band upon which lay jewels green as grass. It shone and gleamed against the gold. He must needs be passing bold, to whom the maid would show her love. The shield the maid should bear was three spans thick beneath the studs, as we are told. Rich enow it was, of steel and eke of gold, the which four chamberlains could scarcely carry.

When the stalwart Hagen saw the shield borne forth, the knight of Troneg spake full grim of mood: "How now, King Gunther? How we shall lose our lives! She you would make your love is the devil's bride, in truth."

Hear now about her weeds; enow of these she had; she wore a surcoat of silk of Azagoue, (3) noble and costly. Many a lordly stone shone in contrast to its color on the person of the queen.

Then was brought forth for the lady a spear, sharp, heavy, and large, the which she cast all time, stout and unwieldy, mickle and broad, which on its edges cut most fearfully. Of the spear's great weight hear wonders told. Three and one half weights (4) of iron were wrought therein, the which scarce three of Brunhild's men could bear. The noble Gunther gan be sore afraid. Within his heart he thought: "What doth this mean? How could the devil from hell himself escape alive? Were I safe and sound in Burgundy, long might she live here free of any love of mine."

Then spake Hagen's brother, the valiant Dankwart: "The journey to this court doth rue me sore. We who have ever borne the name of knights, how must we lose our lives! Shall we now perish at the hands of women in these lands? It doth irk me much, that ever I came unto this country. Had but my brother Hagen his sword in hand, and I mine, too, then should Brunhild's men go softly in their overweening pride. This know for sure, they'd guard against it well. And had I sworn a peace with a thousand oaths, before I'd see my dear lord die, the comely maid herself should lose her life."

"We might leave this land unscathed," spake then his brother Hagen, "had we the harness which we sorely need and our good swords as well; then would the pride of this strong dame become a deal more soft."

What the warrior spake the noble maid heard well. Over her shoulders she gazed with smiling mouth. "Now sith he thinketh himself so brave, bring them forth their coats-of-mail; put in the warriors' hands their sharp-edged swords."

When they received their weapons as the maiden bade, bold Dankwart blushed for very joy. "Now let them play whatso they list," spake the doughty man. "Gunther is unconquered, since now we have our arms."

Mightily now did Brunhild's strength appear. Into the ring men bare a heavy stone, huge and great, mickle and round. Twelve brave and valiant men-at-arms could scarcely bear it. This she threw at all times, when she had shot the spear. The Burgundians' fear now grew amain.

"Woe is me," cried Hagen. "Whom hath King Gunther chosen for a love? Certes she should be the foul fiend's bride in hell."

Upon her fair white arm the maid turned back her sleeves; with her hands she grasped the shield and poised the spear on high. Thus the strife began. Gunther and Siegfried feared Brunhild's hate, and had Siegfried not come to Gunther's aid, she would have bereft the king of life. Secretly Siegfried went and touched his hand; with great fear Gunther marked his wiles. "Who hath touched me?" thought the valiant man. Then he gazed around on every side, but saw none standing there.

"'Tis I, Siegfried, the dear friend of thine. Thou must not fear the queen. Give me the shield from off thy hand and let me bear it and mark aright what thou dost hear me say. Make thou the motions, I will do the deeds."

When Gunther knew that it was Siegfried, he was overjoyed.

Quoth Siegfried: "Now hide thou my arts; tell them not to any man; then can the queen win from thee little fame, albeit she doth desire it. See how fearlessly the lady standeth now before thee."

Then with might and main the noble maiden hurled the spear at a shield, mickle, new, and broad, which the son of Siegelind bore upon his arm. The sparks sprang from the steel, as if the wind did blow. The edge of the mighty spear broke fully through the shield, so that men saw the fire flame forth from the armor rings. The stalwart men both staggered at the blow; but for the Cloak of Darkness they had lain there dead. From the mouth of Siegfried, the brave, gushed forth the blood. Quickly the good knight sprang back again and snatched the spear that she had driven through his shield. Stout Siegfried's hand now sent it back again. He thought: "I will not pierce the comely maid." So he reversed the point and cast it at her armor with the butt, that it rang out loudly from his mighty hand. The sparks flew from the armor rings, as though driven by the wind. Siegmund's son had made the throw with might. With all her strength she could not stand before the blow. In faith King Gunther never could have done the deed.

Brunhild, the fair, how quickly up she sprang! "Gunther, noble knight, I cry you mercy for the shot." She weened that he had done it with his strength. To her had crept a far more powerful man. Then went she quickly, angry was her mood. The noble maid and good raised high the stone and hurled it mightily far from her hand. After the cast she sprang, that all her armor rang, in truth. The stone had fallen twelve fathoms hence, but with her leap the comely maid out-sprang the throw. Then went Sir Siegfried to where lay the stone. Gunther poised it, while the hero made the throw. Siegfried was bold, strong, and tall; he threw the stone still further and made a broader jump. Through his fair arts he had strength enow to bear King Gunther with him as he sprang. The leap was made, the stone lay on the ground; men saw none other save Gunther, the knight, alone. Siegfried had banished the fear of King Gunther's death. Brunhild, the fair, waxed red with wrath. To her courtiers she spake a deal too loud, when she spied the hero safe and sound at the border of the ring: "Come nearer quickly, ye kinsmen and liegemen of mine, ye must now be subject to Gunther, the king."

Then the brave knights laid aside their arms and paid their homage at the feet of mighty Gunther from the Burgundian land. They weened that he had won the games by his own strength alone. He greeted them in loving wise; in sooth he was most rich in virtues.

Then the lovely maiden took him by the hand; full power she granted him within the land. At this Hagen, the bold and doughty knight, rejoiced him. She bade the noble knight go with her hence to the spacious palace. When this was done, they gave the warriors with their service better cheer. With good grace Hagen and Dankwart now must needs submit. The doughty Siegfried was wise enow and bare away his magic cloak. Then he repaired to where the ladies sate. To the king he spake and shrewdly did he this: "Why wait ye, good my lord? Why begin ye not the games, of which the queen doth deal so great a store? Let us soon see how they be played." The crafty man did not as though he wist not a whit thereof.

Then spake the Queen: "How hath it chanced that ye, Sir Siegfried, have seen naught of the games which the hand of Gunther here hath won?"

To this Hagen of the Burgundian land made answer. He spake: "Ye have made us sad of mind, my lady. Siegfried, the good knight, was by the ship when the lord of the Rhineland won from you the games. He knoweth naught thereof."

"Well is me of this tale," spake Siegfried, the knight, "that your pride hath been brought thus low, and that there doth live a wight who hath the power to be your master. Now, O noble maiden, must ye follow us hence to the Rhine."

Then spake the fair-fashioned maid: "That may not be. First must my kith and liegemen learn of this. Certes, I may not so lightly void my lands; my dearest friends must first be fetched."

Then bade she messengers ride on every side. She called her friends, her kinsmen, and her men-at-arms and begged them come without delay to Isenstein, and bade them all be given lordly and rich apparel. Daily, early and late, they rode in troops to Brunhild's castle.

"Welaway," cried Hagen, "what have we done! We may ill abide the coming of fair Brunhild's men. If now they come into this land in force, then hath the noble maid been born to our great rue. The will of the queen is unknown to us; what if she be so wroth that we be lost?"

Then the stalwart Siegfried spake: "Of that I'll have care. I'll not let hap that which ye fear. I'll bring you help hither to this land, from chosen knights the which till now ye have not known. Ye must not ask about me; I will fare hence. Meanwhile may God preserve your honor. I'll return eftsoon and bring you a thousand men, the very best of knights that I have ever known."

"Pray tarry not too long," spake then the king; "of your help we be justly glad."

43

He answered: "In a few short days I'll come again. Tell ye to Brunhild, that ye've sent me hence."

ENDNOTES:
(1) "Palaces". See Adventure III, note 7.
(2) "Surcoat", which here translates the M.H.G. "wafenhemde", is a light garment of cloth or silk worn above the armor.
(3) "Azagouc". See Zazamanc, Adventure VI, note 2. This strophe is evidently a late interpolation, as it contradicts the description given above.
(4) Weights. The M.H.G. "messe" (Lat. "masse") is just as indefinite as the English expression. It was a mass or lump of any metal, probably determined by the size of the melting-pot.

ADVENTURE VIII

How Siegfried Fared To His Men-At-Arms, the Nibelungs (1)

Through the gate Siegfried hied him in his Cloak of Darkness down to the sand, where he found a skiff. Secretly the son of Siegmund embarked and drove it quickly hence, as though the wind did blow it on. None saw the steersman; the bark fared fast, impelled by Siegfried's mighty strength. They weened a seldom strong wind did drive it on. Nay, it was rowed by Siegfried, the son of Siegelind, the fair. In the time of a day and night with might and main he reached a land full hundred rests (2) away, or more. The people hight Nibelungs, where he owned the mighty hoard. The hero rowed alone to a broad isle, where the lusty knight now beached the boat and made it fast full soon. To a hill he hied him, upon which stood a castle, and sought here lodgment, as way-worn travelers do. He came first to a gateway that stood fast locked. In sooth they guarded well their honor, as men still do. The stranger now gan knock upon the door, the which was closely guarded. There within he saw a giant standing, who kept the castle and at whose side lay at all times his arms. He spake: "Who is it who doth knock so rudely on the gate?"

Then bold Siegfried changed his voice and spake: "I am a knight; do up the door, else will I enrage many a one outside to-day, who would liefer lie soft and take his ease."

When Siegfried thus spake, it irked the warder. Meanwhile the giant had donned his armor and placed his helm upon his head. Quickly the mighty man snatched up his shield and opened wide the gate. How fiercely he ran at Siegfried and asked, how he durst wake so many valiant men? Huge blows were dealt out by his hand. Then the lordly stranger gan defend him, but with an iron bar the warder shattered his shield-plates. Then was the hero in dire need. Siegfried gan fear a deal his death, when the warder struck such mighty blows. Enow his master Siegfried loved him for this cause. They strove so sore that all the castle rang and the sound was heard in Nibelung's hall. He overcame the warder and bound him, too.

The tale was noised abroad in all the Nibelungs' land. Alberich, the bold, a savage dwarf, heard the fierce struggle through the mountain. He armed him quick and ran to where he found the noble stranger, as he bound the mighty giant. Full wroth was Alberich and strong enow. On his body he bare helmet and rings of mail and in his hand a heavy scourge of gold. Swift and hard he ran to where Siegfried stood. Seven heavy knobs (3) hung down in front, with which he smote so fiercely the shield upon the bold man's arm, that it brake in parts. The stately stranger came in danger of his life. From his hand he flung

45

the broken shield and thrust into the sheath a sword, the which was long. He would not strike his servant dead, but showed his courtly breeding as his knightly virtue bade him. He rushed at Alberich and with his powerful hands he seized the gray-haired man by the beard. So roughly he pulled his beard, that he screamed aloud. The tugging of the youthful knight hurt Alberich sore.

Loud cried the valiant dwarf: "Now spare my life. And might I be the vassal of any save one knight, to whom I swore an oath that I would own him as my lord, I'd serve you till my death." So spake the cunning (4) man.

He then bound Alberich as he had the giant afore. Full sore the strength of Siegfried hurt him. The dwarf gan ask: "How are ye named?"

"My name is Siegfried," he replied; "I deemed ye knew me well."

"Well is me of these tidings," spake Alberich, the dwarf. "Now have I noted well the knightly deeds, through which ye be by right the sovran of the land. I'll do whatso ye bid, and ye let me live."

Then spake Sir Siegfried: "Go quickly now and bring me the best of knights we have, a thousand Nibelungs, that they may see me here."

Why he wanted this, none heard him say. He loosed the bonds of Alberich and the giant. Then ran Alberich swift to where he found the knights. In fear he waked the Nibelung men. He spake: "Up now, ye heroes, ye must go to Siegfried."

From their beds they sprang and were ready in a trice. A thousand doughty knights soon stood well clad. They hied them to where they saw Sir Siegfried stand. Then was done a fair greeting, in part by deeds. Great store of tapers were now lit up; they proffered him mulled wine. (5) He gave them thanks that they were come so soon. He spake: "Ye must away with me across the flood."

Full ready for this he found the heroes brave and good. Well thirty hundred men were come eftsoon, from whom he chose a thousand of the best. Men brought them their helmets and other arms, for he would lead them to Brunhild's land. He spake: "Ye good knights, this will I tell you, ye must wear full costly garments there at court, for many lovely dames shall gaze upon us. Therefore must ye deck yourselves with goodly weeds."

Early on a morn they started on their way. What a speedy journey Siegfried won! They took with them good steeds and lordly harness, and thus they came in knightly wise to Brunhild's land. The fair maids stood upon the battlements. Then spake the queen: "Knoweth any, who they be whom I see sailing yonder far out upon the sea? They have rich sails e'en whiter than the snow."

Quoth the king of the Rhineland: "They're men of mine, the which I left hard by here on the way. I had them sent for, and now they be come, my lady." All eyes were fixed upon the lordly strangers.

Then one spied Siegfried standing at his vessel's prow in lordly weeds and many other men. The queen spake: "Sir King, pray tell me, shall I receive the strangers or shall I deny them greetings?"

He spake: "Ye must go to meet them out before the palace, that they may well perceive how fain we be to see them here."

Then the queen did as the king advised her. She marked out Siegfried with her greetings from the rest. Men purveyed them lodgings and took in charge their trappings. So many strangers were now come to the land, that everywhere they jostled Brunhild's bands. Now would the valiant men fare home to Burgundy.

Then spake the queen: "My favor would I bestow on him who could deal out to the king's guests and mine my silver and gold, of which I have such store."

To this Dankwart, King Giselher's liegeman, answered: "Most noble queen," spake the brave knight, "let me but wield the keys. I trow to deal it out in fitting wise; whatso of blame I gain, let be mine own." That he was bountiful, he made appear full well.

When now Sir Hagen's brother took the keys in charge, the hero's hand did proffer many a costly gift. He who craved a mark (6) received such store that all the poor might lead a merry life. Full hundred pounds he gave, nor did he stop to count. Enow walked before the hall in rich attire, who never had worn afore such lordly dress. Full sore it rued the queen when this she heard. She spake: "Sir King, I fain would have your aid, lest your chamberlain leave naught of all my store of dress; he squandereth eke my gold. If any would forfend this, I'd be his friend for aye. He giveth such royal gifts, the knight must ween, forsooth, that I have sent for death. I would fain use it longer and trow well myself to waste that which my father left me." No queen as yet hath ever had so bounteous a chamberlain.

Then spake Hagen of Troneg: "My lady, be it told you that the king of the Rhineland hath such great store of gold and robes to give, that we have no need to carry hence aught of Brunhild's weeds."

"Nay, and ye love me," spake the queen, "let me fill twenty traveling chests

47

with gold and silk as well, the which my hand shall give, when we are come across to Gunther's land."

Men filled her chests with precious stones, the while her chamberlains stood by. She would not trust the duty to Giselher's men. Gunther and Hagen began to laugh thereat.

Then spake the queen: "With whom shall I leave my lands? This my hand and yours must first decree."

Quoth the noble king: "Now bid draw near whom ye deem fit and we will make him steward."

The lady spied near by one of her highest kin (it was her mother's brother); to him the maiden spake: "Now let be commended to your care my castles and my lands, till that King Gunther's hand rule here."

Then twenty hundred of her men she chose, who should fare with her hence to Burgundy, together with those thousand warriors from the Nibelung land. They dressed their journey; one saw them riding forth upon the sand. Six and eighty dames they took along and thereto a hundred maids, their bodies passing fair. No longer now they tarried, for they were fain to get them hence. Ho, what great wail was made by those they left at home! In courtly wise she voided thus her land. She kissed her nearest kinsmen who were found at court. After a fair leave-taking they journeyed to the sea. To her fatherland the lady nevermore returned. Many kinds of games were seen upon the way; pastimes they had galore. A real sea breeze did help them on their voyage. Thus they fared forth from the land fully merrily. She would not let her husband court her on the way; this pleasure was deferred until their wedding-tide in the castle, their home, at Worms, to which in good time she came right joyfully with all her knights.

ENDNOTES:
(1) Adventure VIII. This whole episode, in which Siegfried fetches men to aid Gunther in case of attempted treachery on Brunhild's part, is of late origin and has no counterpart in the older versions. It is a further development of Siegfried's fight in which he slew Schilbung and Nibelung and became the ruler of the Nibelung land. The fight with Alberich is simply a repetition of the one in the former episode.
(2) "Rest" (M.H.G. "rast"), originally 'repose', then used as a measure of distance, as here.
(3) "Knobs", round pieces of metal fastened to the scourge.
(4) "Cunning" is to be taken here in the Biblical sense of 'knowing'. The M.H.G. "listig" which it here translates,

denotes 'skilled' or 'learned' in various arts and is a
standing epithet of dwarfs.

(5) "Mulled wine" translates M.H.G. "lutertranc", a claret
mulled with herbs and spice and left to stand until clear.

(6) "Mark". See Adventure V, note 5.

ADVENTURE IX
How Siegfried Was Sent To Worms

When they had thus fared on their way full nine days, Hagen of Troneg spake: "Now mark ye what I say. We wait too long with the tidings for Worms upon the Rhine. Our messengers should be e'en now in Burgundy."

Then spake King Gunther: "Ye have told me true, and none be more fitting for this trip than ye, friend Hagen; now ride ye to my land. None can acquaint them better with our journey home to court."

To this Hagen made answer: "I am no fit envoy. Let me play chamberlan, I'll stay with the ladies upon the flood and guard their robes, until we bring them to the Burgundian land. Bid Siegfried bear the message, he knoweth how to do it well with his mighty strength. If he refuse you the journey, then must ye in courtly and gentle wise pray him of the boon for your sister's sake."

Gunther sent now for the warrior, who came to where he stood. He spake: "Sith we be now nearing my lands at home, it behooveth me to send a messenger to the dear sister of mine and to my mother, too, that we draw near the Rhine. This I pray you, Siegfried; now do my will, that I may requite it to you ever," spake the good knight.

Siegfried, the passing bold man, however said him nay, till Gunther gan beseech him sore. He spake: "Ye must ride for my sake and for Kriemhild's too, the comely maiden, so that the royal maid requite it, as well as I."

When Siegfried heard these words, full ready was the knight. "Now bid me what ye will; naught shall be withheld. I will do it gladly for the fair maid's sake. Why should I refuse her whom I bear in heart? Whatso ye command for love of her, shall all be done."

"Then tell my mother Uta, the queen, that we be of lofty mood upon this voyage. Let my brothers know how we have fared. These tidings must ye let our friends hear, too. Hide naught from my fair sister, give her mine and Brunhild's greetings. Greet the retainers, too, and all my men. How well I have ended that for which my heart hath ever striven! And tell Ortwin, the dear nephew of mine, that he bid seats be built at Worms along the Rhine. Let my other kinsmen know that I am willed to hold with Brunhild a mighty wedding feast. And tell my sister, when she hath heard that I be come with my guests to the land, that she give fair greeting to my bride. For that I will ever render Kriemhild service."

The good Lord Siegfried soon took leave of Lady Brunhild, as beseemed him well, and of all her train; then rode he to the Rhine. Never might there be a better envoy in this world. He rode with four and twenty men-at-arms to Worms; he came without the king. When that was noised about, the courtiers all were grieved; they feared their master had been slain.

Then they dismounted from their steeds, high stood their mood. Giselher, the good young king, came soon to meet them, and Gernot his brother, too. How quickly then he spake, when he saw not Gunther at Siegfried's side: "Be welcome, Siegfried; pray let me know where ye have left the king my brother? The prowess of Brunhild, I ween, hath ta'en him from us. Great scathe had her haughty love then brought us."

"Let be this fear. My battle-comrade sendeth greetings to you and to his kin. I left him safe and sound. He sent me on ahead, that I might be his messenger with tidings hither to this land. Pray have a care, however that may hap, that I may see the queen and your sister, too, for I must let them hear what message Gunther and Brunhild have sent them. Both are in high estate."

Then spake Giselher, the youth: "Now must ye go to her, for ye have brought my much of joy. She is mickle fearful for my brother. I'll answer that the maid will see you gladly."

Then spake Sir Siegfried: "Howsoever I may serve her, that shall be gladly done, in faith. Who now will tell the ladies that I would hie me thither?"

Giselher then became the messenger, the stately man. The doughty knight spake to his mother and his sister too, when that he saw them both: "To us is come Siegfried, the hero from Netherland; him my brother Gunther hath sent hither to the Rhine. He bringeth the news of how it standeth with the king. Pray let him therefore come to court. He'll tell you the right tidings straight from Isenland."

As yet the noble ladies were acquaint with fear, but now for their weeds they sprang and dressed them and bade Sir Siegfried come to court. This he did full gladly, for he was fain to see them. Kriemhild, the noble maid, addressed him fair: "Be welcome, Sir Siegfried, most worshipful knight. Where is my brother Gunther, the noble and mighty king? We ween that we have lost him through Brunhild's strength. Woe is me, poor maid, that ever I was born."

Then spake the daring knight: "Now give me an envoy's guerdon, ye passing fair ladies, ye do weep without a cause. I do you to wit, I left him safe and

51

sound. They have sent me with the tidings to you both. He and his bride do send you kindly greetings and a kinsman's love, O noble queen. Now leave off your weeping, they'll come full soon."

In many a day she had not heard a tale so glad. With her snow-white hem she wiped the tears from her pretty eyes and began to thank the messenger for the tidings, which now were come. Thus her great sorrow and her weeping were taken away. She bade the messenger be seated; full ready he was for this. Then spake the winsome maid: "I should not rue it, should I give you as an envoy's meed my gold. For that ye are too rich, but I will be your friend in other ways."

"And had I alone," spake he, "thirty lands, yet would I gladly receive gifts from your fair hand."

Then spake the courtly maid: "It shall be done." She bade her chamberlain go fetch the meed for tidings. Four and twenty arm-rings, set with goodly gold, she gave him as his meed. So stood the hero's mood that he would not retain them, but gave them straightway to her nearest maidens, he found within the bower. Full kindly her mother offered him her service. "I am to tell you the tale," then spake the valiant man, "of what the king doth pray you, when he cometh to the Rhine. If ye perform that, my lady, he'll ever hold you in his love. I heard him crave that ye should give fair greetings to his noble guests and grant him the boon, that ye ride to meet him out in front of Worms upon the strand. This ye are right truly admonished by the king to do."

Then spake the winsome maid: "For this am I full ready. In whatsoever wise I can serve the king, that will I not refuse; with a kinsman's love it shall be done." Her color heightened for very joy. Never was the messenger of any prince received more fair. The lady would have kissed him, had she but dared. How lovingly he parted from the dames!

The men of Burgundy then did as Siegfried counseled. Sindolt and Hunolt and Rumolt, the knight, must needs be busy with the work of putting up the seats outside of Worms upon the strand. The royal stewards, too, were found at work. Ortwin and Gere would not desist, but sent to fetch their friends on every side, and made known to them the feasting that was to be. The many comely maids arrayed themselves against the feast. Everywhere the palace and the walls were decked out for the guests. Gunther's hall was passing well purveyed for the many strangers. Thus began full merrily this splendid feast.

From every side along the highways of the land pricked now the kinsmen of these three kings, who had been called that they might wait upon those who were coming home. Then from the presses great store of costly weeds was taken. Soon tidings were brought that men saw Brunhild's kinsmen ride along. Great jostling then arose from the press of folk in the Burgundian land. Ho, what bold knights were found on either side!

Then spake fair Kriemhild: "Ye maids of mine, who would be with me at the greeting, seek out from the guests the very best of robes; then will praise and honor be given us by the guests." Then came the warriors, too, and bade the lordly saddles of pure red gold be carried forth, on which the ladies should ride from Worms down to the Rhine. Better trappings might there never be. Ho, what bright gold did sparkle on the jet-black palfreys! From their bridles there gleamed forth many a precious stone. The golden stepping-blocks were brought and placed on shining carpets for the ladies, who were gay of mood. As I have said, the palfreys now stood ready in the courtyard for the noble maids. One saw the steeds wear narrow martingales of the best of silk, of which tale might be told. Six and eighty ladies who wore fillets (1) in their hair were seen come forth. The fair ones came to Kriemhild wearing glittering robes. Then followed many a comely maid in brave attire, fifty and four from the Burgundian land. They were eke the best that might anywhere be found. Men saw them walking with their flaxen hair and shining ribbons. That which the king desired was done with zeal. They wore before the stranger knights rich cloth of silk, the best that could be found, and so many a goodly robe, which well befit their ample beauty. One found there many clothes of sable and ermine fur. Many an arm and hand was well adorned with bracelets over the silken sleeves, which they should wear. None might tell the story of this tiring to the end. Many a hand played with well-wrought girdles, rich and long, above gay colored robes, over costly ferran (2) skirts of silken cloth of Araby. In high spirits were these maids of noble birth. Clasps (3) were sewed in lovely wise upon the dress of many a comely maid. She had good cause to rue it, whose bright color did not shine in contrast to her weeds. No kingly race hath now such fair retainers. When now the lovely maids had donned the garments they should wear, there then drew near a mickle band of high-mettled champions. Together with their shields they carried many an ashen spear.

ENDNOTES:
(1) "Fillets" were worn only by married women.
(2) "Ferran", a gray colored cloth of silk and wool; from O.F. "ferrandine".
(3) "Clasps" or "brooches" were used to fasten the dresses in front.

ADVENTURE X

How Brunhild Was Received At Worms

Across the Rhine men saw the king with his guests in many bands pricking to the shore. One saw the horse of many a maiden, too, led by the bridle. All those who should give them welcome were ready now. When those of Isenland and Siegfried's Nibelung men were come across in boats, they hasted to the shore (not idle were their hands), where the kindred of the king were seen upon the other bank. Now hear this tale, too, of the queen, the noble Uta, how she herself rode hither with the maidens from the castle. Then many a knight and maid became acquaint. Duke Gere led Kriemhild's palfroy by the bridle till just outside the castle gate. Siegfried, the valiant knight, must needs attend her further. A fair maid was she! Later the noble dame requited well this deed. Ortwin, the bold, rode by Lady Uta's side, and many knights and maidens rode in pairs. Well may we aver that so many dames were never seen together at such stately greeting. Many a splendid joust was ridden by worshipful knights (not well might it be left undone) afore Kriemhild, the fair, down to the ships. Then the fair-fashioned ladies were lifted from the palfreys. The king was come across and many a worthy guest. Ho, what stout lances brake before the ladies' eyes! One heard the clash of many hurtling shields. Ho, what costly bucklers rang loudly as they closed! The lovely fair stood by the shore as Gunther and his guests alighted from the boats; he himself led Brunhild by the hand. Bright gems and gleaming armor shone forth in rivalry. Lady Kriemhild walked with courtly breeding to meet Dame Brunhild and her train. White hands removed the chaplets, (1) as these twain kissed each other; through deference this was done.

Then in courteous wise the maiden Kriemhild spake: "Be ye welcome in these lands of ours, to me and to my mother and to all the loyal kin we have."

Low bows were made and the ladies now embraced full oft. Such loving greeting hath one never heard, as the two ladies, Dame Uta and her daughter, gave the bride; upon her sweet mouth they kissed her oft. When now Brunhild's ladies all were come to land, stately knights took many a comely woman by the hand in loving wise. The fair-fashioned maids were seen to stand before the lady Brunhild. Long time elasped or ever the greetings all were done; many a rose-red mouth was kissed, in sooth. Still side by side the noble princesses stood, which liked full well the doughty warriors for to see. They who had heard men boast afore that such beauty had ne'er been seen as these two dames possessed, spied now with all their eyes and must confess the truth. Nor did one see upon their persons cheats of any kind. Those who wot how to judge of women and lovely charms, praised Gunther's bride for beauty; but the wise had seen more clear and spake, that one must give Kriemhild the palm before Brunhild.

Maids and ladies now drew near each other. Many a comely dame was seen arrayed full well. Silken tents and many rich pavilions stood hard by, the which quite filled the plain of Worms. The kinsmen of the king came crowding around, when Brunhild and Kriemhild and with them all the dames were bidden go to where shade was found. Thither the knights from the Burgundian land escorted them.

Now were the strangers come to horse, and shields were pierced in many royal jousts. From the plain the dust gan rise, as though the whole land had burst forth into flames. There many a knight became well known as champion. Many a maiden saw what there the warriors plied. Methinks, Sir Siegfried and his knights rode many a turn afore the tents. He led a thousand stately Nibelungs.

Then Hagen of Troneg came, as the king had counseled, and parted in gentle wise the jousting, that the fair maids be not covered with the dust, the which the strangers willingly obeyed. Then spake Sir Gernot: "Let stand the steeds till the air grow cooler, for ye must be full ready when that the king will ride. Meanwhile let us serve the comely dames before the spacious hall."

When now over all the plain the jousts had ceased, the knights, on pastime bent, hied them to the ladies under many a high pavilion in the hope of lofty joys. There they passed the hours until they were minded to ride away.

Just at eventide, when the sun was setting and the air grew chill, no longer they delayed, but man and woman hasted toward the castle. Many a comely maiden was caressed with loving glances. In jousting great store of clothes were torn by good knights, by the high-mettled warriors, after the custom of the land, until the king dismounted by the hall. Valiant heroes helped the ladies, as is their wont. The noble queens then parted; Lady Uta and her daughter went with their train to a spacious hall, where great noise of merriment was heard on every side.

The seats were now made ready, for the king would go to table with his guests. At his side men saw fair Brunhild stand, wearing the crown in the king's domain. Royal enow she was in sooth. Good broad tables, with full many benches for the men, were set with vitaille, as we are told. Little they lacked that they should have! At the king's table many a lordly guest was seen. The chamberlains of the host bare water forth in basins of ruddy gold. It were but in vain, if any told you that men were ever better served at princes' feasts: I would not believe you that.

Before the lord of the Rhineland took the water to wash his hands, Siegfried did as was but meet, he minded him by his troth of what he had promised, or ever he had seen Brunhild at home in Isenland. He spake: "Ye must remember how ye swore me by your hand, that when Lady Brunhild came to this land, ye would give me your sister to wife. Where be now these oaths? I have suffered mickle hardship on our trip."

Then spake the king to his guest: "Rightly have ye minded me. Certes my hand shall not be perjured. I'll bring it to pass as best I can."

Then they bade Kriemhild go to court before the king. She came with her fair maidens to the entrance of the hall. At this Sir Giselher sprang down the steps. "Now bid these maidens turn again. None save my sister alone shall be here by the king."

Then they brought Kriemhild to where the king was found. There stood noble knights from many princes' lands; throughout the broad hall one bade them stand quite still. By this time Lady Brunhild had stepped to the table, too. Then spake King Gunther: "Sweet sister mine, by thy courtesie redeem my oath. I swore to give thee to a knight, and if he become thy husband, then hast thou done my will most loyally."

Quoth the noble maid: "Dear brother mine, ye must not thus entreat me. Certes I'll be ever so, that whatever ye command, that shall be done. I'll gladly pledge my troth to him whom ye, my lord, do give me to husband."

Siegfried here grew red at the glance of friendly eyes. The knight then proffered his service to Lady Kriemhild. Men bade them take their stand at each other's side within the ring and asked if she would take the stately man. In maidenly modesty she was a deal abashed, yet such was Siegfried's luck and fortune, that she would not refuse him out of hand. The noble king of Netherland vowed to take her, too, to wife. When he and the maid had pledged their troths, Siegfried's arm embraced eftsoon the winsome maid. Then the fair queen was kissed before the knights. The courtiers parted, when that had happed; on the bench over against the king Siegfried was seen to take his scat with Kriemhild. Thither many a man accompanied him as servitor; men saw the Nibelungs walk at Siegfried's side.

The king had seated him with Brunhild, the maid, when she espied Kriemhild (naught had ever irked her so) sitting at Siegfried's side. She began to weep and hot tears coursed down fair cheeks. Quoth the lord of the land: "What aileth you, my lady, that ye let bright eyes grow dim? Ye may well rejoice; my castles and my land and many a stately vassal own your sway."

"I have good cause to weep," spake the comely maid; "my heart is sore because of thy sister, whom I see sitting so near thy vassal's side. I must ever weep that she be so demeaned."

Then spake the King Gunther: "Ye would do well to hold your peace. At another time I will tell you the tale of why I gave Siegfried my sister unto wife. Certes she may well live ever happily with the knight."

She spake: "I sorrow ever for her beauty and her courtesie. I fain would flee, and I wist whither I might; go, for never will I lie close by your side, unless ye tell me through what cause Kriemhild be Siegfried's bride."

Then spake the noble king: "I'll do it you to wit; he hath castles and broad domains, as well as I. Know of a truth, he is a mighty king, therefore did I give him the peerless maid to love."

But whatsoever the king might say, she remained full sad of mood.

Now many a good knight hastened from the board. Their hurtling waxed so passing hard, that the whole castle rang. But the host was weary of his guests. Him-thought that he might lie more soft at his fair lady's side. As yet he had not lost at all the hope that much of joy might hap to him through her. Lovingly he began to gaze on Lady Brunhild. Men bade the guests leave off their knightly games, for the king and his wife would go to bed. Brunhild and Kriemhild then met before the stairway of the hall, as yet without the hate of either. Then came their retinue. Noble chamberlains delayed not, but brought them lights. The warriors, the liegemen of the two kings, then parted on either side and many of the knights were seen to walk with Siegfried.

The lords were now come to the rooms where they should lie. Each of the twain thought to conquer by love his winsome dame. This made them blithe of mood. Siegfried's pleasure on that night was passing great. When Lord Siegfried lay at Kriemhild's side and with his noble love caressed the high-born maid so tenderly, she grew as dear to him as life, so that not for a thousand other women would he have given her alone. No more I'll tell how Siegfried wooed his wife; hear now the tale of how King Gunther lay by Lady Brunhild's side. The stately knight had often lain more soft by other dames. The courtiers now had left, both maid and man. The chamber soon was locked; he thought to caress the lovely maid. Forsooth the time was still far off, ere she became his wife. In a smock of snowy linen she went to bed. Then thought the noble knight: "Now have I here all that I have ever craved in all my days." By rights she must needs please him through her comeliness. The noble king gan shroud the lights and then the bold knight hied him to where the lady lay. He laid him at her side, and great was his joy when in his arms he clasped the lovely fair. Many loving caresses he might have given, had but the noble dame allowed it. She waxed so wroth that he was sore a-troubled; he weened that they were lovers, but he found here hostile hate. She spake: "Sir

Knight, pray give this over, which now ye hope. Forsooth this may not hap, for I will still remain a maid, until I hear the tale; now mark ye that."

Then Gunther grew wroth; he struggled for her love and rumpled all her clothes. The high-born maid then seized her girdle, the which was a stout band she wore around her waist, and with it she wrought the king great wrong enow. She bound him hand and foot and bare him to a nail and hung him on the wall. She forbade him love, sith he disturbed her sleep. Of a truth he came full nigh to death through her great strength.

Then he who had weened to be the master, began to plead. "Now loose my bands, most noble queen. I no longer trow to conquer you, fair lady, and full seldom will I lie so near your side."

She reeked not how he felt, for she lay full soft. There he had to hang all night till break of day, until the bright morn shone through the casements. Had he ever had great strength, it was little seen upon him now.

"Now tell me, Sir Gunther, would that irk you aught," the fair maid spake, "and your servants found you bound by a woman's hand?"

Then spake the noble knight: "That would serve you ill; nor would it gain me honor," spake the doughty man. "By your courtesie, pray let me lie now by your side. Sith that my love mislike you so, I will not touch your garment with my hands."

Then she loosed him soon and let him rise. To the bed again, to the lady he went and laid him down so far away, that thereafter he full seldom touched her comely weeds. Nor would she have allowed it.

Then their servants came and brought them new attire, of which great store was ready for them against the morn. However merry men made, the lord of the land was sad enow, albeit he wore a crown that day. As was the usage which they had and which they kept by right, Gunther and Brunhild no longer tarried, but hied them to the minster, where mass was sung. Thither, too, Sir Siegfried came and a great press arose among the crowd. In keeping with their royal rank, there was ready for them all that they did need, their crowns and robes as well. Then they were consecrated. When this was done, all four were seen to stand joyful 'neath their crowns. Many young squires, six hundred or better, were now girt with sword in honor of the kings, as ye must know. Great joy rose then in the Burgundian land; one heard spear-shafts clashing in the hands of the sworded knights. There at the windows the fair maids sat; they saw shining afore them the gleam of many a shield. But the king had sundered him from his liegemen; whatso others plied, men saw him stand full sad. Unlike stood his and Siegfried's mood. The noble knight and good would fain

58

have known what ailed the king. He hasted to him and gan ask: "Pray let me know how ye have fared this night, Sir King."

Then spake the king to his guest: "Shame and disgrace have I won; I have brought a fell devil to my house and home. When I weened to love her, she bound me sore; she bare me to a nail and hung me high upon a wall. There I hung affrighted all night until the day, or ever she unbound me. How softly she lay bedded there! In hope of thy pity do I make plaint to thee as friend to friend."

Then spake stout Siegfried: "That rueth me in truth. I'll do you this to wit; and ye allow me without distrust, I'll contrive that she lie by you so near this night, that she'll nevermore withhold from you her love."

After all his hardships Gunther liked well this speech. Sir Siegfried spake again: "Thou mayst well be of good cheer. I ween we fared unlike last night. Thy sister Kriemhild is dearer to me than life; the Lady Brunhild must become thy wife to-night. I'll come to thy chamber this night, so secretly in my Cloud Cloak, that none may note at all my arts. Then let the chamberlains betake them to their lodgings and I'll put out the lights in the pages' hands, whereby thou mayst know that I be within and that I'll gladly serve thee. I'll tame for time thy wife, that thou mayst have her love to-night, or else I'll lose my life."

"Unless be thou embrace my dear lady," spake then the king, "I shall be glad, if thou do to her as thou dost list. I could endure it well, an' thou didst take her life. In sooth she is a fearful wife."

"I pledge upon my troth," quoth Siegfried, "that I will not embrace her. The fair sister of thine, she is to me above all maids that I have ever seen."

Gunther believed full well what Siegfried spake.

From the knightly sports there came both joy and woe; but men forbade the hurtling and the shouting, since now the ladies were to hie them to the hall. The grooms-in-waiting bade the people stand aside; the court was cleared of steeds and folk. A bishop led each of the ladies, as they should go to table in the presence of the kings. Many a stately warrior followed to the seats. In fair hope the king sate now full merrily; well he thought on that which Siegfried had vowed to do. This one day thought him as long as thirty days, for all his thoughts were bent upon his lady's love. He could scarce abide the time to leave the board. Now men let fair Brunhild and Kriemhild, too, both go to their rest. Ho, what doughty knights were seen to walk before the queens!

The Lord Siegfried sate in loving wise by his fair wife, in bliss without alloy. With her snow-white hands she fondled his, till that he vanished from before her eyes, she wist not when. When now she no longer spied him, as she toyed, the queen spake to his followers: "Much this wondereth me, whither the king be gone. Who hath taken his hands from mine?"

She spake no other word, but he was gone to where he found many grooms of the chamber stand with lights. These he gan snuff out in the pages' hands. Thus Gunther knew that it was Siegfried. Well wist he what he would; he bade the maids and ladies now withdraw. When that was done, the mighty king himself made fast the door and nimbly shoved in place two sturdy bolts. Quickly then he hid the lights behind the hangings of the bed. Stout Siegfried and the maiden now began a play (for this there was no help) which was both lief and loth to Gunther. Siegfried laid him close by the high-born maid. She spake: "Now, Gunther, let that be, and it be lief to you, that ye suffer not hardship as afore."

Then the lady hurt bold Siegfried sore. He held his peace and answered not a whit. Gunther heard well, though he could not see his friend a bit, that they plied not secret things, for little ease they had upon the bed. Siegfried bare him as though he were Gunther, the mighty king. In his arms he clasped the lovely maid. She cast him from the bed upon a bench near by, so that his head struck loudly against the stool. Up sprang the valiant man with all his might; fain would he try again. When he thought now to subdue her, she hurt him sore. Such defense, I ween, might nevermore be made by any wife.

When he would not desist, up sprang the maid. "Ye shall not rumple thus my shift so white. Ye are a clumsy churl and it shall rue you sore, I'll have you to know fall well," spake the comely maid. In her arms she grasped the peerless knight; she weened to bind him, as she had done the king, that she might have her case upon the bed. The lady avenged full sore, that he had rumpled thus her clothes. What availed his mickle force and his giant strength? She showed the knight her masterly strength of limb; she carried him by force (and that must needs be) and pressed him rudely 'twixt a clothes-press and the wall.

"Alas," so thought the knight, "if now I lose my life at a maiden's hands, then may all wives hereafter bear towards their husbands haughty mien, who would never do it else."

The king heard it well and feared him for his liegeman's life. Siegfried was sore ashamed; wrathful he waxed and with surpassing strength he set himself against her and tried it again with Lady Brunhild in fearful wise. It thought the king full long, before he conquered her. She pressed his hands, till from her strength the blood gushed forth from out the nails: this irked the hero. Therefore he brought the highborn maiden to the pass that she gave over her unruly will, which she asserted there afore. The king heard all, albeit not a word he spake. Siegfried pressed her against the bed, so that she shrieked aloud. Passing sore his strength did hurt her. She grasped the girdle around

60

her waist and would fain have bound him, but his hand prevented it in such a wise that her limbs and all her body cracked. Thus the strife was parted and she became King Gunther's wife.

She spake: "Most noble king, pray spare my life. I'll do thee remedy for whatso I have done thee. I'll no longer struggle against thy noble love, for I have learned full well that thou canst make thee master over women."

Siegfried let the maiden be and stepped away, as though he would do off his clothes. From her hand he drew a golden finger ring, without that she wist it, the noble queen. Thereto he took her girdle, a good stout band. I know not if he did that for very haughtiness. He gave it to his wife and rued it sore in after time.

Then lay Gunther and the fair maid side by side. He played the lover, as beseemed him, and thus she must needs give over wrath and shame. From his embrace a little pale she grew. Ho, how her great strength failed through love! Now was she no stronger than any other wife. He caressed her lovely form in lover's wise. Had she tried her strength again, what had that availed? All this had Gunther wrought in her by his love. How right lovingly she lay beside him in bridal joy until the dawn of day!

Now was Sir Siegfried gone again to where he was given fair greetings by a woman fashioned fair. He turned aside the question she had thought to put and hid long time from her what he had brought, until she ruled as queen within his land. How little he refused to give her what he should!

On the morn the host was far cheerier of mood than he had been afore. Through this the joy of many a noble man was great in all his lands, whom he had bidden to his court, and to whom he proffered much of service. The wedding feast now lasted till the fourteenth day, so that in all this while the sound never died away of the many joys which there they plied. The cost to the king was rated high. The kinsmen of the noble host gave gifts in his honor to the strolling folk, as the king commanded: vesture and ruddy gold, steeds and silver, too. Those who there craved gifts departed hence full merrily. Siegfried, the lord from Netherland, with a thousand of his men, gave quite away the garments they had brought with them to the Rhine and steeds and saddles, too. Full well they wot how to live in lordly wise. Those who would home again thought the time too long till the rich gifts had all been made. Nevermore have guests been better eased. Thus ended the wedding feast; Gunther, the knight, would have it so.

ENDNOTES:
(1) "Chaplet" (O.F. "chaplet", dim. of "chapel", M.H.G. "schapel" or "schapelin") or wreath was the headdress especially of unmarried girls, the hair being worn flowing.

It was often of flowers or leaves, but not infrequently of gold and silver. (See Weinhold, "Deutsche Frauen im Mittelalter", i, 387.)

ADVENTURE XI

How Siegfried Journeyed Homeward With His Wife

When now the strangers had all ridden hence, Siegmund's son spake to his fellowship: "We must make us ready, too, to journey to my lands."

Lief was it to his wife, when the lady heard the tale aright. She spake to her husband: "When shall we ride? I pray thee, make me not haste too sore. First must my brothers share their lands with me."

It was loth to Siegfried, when he heard this from Kriemhild. The lordings hied them to him and all three spake: "Now may ye know, Sir Siegfried, that our true service be ever at your bidding till our death."

Then he made obeisance to the knights, as it was proffered him in such kindly wise. "We shall share with you," spake Giselher, the youth, "both land and castles which we do own and whatever broad realms be subject to our power. Of these ye and Kriemhild shall have a goodly share."

The son of Siegmund spake to the princes, as he heard and saw the lordings' will: "God grant that ye be ever happy with your heritage and the folk therein. My dear bride can well forego in truth the share which ye would give. There where she shall wear a crown, she shall be mightier than any one alive, and live to see the day. For whatsoever else ye do command, I stand ready to your bidding."

Then spake the Lady Kriemhild: "Though ye forego my heritage, yet is it not so light a matter with the Burgundian men-at-arms. A king might gladly lead them to his land. Forsooth my brothers' hands must share them with me."

Then spake the Lord Gernot: "Now take whomsoever thou dost wish. Thou wilt find here really a one who'll gladly ride with thee. We will give thee a thousand of our thirty hundred warriors; be they thy court retainers."

Kriemhild then gan send for Hagen of Troneg and also for Ortwin, to ask if they and their kinsfolk would be Kriemhild's men.

At this Hagen waxed wonderly wroth. He spake: "Certes, Gunther may not give us to any in the world. Let others follow as your train. Ye know full well

63

the custom of the men of Troneg: we must in duty bound remain here with the kings at court. We must serve them longer, whom we till now have followed."

They gave that over and made them ready to ride away. Lady Kriemhild gained for herself two and thirty maids and five hundred men, a noble train. The Margrave Eckewart (1) followed Kriemhild hence. They all took leave, both knights and squires and maids and ladies, as was mickle right. Anon they parted with a kiss and voided merrily King Gunther's land. Their kinsmen bare them company far upon the way and bade them pitch their quarters for the night, whereso they listed, throughout the princes' land.

Then messengers were sent eftsoon to Siegmund, that he might know, and Siegelind, too, that his son would come with Lady Uta's child, Kriemhild, the fair, from Worms beyond the Rhine. Liefer tidings might they never have. "Well for me," spake then Siegmund, "that I have lived to see fair Kriemhild here as queen. My heritage will be thereby enhanced. My son, the noble Siegfried, shall himself be king."

Then the Lady Siegelind gave much red velvet, silver, and heavy gold; this was the envoy's meed. The tale well liked her, which then she heard. She clad her and her handmaids with care, as did beseem them. Men told who was to come with Siegfried to the land. Anon they bade seats be raised, where he should walk crowned before his friends. King Siegmund's liegemen then rode forth to meet him. Hath any been ever better greeted than the famous hero in Siegmund's land, I know not. Siegelind, the fair, rode forth to meet Kriemhild with many a comely dame (lusty knights did follow on behind), a full day's journey, till one espied the guests. Home-folk and the strangers had little easement till they were come to a spacious castle, hight Xanten, (2) where they later reigned.

Smilingly Siegelind and Siegmund kissed Kriemhild many times for joy and Siegfried, too; their sorrow was taken from them. All their fellowship received great welcome. One bade now bring the guests to Siegmund's hall, and lifted the fair young maids down from the palfreys. Many a knight gan serve the comely dames with zeal. However great the feasting at the Rhine was known to be, here one gave the heroes much better robes than they had worn in all their days. Of their splender great marvels might be told. When now they sate in lofty honors and had enow of all, what gold-hued clothes their courtiers wore with precious stones well worked thereon! Thus did Siegelind, the noble queen, purvey them well.

Then to his friends Lord Siegmund spake: "I do all Siegfried's kin to wit, that he shall wear my crown before these knights." Those of Netherland heard full fain the tale. He gave his son the crown, the cognizance, (3) and lands, so that he then was master of them all. When that men went to law and Siegfried

64

uttered judgment, that was done in such a wise that men feared sore fair Kriemhild's husband.

In these high honors Siegfried lived, of a truth, and judged as king, till the tenth year was come, when his fair lady bare a son. This was come to pass after the wish of the kinsmen of the king. They hastened to baptize and name him Gunther for his uncle; nor had he need to be ashamed of this. Should he grow like to his kinsman, he would fare full well. They brought him up with care, as was but due. In these same times the Lady Siegelind died, and men enow made wail when death bereft them of her. Then the child of the noble Uta held withal the power over the lands, which well beseemed such high-born dames. (4)

Now also by the Rhine, as we hear tell, at mighty Gunther's court, in the Burgundian land, Brunhild, the fair, had born a son. For the hero's sake they named him Siegfried. With what great care they bade attend him! The noble Gunther gave him masters who well wot how to bring him up to be a doughty man. Alas, what great loss of kin he later suffered through misfortune!

Many tales were told all time, of how right worshipfully the lusty knights dwelt alway in Siegmund's land. Gunther dealt the same with his distinguished kin. The Nibelung land and Schilbung's knights and the goods of both served Siegfried here (none of his kinsmen ever waxed mightier than he). So much the higher rose the mood of the valiant man. The very greatest heard that any hero ever gained, save those who owned it aforetime, the bold man had, the which he had won by his own hand hard by a hill, and for which he did many a lusty knight to death. He had honors to his heart's desire, and had this not been so, yet one must rightly aver of the noble champion, that he was one of the best that ever mounted horse. Men feared his might and justly, too.

ENDNOTES:
(1) "Eckewart", see Adventure I, note 15.
(2) "Xanten", see Adventure II, note 3.
(3) "Cognizance", 'jurisdiction.'
(4) "Dames", i.e., Siegelind and Kriemhild.

ADVENTURE XII

How Gunther Bade Siegfried To The Feasting

Now Gunther's wife thought alway: "How haughtily doth Lady Kriemhild bear her! Is not her husband Siegfried our liegeman? Long time now hath he done us little service." This she bare within her heart, but held her peace. It irked her sore that they did make themselves such strangers and that men from Siegfried's land so seldom served her. Fain would she have known from whence this came. She asked the king if it might hap that she should see Kriemhild again. Secretly she spake what she had in mind. The speech like the king but moderately well. "How might we bring them," quoth he, "hither to our land? That were impossible, they live too far away; I dare not ask them this."

To this Brunhild replied in full crafty wise: "However high and mighty a king's vassal be, yet should he not leave undone whatsoever his lord command him."

King Gunther smiled when she spake thus. However oft he saw Siegfried, yet did he not count it to him as service.

She spake: "Dear lord, for my sake help me to have Siegfried and thy sister come to this land, that we may see them here. Naught liefer might ever hap to me in truth. Whenso I think on thy sister's courtesie and her well-bred mind, how it delighteth me! How we sate together, when I first became thy wife! She may with honor love bold Siegfried."

She besought so long, till the king did speak: "Now know that I have never seen more welcome guests. Ye need but beg me gently. I will send my envoys for the twain, that they may come to see us to the Rhine."

Then spake the queen: "Pray tell me then, when ye are willed to send for them, or in what time our dear kinsmen shall come into the land. Give me also to know whom ye will send thither."

"That will I," said the prince. "I will let thirty of my men ride thither."

He had these come before him and bade them carry tidings to Siegfried's land. To their delight Brunhild did give them full lordly vesture.

Then spake the king: "Ye knights must say from me all that I bid you to mighty

66

Siegfried and the sister of mine; this must ye not conceal: that no one in the world doth love them more, and beg them both to come to us to the Rhine. For this I and my lady will be ever at your service. At the next Midsummer's Day shall he and his men gaze upon many here, who would fain do them great honor. Give to the king Siegmund my greetings, and say that I and my kinsmen be still his friends, and tell my sister, too, that she fail not to ride to see her kin. Never did feasting beseem her better."

Brunhild and Uta and whatever ladies were found at court all commended their service to the lovely dames and the many valiant men in Siegfried's land. With the consent of the kinsmen of the king the messengers set forth. They rode as wandering knights; their horses and their trappings had now been brought them. Then they voided the land, for they had haste of the journey, whither they would fare. The king bade guard the messengers well with convoys. In three weeks they came riding into the land, to Nibelung's castle, in the marches of Norway, (1) whither they were sent. Here they found the knight. The mounts of the messengers were weary from the lengthy way.

Both Siegfried and Kriemhild were then told that knights were come, who wore such clothes as men were wont to wear at Burgundy. She sprang from a couch on which she lay to rest and bade a maiden hie her to the window. In the court she saw bold Gere standing, him and the fellowship that had been sent thither. What joyful things she there found against her sorrow of heart! She spake to the king: "Now behold where they stand, who walk in the court with the sturdy Gere, whom my brother sendeth us adown the Rhine."

Spake Then the valiant Siegfried: "They be welcome to us."

All the courtiers ran to where one saw them. Each of them in turn then spake full kindly, as best he could to the envoys. Siegmund, the lord, was right blithe of their coming. Then Gere and his men were lodged and men bade take their steeds in charge. The messengers then went hence to where Lord Siegfried sate by Kriemhild. This they did, for they had leave to go to court. The host and his lady rose from their seats at once and greeted well Gere of the Burgundian land with his fellowship, Gunther's liegemen. One bade the mighty Gere go and sit him down.

"Permit us first to give our message, afore we take our seats; let us way-worn strangers stand the while. We be come to tell you tidings which Gunther and Brunhild, with whom all things stand well, have sent you, and also what Lady Uta, your mother, sendeth. Giselher, the youth, and Sir Gernot, too, and your dearest kin, they have sent us hither and commend their service to you from out the Burgundian land."

"Now God requite them," quoth Siegfried; "I trow them much troth and good, as one should to kinsfolk; their sister doth the same. Ye must tell us more, whether our dear friends at home be of good cheer? Since we have been parted from them, hath any done amiss to my lady's kinsmen? That ye must let me know. If so, I'll ever help them bear it in duty bound, until their foes must rue my service."

Then spake the Margrave Gere, a right good knight: "They are in every virtue of such right high mood, that they do bid you to a feasting by the Rhine. They would fain see you, as ye may not doubt, and they do beg my lady that she come with you, when the winter hath taken an end. They would see you before the next Midsummer's Day."

Quoth the stalwart Siegfried: "That might hardly hap."

Then answered Gere from the Burgundian land: "Your mother Uta, Gernot, and Giselher have charged you, that ye refuse them not. I hear daily wail, that ye do live so far away. My Lady Brunhild and all her maids be fain of the tidings, if that might be that they should see you again; this would raise their spirits high." These tidings thought fair Kriemhild good.

Gere was of their kin; the host bade him be seated and had wine poured out for the guests; no longer did they tarry. Now Siegmund was come to where he saw the messengers. The lord said to the Burgundians in friendly wise: "Be welcome, Sir Knights, ye men of Gunther. Sith now Siegfried, my son, hath won Kriemhild to wife, one should see you more often here in this our land, if ye would show your kinship."

They answered that they would gladly come, when so he would. Of their weariness they were cased with joyous pastime. Men bade the messengers be seated and brought them food, of which Siegfried had them given great store. They must needs stay there full nine days, till at last the doughty knights made plaint, that they durst not ride again to their land.

Meantime king Siegfried had sent to fetch his friends; he asked them what they counseled, whether or no they should to the Rhine. "My kinsman Gunther and his kin have sent to fetch me for a feasting. Now I would go full gladly, but that his land doth lie too far away. They beg Kriemhild, too, that she journey with me. Now advise, dear friends, in what manner she shall ride thither. Though I must harry for them through thirty lands, yet would Siegfried's arm fain serve them there."

Then spake his warriors: "And ye be minded to journey to the feasting, we will advise what ye must do. Ye should ride to the Rhine with a thousand knights, then can ye stand with worship there in Burgundy land."

Up spake then Lord Siegmund of Netherland: "Will ye to the feasting, why make ye it not known to me? If ye scorn it not, I will ride thither with you and will take a hundred knights, wherewith to swell your band."

"And will ye ride with us, dear father mine," quoth brave Siegfried, "glad shall I be of that. Within a twelfth night I will quit my lands."

All who craved it were given steeds and vesture, too.

Since now the noble king was minded for the journey, men bade the good and speedy envoys ride again. He sent word to his wife's kindred on the Rhine, that he would full fain be at their feasting. Siegfried and Kriemhild, as the tale doth tell, gave the messengers such store of gifts that their horses could not bear them to their native land. A wealthy man was he. They drove their sturdy sumpters merrily along.

Siegfried and Siegmund arrayed their men. Eckewart, the margrave, that very hour bade seek out ladies' robes, the best that were at hand or might be found throughout all Siegfried's land. Men gan prepare the saddles and the shields. To knights and ladies who should go hence with him was given whatso they would, so that they wanted naught. He brought to his kinsfolk many a lordly stranger.

The messengers pricked fast upon their homeward way. Now was Gere, the knight, come to Burgundy and was greeted fair. Then they dismounted from their steeds and from the nags in front of Gunther's hall. Young and old did hie them, as people do, to ask the tidings. Quoth the good knight: "When I tell them to the king, thou be at hand a hear."

With his fellowship he went to where he found King Gunther. For very joy the king sprang from his seat. Fair Brunhild cried them mercy, that they were come so quick. Gunther spake to the envoys: "How fareth Siegfried, from whom so much of gladness hath happed to me?"

Brave Gere spake: "He blushed for joy, he and your sister; no truer tidings did ever any man send to friends, than the Lord Siegfried and his father, too, have sent to you."

Then to the margrave spake the noble queen: "Now tell me, cometh Kriemhild to us? Hath the fair still kept the graces which she knew how to use?"

"She cometh to you surely," quoth Gere, the knight.

Then Uta bade the messenger come quickly to her. By her question one might note full well that she was fain to hear if Kriemhild still were well. He told how he had found her and that she would shortly come. Nor were the gifts concealed by them at court, which Siegfried gave them, gold and vesture; these they brought for the vassals of the three kings to see. For their passing great bounty men gave them thanks.

"He may lightly give great gifts," spake then Hagen; "he could not squander all his wealth, and he should live for aye. His hand hath closed upon the hoard of the Nibelungs. Ho, let him only come to the Burgundian land!"

All the courtiers were glad that they should come. Early and late the men of the three kings were busy. Many benches they gan raise for the folk. The valiant Hunolt and the knight Sindolt had little rest. All time they had to oversee the stewards and the butlers and raise many a bench. Ortwin helped them, too, at this, and Gunther said them thanks. Rumolt, the master cook, how well he ruled his underlings! Ho, how many a broad kettle, pot, and pan they had! They made ready the vitaille for those who were coming to the land.

ENDNOTES:
(1) "Norway". The interpolated character of the Adventures XI to XIII, which are not found in the earlier versions, is shown by the confusion in the location of Siegfried's court. The poet has forgotten that Xanten is his capital, and locates it in Norway. No mention is made, however, of the messengers crossing the sea; on the contrary, Kriemhild speaks of their being sent down the Rhine.

ADVENTURE XIII

How They Journeyed To The Feasting

Let us now take leave of all their bustling, and tell how Lady Kriemhild and her maidens journeyed from the Nibelung land down toward the Rhine. Never did sumpters bear so much lordly raiment. They made ready for the way full many traveling chests. Then Siegfried, the knight, and the queen as well, rode forth with their friends to where they had hope of joys. Later it sped them all to their great harm. They left Siegfried's little child, Kriemhild's son, at home. That must needs be. Great grief befell him through their journey to the court. The bairn never saw his father and his mother more. With them, too, there rode Lord Siegmund. Had he known aright how he would fare at the feasting, no whit of it would he have seen. No greater woe might ever hap to him in loving friends.

Messengers were sent ahead, who told the tale. Then with a stately band there rode to meet them many of Uta's kith and Gunther's liegemen. The host gan bestir him for his guests. He went to where Brunhild sate and asked: "How did my sister greet you when ye came to our land? In like manner must ye greet Siegfried's wife."

"That will I gladly," quoth she, "for I have good cause to be her friend."

The mighty king spake further: "They come to us early on the morrow; if ye would greet them, set quickly to work, that we abide them not within the castle. At no time have such welcome guests ever come to see me."

At once she bade her maids and ladies hunt out goodly raiment, the best they had, the which her train should wear before the guests. One may lightly say, they did this gladly. Gunther's men hasted also for to serve them, and around him the host did gather all his knights. Then the queen rode forth in princely wise and mickle greeting of the welcome guests was done. With what great joy did they receive them! It thought them as though Lady Kriemhild had not greeted Lady Brunhild so fair in the Burgundian land. Those who had never seen her became acquaint with lofty mood.

Now was Siegfried come with his liegemen. One saw the heroes wending to and fro upon the plain in unwieldy bands. None might guard him there against the jostling and the dust.

When that the ruler of the land spied Siegfried and Siegmund, how lovingly he spake: "Now be ye full welcome to me and all my friends; we shall be of good cheer because of this your journey to our court."

"Now God requite you," quoth Siegmund, the honor-seeking man; "sith my son Siegfried won you to kinsman, my heart hath urged that I should go to see you."

At this spake Gunther: "Now hath joy happed to me thereby."

Siegfried was received with much great worship as beseemed him; none bare him hatred there. Giselher and Gernot helped thereby with great courtesie. I ween, never have guests been greeted in such goodly wise.

Then the wives of the two kings drew near each other. Emptied were many saddles, as fair ladies were lifted down by knightly hands upon the sward. How busy were those who gladly served the dames! The lovely women now drew near each other, and many a knight was blithe, that such fair greeting passed between the twain. Then one saw great press of warriors standing by the high-born maids. The lordly meiny (1) grasped each other by the hand. Much courteous bowing was seen and loving kisses from fair-fashioned dames. This liked well Gunther's and Siegfried's liegemen for to see. They bided now no longer, but rode to town. The host bade show his guests full well that all were fain to see them in the Burgundian land. Many a royal joust took place before the high-born maids. Hagen of Troneg and Ortwin, too, proved full well their prowess. One durst not leave undone whatso they would command. Much service was rendered by them to the welcome guests. Many shields were heard resound from thrusts and blows before the castle gate. The host and his guests tarried long time without, or ever they came within. Forsooth the hours passed quickly for them with their sports. Merrily they rode before the royal palace. Many cunning housings (2) of good cloth and well cut were seen hanging on either side from the saddles of the fair-fashioned dames.

Then came Gunther's liegemen. Men bade lead the strangers quickly to their easement. At times one saw Brunhild glance at Lady Kriemhild, who was passing fair enow. Her color against the gold gave back the gleam in lovely wise. On every side in Worms one heard the courtiers shout. Gunther bade Dankwart, his marshal, have them in his care, who then gan lodge the retinue in goodly wise. One let them eat within and eke without. Never were stranger guests better cared for. Men gave them gladly all they craved; so rich was the king, that not a wish was there denied. Men served them in friendly wise without all hate. The host now took his seat at table with his guests. One bade Siegfried be seated where he sate afore. Then many a stately man went with him to the seats. Twelve hundred warriors in sooth did sit at his round table.

Brunhild thought her that a vassal could not be mightier than he; yet she was still so friendly to him that she did not wish his death.

On an evening when the king was seated at the board, many costly robes were wet with wine, as the butlers hied them to the tables. Full service was given there with mickle zeal. As hath long been the wont at feasts, men bade the ladies and the maids be given fair lodgment. From wherever they were come, the host bare them right good will. One gave them all enow with goodly honors.

When the night had an end and the day appeared, many a precious stone from the sumpter chests sparkled on goodly weeds, as they were touched by woman's hand. Many a lordly robe was taken forth. Or ever the day had fully dawned, many knights and squires came out before the hall. Then rose a merry rout before the early mass, which was sung for the king. There young heroes rode so well that the king did cry them mercy. Many a trumpet rang out passing loud, and the noise of drums and flutes did grow so great that the broad town of Worms reechoed with the sound. The high-mettled heroes horsed them everywhere. Then there rose in the land high knightly play from many a doughty champion; one saw a great rout of them whose youthful hearts beat high, and many a dapper knight and a good stood armed with shield. At the easements sate the high-born dames and many comely maids, decked out in brave attire. They watched the pastimes of the many valiant men. The host himself gan tilt there with his friends. Thus they passed the time, the which seemed aught but long.

Then from the dome was heard the sound of many bells. The palfreys came, the ladies rode away; but many a bold man followed the noble queens. They alighted on the green before the minster; Brunhild was still friendly to her guests. Wearing crowns, they entered the spacious church. Later their love was parted, which caused great hate. When they had heard the mass, they rode away again with many honors and were soon seen going merrily to table. Their pleasure at the feasting did not flag until the eleventh day.

ENDNOTES:
(1) "Meiny" (M.E. "meiny", O.F. "mesnee"), 'courtiers', 'serving folk'.
(2) "Housings", 'saddle cloths'.

On a day before the vesper tide a great turmoil arose, which many knights made in the court, where they plied their knightly sports for pastime's sake, and a great throng of men and women hasted there to gaze. The royal queens had sat them down together and talked of two worshipful knights.

Then spake the fair Kriemhild: "I have a husband who by right should rule over all these kingdoms."

Quoth Lady Brunhild: "How might that be? If none other lived but he and thou, then might these kingdoms own his sway, but the while Gunther liveth, this may never hap."

Kriemhild replied: "Now dost thou see, how he standeth, how right royally he walketh before the knights, as the moon doth before the stars? Therefore must I needs be merry of mood."

Said Lady Brunhild: "However stately be thy husband, howso worthy and fair, yet must thou grant the palm to Knight Gunther, the noble brother of thine. Know of a truth, he must be placed above all kings."

Then Kriemhild spake again: "So doughty is my husband, that I have not lauded him without good cause. His worship is great in many things. Dost thou believe it, Brunhild, he is easily Gunther's peer."

"Forsooth thou must not take it amiss of me, Kriemhild, for I have not spoken thus without good reason. I heard them both aver, when I saw them first of all, and the king was victor against me in the games, and when he won my love in such knightly wise, that he was liegeman to the king, and Siegfried himself declared the same. I hold him therefore as my vassal, sith I heard him speak thus himself."

Then spake fair Kriemhild: "Ill had I then sped. How could my noble brothers have so wrought, that I should be a mere vassal's bride? Therefore I do beseech thee, Brunhild, in friendly wise, that for my sake thou kindly leave off this speech."

"I'll not leave it off," quoth the king's wife. "Why should I give up so many a knight, who with the warrior doth owe us service?"

Kriemhild, the passing fair, waxed wroth out of wit. "Thou must forego that ho ever do you a vassal's service; he is worthier than my brother Gunther, the full noble man. Thou must retract what I have heard thee say. Certes, it wondereth me, sith he be thy vassal and thou hast so much power over us twain, why he hath rendered thee no tribute so long a time. By right I should be spared thy overweening pride."

"Thou bedrest thee too high," spake the king's wife. "I would fain see whether men will hold thee in such high honor as they do me."

The ladies both grew wonderly wroth of mood. Then spake the Lady Kriemhild: "This must now hap. Sith thou hast declared my husband for thy liegeman, now must the men of the two kings perceive to-day whether I durst walk before the queen to church. Thou must see to-day that I am noble and free and that my husband is worthier than thine; nor will I myself be taxed therewith. Thou shalt mark to-day how thy liegewoman goeth to court before the knights of the Burgundian land. I myself shall be more worshipful than any queen was known to be, who ever wore a crown." Great hate enow rose then betwixt the ladies.

Then Brunhild answered: "Wilt thou not be a liegewoman of mine, so must thou sunder thee with thy ladies from my train when that we go to church."

To this Kriemhild replied: "In faith that shall be done."

"Now array you, my maids," spake Siegfried's wife. "I must be here without reproach. Let this be seen to-day, and ye do have rich weeds. Brunhild shall fain deny what she hath here averted."

They needed not much bidding, but sought rich robes and many a dame and maid attired her well. Then the wife of the noble king went forth with her train. Fair Kriemhild, too, was well arrayed and three and forty maidens with her, whom she had brought hither to the Rhine. They wore bright vesture wrought in Araby, and thus the fair-fashioned maids betook them to the minster. All Siegfried's men awaited them before the house. The folk had marvel whence it chanced that the queens were seen thus sundered, so that they did not walk together as afore. From this did many a warrior later suffer dire distress. Here before the minster stood Gunther's wife, while many a good knight had pastime with the comely dames whom they there espied.

Then came the Lady Kriemhild with a large and noble train. Whatever kind of clothes the daughters of noble knights have ever worn, these were but the wind against her retinue. She was so rich in goods, that what the wives of thirty kings could not purvey, that Kriemhild did. An' one would wish to, yet he could not aver that men had ever seen such costly dresses as at this time her fair-fashioned maidens wore. Kriemhild had not done it, save to anger Brunhild. They met before the spacious minster. Through her great hate the mistress of the house in evil wise bade Kriemhild stand: "Forsooth no vassaless should ever walk before the queen."

Then spake fair Kriemhild (angry was her mood): "Couldst thou have held thy peace, 'twere well for thee. Thou hast disgraced thee and the fair body of thine. How might a vassal's leman (1) ever be the wife of any king?"

"Whom callest thou here leman?" spake the queen.

"That call I thee," quoth Kriemhild. "Thy fair person was first caressed by Siegfried, my dear husband. Certes, it was not my brother who won thy maidhood. Whither could thy wits have wandered? It was an evil trick. Wherefore didst thou let him love thee, sith he be thy vassal? I hear thee make plaint without good cause," quoth Kriemhild.

"I' faith," spake then Brunhild, "Gunther shall hear of this."

"What is that to me?" said Kriemhild. "Thy pride hath bewrayed thee. With words thou hast claimed me for thy service. Know, by my troth, it will ever grieve me, for I shall be no more thy faithful friend."

Then Brunhild wept. Kriemhild delayed no longer, but entered the minster with her train before the queen. Thus there rose great hatred, from which bright eyes grew dim and moist.

Whatso men did or sang to God's service there, the time seemed far too long for Brunhild, for she was sad of heart and mood. Many a brave knight and a good must later rue this day. Brunhild with her ladies now went forth and stopped before the minster. Her-thought: "Kriemhild must tell me more of what this word-shrewd woman hath so loudly charged me. Hath Siegfried made boast of this, 'twill cost his life."

Now the noble Kriemhild came with many a valiant liegeman. Lady Brunhild spake: "Stand still a while. Ye have declared me for a leman, that must ye let be seen. Know, that through thy speech, I have fared full ill."

Then spake the Lady Kriemhild: "Ye should have let me pass. I'll prove it by the ring of gold I have upon my hand, and which my lover brought me when he first lay at your side."

Brunhild had never seen so ill a day. She spake: "This costly hoop of gold was stolen from me, and hath been hid full long a time from me in evil wise. I'll find out yet who hath ta'en it from me."

Both ladies now had fallen into grievous wrath.

Kriemhild replied: "I'll not be called a thief. Thou hadst done better to have held thy peace, an' thou hold thine honor dear. I'll prove it by the girdle which I wear about my waist, that I lie not. Certes, my Siegfried became thy lord."

She wore the cord of silk of Nineveh, set with precious stones; in sooth 'twas fair enow. When Brunhild spied it, she began to weep. Gunther and all the Burgundian men must needs now learn of this.

Then spake the queen: "Bid the prince of the Rhineland come hither. I will let him hear how his sister hath mocked me. She saith here openly that I be Siegfried's wife."

The king came with knights, and when he saw his love a-weeping, how gently he spake: "Pray tell me, dear lady, who hath done you aught?"

She answered to the king: "I must stand unhappy; thy sister would fain part me from all mine honors. I make here plaint to thee she doth aver that Siegfried, her husband hath had me as his leman."

Quoth King Gunther: "Then hath she done ill."

"She weareth here my girdle, which I have lost, and my ring of ruddy gold. It doth repent me sore that I was ever born, unless be thou clearest me of this passing great shame, for that I'll serve thee ever."

King Gunther spake: "Have him come hither. He must let us hear if he hath made boast of this, or he must make denial, the hero of Netherland." One bade fetch at once Kriemhild's love.

When Siegfried saw the angry dames (he wist not of the tale), how quickly then he spake: "I fain would know why these ladies weep, or for what cause the king hath had me fetched."

Then King Gunther spake: "It doth rue me sore, forsooth. My Lady Brunhild hath told me here a tale, that thou hast boasted thou wast the first to clasp her lovely body in thine arms; this Lady Kriemhild, thy wife, doth say."

Then spake Lord Siegfried: "And she hath told this tale, she shall rue it sore, or ever I turn back, and I'll clear me with solemn oaths in front of all thy men, that I have not told her this."

Quoth the king of the Rhineland: "Let that be seen. The oath thou dost offer, and let it now be given, shall free thee of all false charges."

They bade the proud Burgundians form a ring. Siegfried, the bold, stretched out his hand for the oath; then spake the mighty king: "Thy great innocence is so well known to me, that I will free thee of that of which my sister doth accuse thee and say, thou hast never done this thing."

Siegfried replied: "If it boot my lady aught to have thus saddened Brunhild, that will surely cause me boundless grief."

Then the lusty knights and good gazed one upon the other. "One should so train women," spake again Siegfried, the knight, "that they leave haughty words unsaid. Forbid it to thy wife, and I'll do the same to mine. In truth, I do shame me of her great discourtesie."

Many fair ladies were parted by the speech. Brunhild mourned so sore, that it moved King Gunther's men to pity. Then came Hagen of Troneg to his sovran lady. He found her weeping, and asked what grief she had. She told him then the tale. On the spot he vowed that Kriemhild's lord should rue it sore, or he would nevermore be glad. Ortwin and Gernot joined their parley and these heroes counseled Siegfried's death. Giselher, the son of the noble Uta, came hither too. When he heard the talk, he spake full true: "Ye trusty knights, wherefore do ye this? Siegfried hath not merited forsooth such hate, that he should therefore lose his life. Certes, women oft grow angry over little things."

"Shall we then raise cuckolds?" answered Hagen; "such good knights would gain from that but little honor. Because he hath boasted of my liege lady, I will rather die, an' it cost him not his life."

Then spake the king himself: "He hath shown us naught but love and honor, so let him live. What booteth it, if I now should hate the knight? He was ever faithful to us and that right willingly."

Knight Ortwin of Metz then spake: "His great prowess shall not in sooth avail him aught. If my lord permit, I'll do him every evil."

So without cause the heroes had declared a feud against him. In this none followed, save that Hagen counselled all time Knight Gunther the that if Siegfried no longer lived, then many kingly lands would own his sway. At this the king grew sad, so they let it rest.

Jousting was seen once more. Ho, what stout shafts they splintered before the minster in the presence of Siegfried's wife, even down to the hall! Enow of Gunther's men were now in wrath. The king spake: "Let be this murderous rage, he is born to our honor and to our joy. Then, too, the wonderly bold man is so fierce of strength, that none durst match him, if he marked it."

"No, not he," spake Hagen then, "Ye may well keep still; I trow to bring it to pass in secret, that he rue Brunhild's tears. Certes, Hagen hath broken with him for all time."

Then spake King Gunther: "How might that chance?"

To this Hagen made answer: "I'll let you hear. We'll bid messengers, that be not known to any here, ride into our land, to declare war upon us openly. Then do ye say before your guests that ye and your men will take the field. When that is done, he will vow to serve you then and from this he shall lose his life, an' I learn the tale from the bold knight's wife."

The king followed his liegeman Hagen in evil wise. These chosen knights gan plan great faithlessness, or ever any one was ware. From two women's quarreling full many a hero lost his life.

ENDNOTES:
(1) "Leman" (M.E. "lemman", O.E. "leof mann", 'lief man', i.e., 'dear one'), 'mistress' in a bad sense.

ADVENTURE XV
How Siegfried Was Betrayed

Upon the fourth morning two and thirty men were seen to ride to court and the tale was brought to mighty Gunther that war had been declared. The very direst woes befell fair women from a lie. They gained leave to come before the king and say that they were Liudeger's men, whom Siegfried's hand had conquered afore and had brought as hostages to Gunther's land. He greeted then the messengers and bade them go and seat them. One among them spake: "My lord, pray let us stand till we have told the message we do bear you. This know, ye have of a truth many a mother's son as foe. Liudegast and Liudeger, whom ye one time gave grievous sores, declare a feud against you and are minded to ride with an army to this land." The king waxed wroth when he heard This tale.

Men bade lead the perjurers to their lodgings. How might Siegfried, or any else against whom they plotted, ware himself against their wiles? This later brought great sorrow to them all. The king walked whispering with his friends; Hagen of Troneg never let him rest. Enow of the king's liegemen would fain have parted the strife, but Hagen would not give up his plan. On a day Siegfried found them whispering. The hero of Netherland gan ask: "How go the king and his men so sadly? I'll help avenge it, hath any done you aught."

Then spake King Gunther: "I am rightly sad. Liudegast and Liudeger have challenged me to war; they are minded to ride openly into my land."

At this the bold knight said: "Siegfried's hand shall hinder that with zeal, as beseemeth all your honors. I'll do yet to these knights as I did before; I'll lay waste their lands, or ever I turn again. Be my head your pledge of this. Ye and your warriors shall stay at home and let me ride to meet them with those I have. I'll let you see how fain I serve you. This know, through me it shall go evil with your foes."

"Well is me of these tidings," spake then the king, as though he were glad in earnest of this aid. With guile the faithless man bowed low.

Quoth Lord Siegfried: "Ye shall have small care."

Then they made ready for the journey hence with the men-at-arms. This was done for Siegfried and his men to see. He, too, bade those of Netherland get them ready. Siegfried's warriors sought out warlike weeds. Then the stalwart Siegfried spake: "My father Siegmund, ye must stay here. We shall return in short space hither to the Rhine, and God give us luck. Ye must here make merry with the king."

They tied fast their banners, as though they would away, and there were enow of Gunther's men who wist not wherefore this was done. Great rout of men was seen at Siegfried's side. They bound their helmets and their breastplates upon the steeds, and many a stout knight made ready to quit the land. Then Hagen of Troneg went to find Kriemhild and asked for leave; sith they would void the land.

"Now well is me," spake Kriemhild, "that I have won a husband who dare protect so well my loving kinsfolk, as my Lord Siegfried doth here. Therefore," spake the queen, "will I be glad of heart. Dear friend Hagen, think on that, that I do serve you gladly and never yet did bear you hate. Requite this now to me in my dear husband. Let him not suffer, if I have done to Brunhild aught. I since have rued it," spake the noble wife. "Moreover, he since hath beaten me black and blue; the brave hero and a good hath well avenged that ever I spake what grieved her heart."

"Ye'll be friends once more after some days. Kriemhild, dear lady, pray tell me how I may serve you in your husband Siegfried. Liefer will I do this for you than for any else."

"I should be without all fear," quoth the noble dame, "that any one would take his life in the fray, if he would not follow his overweening mood; then the bold knight and a good were safe."

"Lady," spake then Hagen, "an' ye do think that men might wound him, pray let me know with what manner of arts I can prevent this. On foot, on horse, will I ever be his guard."

She spake: "Thou art my kinsman and I am thine. I'll commend to thee trustingly the dear lover of mine, that thou mayst guard him well, mine own dear husband." She made him acquaint with tales which had been better left unsaid. She spake: "My husband is brave and strong enow. When he slew the dragon on the hill, the lusty warrior bathed him of a truth in the blood, so that since then no weapon ever cut him in the fray. Yet am I in fear, whenever he standeth in the fight and many javelins are cast by heroes' hands, that I may lose this dear husband of mine. Alas, how oft I suffer sore for Siegfried's sake! Dear kinsman, in the hope that thou wilt hold thy troth with me, I'll tell thee where men may wound the dear lord of mine. I let thee hear this, 'tis done in faith. When the hot blood gushed from the dragon's wounds and the bold hero

81

and a good bathed him therein, a broad linden leaf did fall betwixt his shoulder blades. Therefore am I sore afraid that men may cut him there."

Then spake Hagen of Troneg: "Sew a small mark upon his coat, whereby I may know where I must guard him, when we stand in battle."

She weened to save her knight, but 'twas done unto his death. She spake: "With fine silk I'll sew a secret cross upon his vesture. There, knight, thy hand must guard my husband, when the strife is on and he standeth in the battle before his foes."

"That will I well, dear my lady," Hagen then replied.

The lady weened that it would boot him aught, but Kriemhild's husband was thereby betrayed. Hagen then took leave; merrily he hied him hence. The king's liegeman was blithe of mood. I ween that nevermore will warrior give such false counsel, as was done by him when Kriemhild trusted in his troth.

Next morning Siegfried with a thousand of his men rode merrily forth. He weened he should avenge the grievance of his kinsmen. Hagen rode so near him that he could eye his clothes. When he saw the sign, he sent in secret twain of his men, who should tell another tale: that Gunther's land should still have peace and that Liudeger had sent them to the king. How loth Siegfried now rode home again, or ever he had avenged his kinsmen's wrongs! Gunther's men could hardly turn him back. He rode then to the king; the host gan thank him. "Now God requite you of your will, friend Siegfried, that ye do so willingly what I bid you. For this I'll ever serve you, as I rightly should. I trust you more than all my friends. Now that we be rid of this foray, I am minded to ride a-hunting for bears and boars to the Vosges forest, as I have done oft-time." That Hagen, the faithless knight, had counseled. "Let it be told to all my guests, that we ride betimes. Those that would hunt with me must make them ready. If any choose to stay at home to court the ladies, that liketh me as well."

Then spake Sir Siegfried in lordly wise: "And ye would a-hunting, I'd fain go with you. Pray lend me a huntsman and some brach, (1) and I will ride to the pines."

"Will ye have but one?" spake the king anon. "I'll lend you, an' ye will, four men to whom both wood and paths be known where the game is wont to go, and who will not let you miss the camp."

Then rode the full lusty warrior to his wife, whilst Hagen quickly told the king how he thought to trap the doughty knight. A man should never use such faithlessness.

ENDNOTES:
(1) "Brach", 'hunting dog', cognate with M.H.G. "braeke", used
here.

ADVENTURE XVI

How Siegfried Was Slain

Gunther and Hagen, the passing bold knights, faithlessly let cry a-hunting in the woods, that with sharp spears they would hunt boars and bears and bison. What might be braver? With them rode Siegfried in lordly guise; many kinds of victual did they take along. At a cool spring he later lost his life, the which Brunhild, King Gunther's wife, had counseled. The bold knight then went to where he found Kriemhild. His costly hunting garb and those of his fellowship were already bound upon the sumpters, for they would cross the Rhine. Never could Kriemhild have been more sorrowful. He kissed his love upon her mouth. "God let me see thee, lady, still in health and grant that thine eyes may see me too. Thou shalt have pastime with thy loving kinsmen. I may not stay at home."

Then she thought of the tale she had told to Hagen, though she durst not say a whit. The noble queen began to rue that she was ever born. Lord Siegfried's wife wept out of measure. She spake to the knight: "Let be your hunting. I had an evil dream last night, how two wild boars did chase you across the heath; then flowers grew red. I have in truth great cause to weep so sore. I be much adread of sundry plans and whether we have not misserved some who might bear us hostile hate. Tarry here, dear my lord, that I counsel by my troth."

He spake: "Dear love, I'll come back in a few short days. I wot not here of people who bear me aught of hate. Each and all of thy kinsmen be my friends, nor have I deserved it other of the knights."

"No, no, Sir Siegfried, in truth I fear thy fall. I had last night an evil dream, how two mountains fell upon thee. I saw thee nevermore. It doth cut me to the heart, that thou wilt part from me."

In his arms he clasped his courteous wife and kissed her tenderly. Then in a short space he took his leave and parted hence. Alas, she never saw him in health again.

Then they rode from thence into a deep wood for pastime's sake. Many bold knights did follow Gunther and his men, but Gernot and Giselher stayed at home. Many laden sumpters were sent before them across the Rhine, the which bare for the hunting fellowship bread and wine, meat and fish, and great store of other things, which so mighty a king might rightly have. They bade the proud huntsmen and bold halt before a green wood over against the courses of the game, upon a passing broad glade where they should hunt. The king was told that Siegfried, too, was come. The hunting fellowship now took their stand on every side. Then the bold knight, the sturdy Siegfried, asked: "Ye heroes bold and brave, who shall lead us to the game within the wood?"

"Let us part," spake Hagen, "ere we begin the chase. Thereby my lords and I may know who be the best hunter on this woodland journey. Let us divide the folk and hounds and let each turn whithersoever he list. He who doth hunt the best shall have our thanks." Short time the huntsmen bided by another after that.

Then spake Lord Siegfried: "I need no dogs save one brach that hath been trained that he can tell the track of the beasts through the pine woods." Quoth Kriemhild's husband: "We'll find the game."

Then an old huntsman took a good sleuth-hound and in a short space brought the lord to where many beasts were found. Whatso rose from its lair the comrades hunted as good hunters still are wont to do. Whatever the brach started, bold Siegfried, the hero of Netherland, slew with his hand. His horse did run so hard that none escaped him. In the chase he gained the prize above them all. Doughty enow he was in all things. The beast which he slew with his hands was the first, a mighty boar; after which he found full soon a monstrous lion. (1) When the brach started this from its lair, he shot it with his bow, in which he had placed a full sharp arrow. After the shot the lion ran the space of but three bounds. The hunting fellowship gave Siegfried thanks. Thereafter he speedily slew a bison and an elk, four strong ure-oxen, (2) and a savage shelk. (3) His horse bare him so swiftly that naught escaped him, nor could hart or hind avoid him. Then the sleuth-hound found a mighty boar; when he began to flee, at once there came the master of the hunt and encountered him upon his path. Wrathfully the boar did run against the valiant hero, but Kriemhild's husband slew him with his sword. Another huntsman might not have done this deed so lightly. When he had felled him, they leashed the sleuth-hound; his rich booty was soon well known to the Burgundian men.

Then spake his huntsman: "Sir Siegfried, if might so be, let us leave a deal of the beasts alive. Ye'll empty both our hill and woods to-day."

At this the brave knight and a bold gan smile. Then the calls of men and the baying of hounds were heard on every side; so great was the noise that both hill and pine woods echoed with the sound. The huntsmen had let loose full four and twenty packs. Then passing many beasts must needs lose their lives. Each man weened to bring it to pass that men should give him the prize of the hunt; that might not be, for the stalwart Siegfried was already standing by the fire. The chase was over, and yet not quite. Those who would to the camp-fire brought with them thither hides of many beasts and game in plenty. Ho, how much the king's meiny bare then to the kitchen!

Then bade the king announce to the huntsman that he would dismount. A horn was blown full loud just once, that all might know that one might find the noble prince in camp. Spake then one of Siegfried's huntsmen: "My lord, I heard by the blast of a horn that we must now hie us to the quarters; I'll now give answer."

Thus by many blasts of horns they asked about the hunters. Then spake Sir Siegfried: "Now let us leave the pine wood!" His steed bare him smoothly and with him they hasted hence. With their rout they started up a savage beast; a wild bear it was. Quoth then the knight to those behind: "I'll give our fellowship a little pastime. Let loose the brach. Forsooth I spy a bear which shall journey with us to the camp. Flee he never so fast, he shall not escape us."

The brach was loosed, the bear sprang hence; Kriemhild's husband would fain overtake him. He reached a thicket, where none could follow. The mighty beast weened now to escape from the hunter with his life, but the proud knight and a good leaped from his steed and began to chase him. The bear was helpless and could not flee away. At once the hero caught it and bound it quickly with not a wound, so that it might neither scratch nor bite the men. The doughty knight then tied it to his saddle and horsed him quickly. Through his overweening mood the bold warrior and a good brought it to the camp-fire as a pastime. In what lordly wise he rode to the quarters! Mickle was his boar-spear, strong and broad. A dainty sword hung downward to his spurs. The lord bare also a fair horn of ruddy gold. Never heard I tale of better hunting weeds. One saw him wear a coat of black and silky cloth and a hat of sable: rich enow it was. Ho, what costly bands he wore upon his quiver! A panther's skin was drawn over it for its sweet fragrance' (4) sake. He bare a bow, which any but the hero must needs draw back with a windlass, and he would bend it. His vesture was befurred with otter skin (5) from head to toe. From the bright fur shone out on both sides of the bold master of the hunt many a bar of gold. Balmung (6) he also bare, a good broad sword, that was so sharp that it never failed when 'twas wielded 'gainst a helmet; its edge was good. In high spirits was the lordly huntsman. Sith I must tell you all the tale, his costly quiver was full of goodly darts, the heads a full hand's breadth, on golden shafts. What he pierced therewith must needs die soon.

Thus the noble knight rode hence in hunter's garb. Gunther's men espied him coming and ran out to meet him and took his horse in charge. On his saddle he carried a large bear and a strong. When he had dismounted, he loosed the bonds from feet and snout. Those of the pack bayed loudly, that spied the bear. The beast would to the woods; the serving folk had fear. Dazed by the din, the bear made for the kitchen. Ho, how he drove the scullions from the fire! Many a kettle was upset and many a firebrand scattered. Ho, what good victual men found lying in the ashes! Then the lordings and their liegemen sprang from their scats. The bear grew furious and the king bade loose the pack that lay enleashed. Had all sped well, they would have had a merry day. No longer the doughty men delayed, but ran for the bear with bows and pikes. There was such press of dogs that none might shoot, but from the people's shouts the whole hill rang. The bear began to flee before the dogs; none could follow him but Kriemhild's husband, who caught and slew him with his sword. Then they bore the bear again to the fire. Those that saw it, averred he was a mighty man.

Men bade now the proud hunting fellowship seat them at the tables. Upon a fair mead there sate a goodly company. Ho, what rich viands they bare there to the noble huntsmen! The butlers who should bring the wine delayed; else might never heroes have been better served. Had they not been so falsely minded, then had the knights been free of every blame.

Now the Lord Siegfried spake: "Me-wondereth, since men do give us such great store from the kitchen, why the butlers bring us not the wine. Unless men purvey the hunters better, I'll be no more your hunting-fellow. I have well deserved that they regard me, too."

The king addressed him from his seat with guile: "We fain would do you remedy of what we lack. It is Hagen's fault, who is willed to let us die of thirst."

Then spake Hagen: "Dear my lord, I weened that the hunt should be in the Spessart (7) wood, therefore sent I thither the wine. Though we may not drink today, how well will I avoid this in the future!"

At this Lord Siegfried spake: "Small thanks ye'll get for that. One should have brought me hither seven sumpter loads of mead and mulled wine. (8) If that might not be, then men should have placed our benches nearer to the Rhine."

Then spake Hagen of Troneg: "Ye noble knights and bold, I wot near by a good cold spring. Let us go thither, that ye wax not wroth."

To the danger of many a knight was this counsel given. The pangs of thirst now plagued the warrior Siegfried. He bade the tables be borne away the sooner, for he would go to the spring in the mountains. With false intent the counsel was then given by the knights. They bade the game which Siegfried's hand had slain, be carried home on wains. Whoever saw it gave him great laud. Hagen of Troneg now foully broke his troth to Siegfried. When they would hence to the broad linden, he spake: "It hath oft been told me, that none can keep pace with Kriemhild's husband when he be minded for to race. Ho, if he would only let us see it here!"

Bold Siegfried from Netherland then answered: "Ye can well test that, and ye will run a race with me to the spring. When that is done, we call give the prize to him who winneth."

"So let us try it then," quoth Hagen, the knight.

Spake the sturdy Siegfried: "Then will I lay me down on the green sward at your feet." (9)

How lief it was to Gunther, when he heard these words! Then the bold knight spake again: "I'll tell you more. I'll take with me all my trappings, my spear and shield and all my hunting garb." Around him he quickly girded his quiver and his sword.

Then they drew the clothes from off their limbs; men saw them stand in two white shifts. Like two wild panthers through the clover they ran, but men spied bold Siegfried first at the spring. In all things he bare away the prize from many a man. Quickly he ungirt his sword and laid aside his quiver and leaned the stout spear against a linden bough. The lordly stranger stood now by the flowing spring. Passing great was Siegfried's courtesie. He laid down his shield where the spring gushed forth, but the hero drank not, albeit he thirsted sore until the king had drunk, who gave him evil thanks. Cool, clear, and good was the spring. Gunther stooped down then to the flowing stream, and when he had drunken straightened up again. Bold Siegfried would fain also have done the same, but now he paid for his courtesie. Hagen bare quite away from him both bow and sword and bounded then to where he found the spear; then he looked for the mark on bold Siegfried's coat. As Lord Siegfried drank above the spring, he pierced him through the cross, so that his heart's blood spurted from the wounds almost on Hagen's clothes. Nevermore will hero do so foul a deed. Hagen left the spear a-sticking in his heart and fled more madly than he ever in the world had run from any man.

When Lord Siegfried felt the mighty wound, up from the spring he started in a rage. From betwixt his shoulder blades a long spear-shaft towered. He weened to find his bow or his sword, and then had Hagen been repaid as he deserved. But when the sorely wounded hero found no trace of his sword, then had he naught else but his shield. This he snatched from the spring and ran at Hagen; nor could King Gunther's man escape him. Albeit he was wounded unto death, yet he smote so mightily that a plenty of precious stones were shaken from the shield. The shield itself burst quite apart. Fain would the lordly stranger have avenged him. Now was Hagen fallen to the ground at his hands, and from the force of the blow the glade rang loudly. Had he had a sword in hand, then had it been Hagen's death, so sore enraged was the wounded man. Forsooth he had good cause thereof. His hue grew pale, he could not stand; his strength of body melted quite away, for in bright colors he bore the signs of death. Thereafter he was bewailed by fair dames enow.

88

Kriemhild's husband fell now among the flowers. Fast from his wounds his blood was seen to gush. He began to rail, as indeed he had great cause, at those who had planned this treacherous death. The deadly wounded spake: "Forsooth, ye evil cowards, what avail my services now that ye have slain me? This is my reward that I was always faithful to you. Alas, ye have acted ill against your kinsmen. Those of them who are born in after days will be disgraced. Ye have avenged your wrath too sore upon me. With shame shall ye be parted from all good warriors."

The knights all ran to where he lay slain. For enow of them it was a hapless day. He was bewailed by those who had aught of loyalty, and this the brave and lusty knight had well deserved. The king of the Burgundians bemoaned his death. Quoth the deadly wounded: "There is no need that he should weep who hath done the damage; he doth merit mickle blame. It had been better left undone."

Then spake the fierce Hagen: "Forsooth I wot not what ye now bewail. All our fear and all our woe have now an end. We shall find scant few who dare withstand us now. Well is me, that to his rule I have put an end."

"Ye may lightly boast you," Siegfried then replied. "Had I wist your murderous bent, I had well guarded my life against you. None doth rue me so sore as Lady Kriemhild, my wife. Now may God have pity that I ever had a son to whom the reproach will be made in after days, that his kindred have slain a man with murderous intent. If I might," so spake Siegfried, "I should rightly make complaint of this." Piteously the deadly wounded spake again: "Noble king, if ye will keep your troth to any in the world, then let my dear love be commended to your grace and let it avail her that she be your sister. For the sake of your princely courtesie protect her faithfully. My father and my men must wait long time for me. Never was woman sorer wounded in a loving friend."

The flowers on every side were wot with blood. With death he struggled, but not for long, sith the sword of death had cut him all too sorely. Then the lusty warrior and a brave could speak no more.

When the lordlings saw that the knight was dead, they laid him on a shield of ruddy gold and took counsel how they might conceal that Hagen had done the deed. Enow of them spake: "Ill hath it gone with us. Ye must all hide it and aver alike that robbers slew Kriemhild's husband as he rode alone a-hunting through the pine wood."

Then Hagen of Troneg spake: "I'll bring him home; I care not if it be known to her, for she hath saddened Brunhild's heart. Little doth it trouble me however much she weep."

ENDNOTES:

(1) "Lion." It is hardly necessary to state that lions did not roam at large in the forests of Germany. They were, however, frequently exhibited in the Middle Ages, and the poet introduced one here to enhance Siegfried's fame as a hunter.

(2) "Ure-oxen", the auerochs, or European bison, now practically extinct.

(3) "Shelk" (M.H.G. "schelch"), probably a species of giant deer.

(4) "Fragrance". It was believed that the odor of the panther attracted the game. Compare the description of the panther in the older "Physiologus", where the odor is said to surpass that of all ointments.

(5) "Otter" translates here M.H.G. "ludem", whose exact connotation is not known. Some interpret it to meau the fish otter, others the "Waldschrat", a kind of faun.

(6) "Balmung", see Adventure III, note 7.

(7) "Spessart wood" lies forty to fifty miles east of Worms and is therefore too distant for a day's hunt, but such trifles did not disturb the poet.

(8) "Mulled wine", see Adventure VIII, note 5.

(9) "Feet". This was probably done as a handicap. The time consumed in rising to his feet would give his opponent quite a start.

ADVENTURE XVII

How Kriemhild Mourned Her Husband And How He Was Buried

Then they waited for the night and crossed the Rhine. Never had heroes hunted worse. Noble maids bewept the game they slew. Forsooth many good warriors must needs atone for this in after days. Now ye may hear a tale of great overweening and dire revenge. Hagen bade carry Siegfried of the Nibelung land, thus dead, before the bower where Kriemhild lodged. He bade place him stealthily against the door, that she might find him when she went forth before the break of day to matins, which Lady Kriemhild full seldom missed through sleep.

Men rang the minster bells according to their custom. Lady Kriemhild, the fair, now waked her many maids and bade them bring a light and her vesture, too. Then came a chamberlain and found Siegfried there. He saw him red with blood, his clothes all wet. He wist not it was his lord, but with the light in his hand he hasted to the bower and through this Lady Kriemhild learned the baneful tale. As she would set out with her ladies for the minster, the chamberlain spake: "Pray stay your feet, there doth lie before the chamber a knight, slain unto death."

Kriemhild gan make passing sore wail, or ever she heard aright that it was her husband. She began to think of Hagen's question, of how he might protect him. Then first she suffered dole; she renounced all pleasure at his death. To the earth she sank, not a word she spake, and here they found lying the hapless fair. Passing great grew Kriemhild's woe. After her faint, she shrieked, that all the chamber rang. Then her meiny said: "Perchance it is a stranger knight."

The blood gushed from her mouth, from dole of heart; she spake: "'Tis Siegfried, mine own dear husband. Brunhild hath counseled this and Hagen hath done the deed."

The lady bade them lead her to where the hero lay. With her white hand she raised his head, and though it was red with blood, she knew him soon. There lay the hero of the Nibelung land in piteous guise. The gracious queen cried sadly: "Oh, woe is me of my sorrow! Thy shield is not carved with swords, thou liest murdered here. Wist I who hath done the deed, I'd ever plot his death."

All her maids made mourn and wailed with their dear lady, for they grieved full sore for their noble lord whom they had lost. Hagen had cruelly avenged the wrath of Brunhild.

Then spake the grief-stricken dame: "Go now and wake with haste all Siegfried's men. Tell Siegmund also of my grief, mayhap he'll help me bewail brave Siegfried."

A messenger ran quickly to where lay Siegfried's warriors from the Nibelung land, and with his baleful tidings stole their joy. They could scarce believe it, till they heard the weeping. Right soon the messenger came to where the king did lie. Siegmund, the lord, was not asleep. I trow his heart did tell him what had happed. Never again might he see his dear son alive.

"Awake, Sir Siegmund; Kriemhild, my lady, bade me go to fetch you. A wrong hath been done her that doth cut her to the heart, more than all other ills. Ye must help her mourn, for much it doth concern you."

Siegmund sat up; he spake: "What are fair Kriemhild's ills, of which thou tellest me?"

Weeping the messenger spake: "I cannot hide them from you; alas, bold Siegfried of Netherland is slain."

Quoth Siegmund: "For my sake let be this jesting and such evil tales, that thou shouldst tell any that he be dead, for I might never bewail him fully before my death."

"If ye will believe naught of what ye hear me say, then you may hear yourself Kriemhild and all her maids bewailing Siegfried's death."

Siegmund then was sore affrighted, as indeed he had great need, He and a hundred of his men sprang from their beds and grasped with their hands their long sharp swords. In sorrow they ran toward the sound of wail. Then came a thousand men-at-arms, bold Siegfried's men. When they heard the ladies wail so pitifully, some first grew ware that they should dress them. Forsooth they lost their wits for very sorrow. Great heaviness was buried in their hearts.

Then King Siegmund came to where he found Kriemhild. He spake: "Alas for the journey hither to this land! Who hath so foully bereft me of my child and you of your husband among such good friends?"

"Oh, if I knew him," spake the noble wife, "neither my heart nor soul would ever wish him well. I would plan such ill against him that his kin must ever weep because of me."

Around the prince Lord Siegmund threw his arms. So great grew the sorrow of his kin, that the palace, the hall, and the town of Worms resounded from the mighty wail and weeping. None might now comfort Siegfried's wife. They stripped off the clothes from his fair body; they washed his wounds and laid him on the bier. Woe were his people from their mighty grief. Then spake his warriors from the Nibelung land: "Our hands be ever ready to avenge him; he liveth in this castle who hath done the deed."

All of Siegfried's men hasted then to arms. These chosen knights came with their shields, eleven hundred men-at-arms, whom Lord Siegmund had in his troop. He would fain avenge the death of his son, as indeed he had great need. They wist not to whom they should address their strife, unless it be to Gunther and his men, with whom Lord Siegfried had ridden to the hunt.

Kriemhild saw them armed, which rued her sore. However great her grief and how dire her need, yet she did so mightily fear the death of the Nibelungs at the hands of her brothers' liegemen, that she tried to hinder it. In kindly wise she warned them, as kinsmen do to loving kin. The grief-stricken woman spake: "My Lord Siegmund, what will ye do? Ye wot naught aright; forsooth King Gunther hath so many valiant men, ye will all be lost, and ye would encounter these knights."

With their shields uncovered, the men stood eager for the fight. The noble queen both begged and bade that the lusty knights avoid it. When they would not give it over, sorely it grieved her. She spake: "Lord Siegmund, ye must let it be until more fitting time, then I'll avenge my husband with you. An' I receive proof who hath bereft me of him, I'll do him scathe. There be too many haughty warriors by the Rhine, wherefore I will not counsel you to fight. They have full well thirty men to each of ours. Now God speed them, as they deserve of us. Stay ye here and bear with me my dole. When it beginneth to dawn, help me, ye lusty knights, to coffin the dear husband of mine."

Quoth the knights: "That shall be done."

None might tell you all the marvel of knights and ladies, how they were heard to wail, so that even in the town men marked the sound of weeping. The noble burghers hasted hither. With the guests they wept, for they, too, were sore aggrieved. None had told them of any guilt of Siegfried, or for what cause the noble warrior lost his life. The wives of the worthy burghers wept with the ladies of the court. Men bade smiths haste to work a coffin of silver and of gold, mickle and strong, and make it firm with strips of good hard steel. Sad of heart were all the folk.

The night was gone, men said the day was dawning. Then the noble lady bade them bear Lord Siegfried, her loved husband, to the minster. Whatever friends he had there were seen weeping as they went. Many bells were ringing as they brought him to the church. On every side one heard the chant of many priests. Then came King Gunther with his men and grim Hagen also toward the sound of wail. He spake: "Alas for thy wrongs, clear sister, that we may not be free from this great scathe. We must ever lament for Siegfried's death."

"That ye do without cause," spake the sorrow-laden wife. "Were this loth to you, it never would have happed. I may well aver, ye thought not on me, when I thus was parted from my dear husband. Would to God," quoth Kriemhild, "that it had happed to me."

Firmly they made denial. Kriemhild gan speak: "Whoso declareth him guiltless, let him show that now. He must walk to the bier before all the folk; thereby one may know the truth eftsoon."

This is a great marvel, which oft doth hap; whenever the blood-stained murderer is seen to stand by the dead, the latter's wounds do bleed, (1) as indeed happed here, whereby one saw the guilt was Hagen's. The wounds bled sore, as they had done at first. Much greater grew the weeping of those who wailed afore.

Then spake King Gunther: "I'd have you know that robbers slew him; Hagen did not do the deed."

"I know these robbers well," quoth she. "Now may God yet let his friends avenge it. Certes, Gunther and Hagen, 'twas done by you."

Siegfried's knights were now bent on strife. Then Kriemhild spake again: "Now share with me this grief."

Gernot, her brother, and young Giselher, these twain now came to where they found him dead. They mourned him truly with the others; Kriemhild's men wept inly. Now should mass be sung, so on every side, men, wives, and children did hie them to the minster. Even those who might lightly bear his loss, wept then for Siegfried. Gernot and Giselher spake: "Sister mine, now comfort thee after this death, as needs must be. We'll try to make it up to thee, the while we live."

Yet none in the world might give her comfort. His coffin was ready well towards midday. From the bier whereon he lay they raised him. The lady would not have that he be buried, so that all the folk had mickle trouble. In a rich cloth of silk they wound the dead. I ween, men found none there that did not weep. Uta, the noble dame, and all her meiny mourned bitterly the stately

94

man. When it was noised abroad that men sang in the minster and had encoffined him, then rose a great press of folk. What offerings they made for his soul's sake! He had good friends enow among these foes. Poor Kriemhild spake to her chamberlains: "Ye must now be put to trouble for my sake, ye who wished him well and be my friends. For Siegfried's soul shall ye deal out his gold."

No child, however small, that had its wits, but must go to service, or ever he was buried. Better than a hundred masses were sung that day. Great throng was there of Siegfried's friends.

When that mass was sung, the folk went hence. Then Lady Kriemhild spake: "Pray let me not hold vigil over the chosen knight this night alone. With him all my joys have come to fall. I will let him lie in state three days and nights, until I sate me with my dear lord. What if God doth bid that death should take me too. Then had ended well the grief of me, poor Kriemhild."

The people of the town returned now to their lodgeings. She begged the priests and monks and all his retinue, that served the knight, to stay. They spent full evil nights and toilsome days; many a man remained without all food and drink. For those who would partake, it was made known that men would give them to the full. This Sir Siegmund purveyed. Then were the Nibelungs made acquaint with mickle toil. During the three days, as we hear tell, those who knew how to sing, were made to bear a deal of work. What offerings men brought them! Those who were very poor, grew rich enow. Whatever of poor men there were, the which had naught, these were bid go to mass with gold from Siegfried's treasure chamber. Since he might not live, many thousand marks of gold were given for his soul. She dealt out well-tilled lands, wherever cloisters and pious folk were found. Enow of gold and silver was given to the poor. By her deeds she showed that she did love him fondly.

Upon the third morning at time of mass, the broad churchyard by the minster was full of weeping country folk. They served him after death, as one should do to loving kin. In the four days, as hath been told, full thirty thousand marks or better still were given to the poor for his soul's sake. Yet his great beauty and his life lay low. When God had been served and the chants were ended, much people fought 'gainst monstrous grief. Men bade bear him from the minster to the grave. Those were seen to weep and wail who missed him most. With loud laments the people followed hence; none was merry, neither wife nor man. They sang and read a service before they buried him. Ho, what good priests were present at his burial! Ere Siegfried's wife was come to the grave, her faithful heart was rung with grief, so that they must needs oft sprinkle her with water from the spring. Her pain was passing great; a mickle wonder it was that she ever lived. Many a lady helped her in her plaint.

Then spake the queen: "Ye men of Siegfried, by your loyalty must ye prove your love to me. Let me receive this little favor after all my woe, that I may see once more his comely head."

She begged so long, with griefs strong will, that they must needs break open the lordly casket. Then men brought the lady to where he lay. With her white hand she raised his fair head and kissed the noble knight and good, thus dead. Tears of blood her bright eyes wept from grief. Then there happed a piteous parting. Men bare her hence, she could not walk, and soon they found the high-born lady lying senseless. Fain would the lovely fair have died of grief.

When they had now buried the noble lord, those who were come with him from the Nibelung land were seen to suffer from unmeasured grief. Men found Siegmund full seldom merry then. There were those that for three days would neither eat nor drink for passing grief. Yet might they not so waste away their bodies, but that they recovered from their sorrows, as still happeneth oft enow.

ENDNOTES:
(1) "Bleed". This was not only a popular superstition, but also a legal practice in case of a murder when the criminal had not been discovered, or if any one was suspected. The suspected person was requested to approach the bier and touch the body, in the belief that the blood would flow afresh if the one touching the body were guilty. Our passage is the first instance of its mention in German literature. A similar one occurs in "Iwein", 1355-1364. The usage was also known in France and England. See the instances quoted by Jacob Grimm in his "Rechtsaltertumer", 930.

ADVENTURE XVIII

How Siegmund Journeyed Home Again

Kriemhild's husband's father went to where he found her. Unto the queen he spake: "We must unto our land; by the Rhine, I ween, we be unwelcome guests. Kriemhild, dear lady, now journey with me to my lands. Albeit treachery here in these lands hath bereft us of your noble husband, yet should ye not requite this. I will be friendly to you for my dear son's sake, of this shall ye have no doubt. Ye shall have, my lady, all the power which Siegfried, the bold knight, gave you aforetime. The land and also the crown shall be subject to you. All Siegfried's men shall serve you gladly."

Then the squires were told that they must ride away. A mickle hurrying for steeds was seen, for they were loth to stay with their deadly foes. Men bade dames and maidens seek their robes. When that King Siegmund would fain have ridden forth, Kriemhild's mother gan beg her that she stay there with her kindred.

The royal lady answered: "That might hardly hap. How could I bear the sight of him from whom such great wrong hath happed to me, poor wife?"

Then spake young Giselher: "Dear sister mine, by thy troth thou shouldst stay here with thy mother. Thou dost need no service of them that have grieved thee and saddened thy mood. Live from my goods alone."

To the warrior she spake: "Certes, it may not hap, for I should die of dole whenever I should gaze on Hagen."

"I'll give thee rede for that, dear sister mine. Thou shalt live with thy brother Giselher, and of a truth I'll comfort thee of thy husband's death."

Then answered the hapless wife: "Of that hath Kriemhild need."

When the youth had made her such kindly offer, then gan Uta and Gernot and her faithful kin entreat. They begged her to tarry there, for but little kith she had among Siegfried's men.

"They be all strangers to you," spake Gernot; "none that liveth is so strong but that he must come to die. Consider that, dear sister, and console your mind. Stay with your kinsfolk; ye shall fare well in truth."

Then she made vow to Giselher that she would stay. The steeds were brought for Siegfried's men, sith they would ride to the Nibelung land. Also all the trappings of the knights were packed upon the sumpters. Then the Lord Siegmund hied him to Kriemhild's side. To the lady he spake: "Siegfried's men are waiting by the steeds. Now must we ride away, for I be ill content in Burgundy."

The Lady Kriemhild then replied: "All that I have of faithful kin advise me that I stay here with them; I have no kith in the Nibelung land."

Loth it was to Siegmund, when that he found Kriemhild of this mind. He spake: "Let no one tell you that. Before all my kinsmen ye shall wear the crown with such sovran power as ye did aforetime. Ye shall not suffer, because we have lost the knight. Ride also with us home again, for the sake of your little child. Lady, ye should not leave him orphaned. When your son groweth up, he will comfort your heart. Meanwhile many bold heroes and good shall serve you."

"Sir Siegmund," quoth she, "forsooth I like not for to ride. Whatever fortune, here must I tarry with my kindred, who help me mourn."

These tales gan now displease the doughty warriors. All spake alike: "We might well aver that now first hath ill befallen us. If ye would stay here with our foes, then have heroes never ridden to court more sorrowfully."

"Ye shall journey free of care, commended unto God; ye shall be given safe-conduct to Siegmund's land, I'll bid them guard you well. To the care of you knights shall my dear child be given."

When they marked that she would not go hence, then wept all of Siegmund's men alike. How right sorrowfully Siegmund parted then from Lady Kriemhild! He became acquaint with grief. "Woe worth this courtly feasting," spake the noble king. "Through pastime will nevermore hap to king or to his kinsmen, what here hath happed to us. Men shall see us nevermore in Burgundy."

Then Siegfried's men spake openly: "A journey to this land might still take place, if we discovered aright him who slew our lord. Enow of his kinsmen be their deadly foes."

He kissed Kriemhild; how sorrowfully he spake, when he perceived aright that she would stay: "Now let us ride joyless home unto our land, now first do I feel all my sorrow."

Down to the Rhine from Worms they rode without an escort. They were surely of the mind that they, the bold Nibelungs, could well defend them, should they be encountered in hostile wise. Leave they asked of none, but Gernot and Giselher were seen to go to Siegmund in loving wise. These brave and lusty knights convinced him that they mourned his loss. Courteously Prince Gernot spake: "God in heaven knoweth well that I be not to blame for Siegfried's death, nor heard I ever that any was his foe. I mourn him justly."

Giselher, the youth, gave them then safe-conduct. Sorrowly he led them from the land home to Netherland. How few kinsman were found joyous then!

How they now fared at Worms I cannot tell. All time men heard Kriemhild mourn, so that none might comfort her heart nor mind, save Giselher alone; loyal he was and good. Brunhild, the fair, sate in overweening pride. How Kriemhild wept, she recked not, nor did she ever show her love or troth. Lady Kriemhild wrought her in after days the bitterest woe of heart.

How The Nibelung Hoard Was Brought to Worms

When the noble Kriemhild thus was widowed, the Margrave Eckewart with his vassals stayed with her in the land, and served her alway. He also often helped his mistress mourn his lord. At Worms, hard by the minster, they built for her a dwelling, broad and passing large, costly and great, where, with her maids, she since dwelt joyless. She liked for to go to church and did this willingly. Where her love lay buried, thither she went all time in mournful mood (how seldom she gave that over). She prayed the good God to have mercy on her soul. With great fidelity she bewept the knight full oft. Uta and her meiny comforted her all time, but so sorely wounded was her heart, that it booted naught, whatever comfort men did offer her. She had the greatest longing for her dear love, that ever wife did have for loving husband. One might see thereby her passing virtue; until her end she mourned, the while life lasted. In after days brave Siegfried's wife avenged herself with might.

Thus she dwelt after her sorrow, after her husband's death, and this is true, well three and one half years, that she spake no word to Gunther, nor did she see her foeman Hagen in all this time.

Then spake Hagen of Troneg: "If ye could compass it to make your sister friendly, then might come to these lands the gold of Nibelung. Of this might ye win great store, an' the queen would be our friend."

The king made answer: "Let us try. My brothers bide with her; we will beg them to bring it to pass that she be our friend, if perchance she might gladly see us win the hoard."

"I trow not," spake Hagen, "that it will ever hap."

Then he bade Ortwin and the Margrave Gere go to court. When that was done, Gernot and Giselher, the youth, were also brought. They tried it with the Lady Kriemhild in friendly wise. Brave Gernot of Burgundy spake: "Lady, ye mourn too long for Siegfried's death. The king will give you proof that he hath not slain him. We hear you mourn all time so greatly."

She spake: "None chargeth him with this. 'Twas Hagen's hand that struck him, where he could be wounded. When he learned this of me, how could I think that he did bear him hate? Else had I guarded against this full well," spake the queen, "so that I had not betrayed his life; then would I, poor wife, leave off my weeping. I'll never be a friend of him that did the deed." Then Giselher, the full stately man, began implore.

When at last she spake: "I will greet the king," men saw him stand before her with his nearest kin, but Hagen durst not come before her. Well he wot his guilt; 'twas he had caused her dole. When now she would forego her hate of Gunther, so that he might kiss her, it had befitted him better had she not been wronged by his advice; then might he have gone boldly unto Kriemhild. Nevermore was peace between kindred brought to pass with so many tears; her loss still gave her woe. All, save the one man alone, she pardoned. None had slain him, had not Hagen done the deed.

Not long thereafter they brought it to pass that Lady Kriemhild gained the hoard from the Nibelung land and brought it to the Rhine. It was her marriage morning gift (1) and was hers by right. Giselher and Gernot rode to fetch it. Kriemhild ordered eighty hundred men, that they should bring it from where it lay hid, where it was guarded by the knight Alberich (2) and his nearest kin. When they saw those from the Rhine coming for the hoard, Alberich, the bold, spake to his friends: "Naught of the treasure dare we withhold from her, sith the noble queen averreth it to be her marriage morning gift. Yet should this never be done," quoth Alberich, "but that with Siegfried we have foully lost the good Cloud Cloak, for fair Kriemhild's love did wear it alway. Now, alas, it hath fared ill with Siegfried, that the hero bereft us of the Cloud Cloak and that all this land did have to serve him."

Then went the warder to where he found the keys. Before the castle stood Kriemhild's liegemen and a deal of her kinsfolk. Men bade carry the treasure hence to the sea, down to the boats; one bare it then upon the waves to the mountains on the Rhine. Now may ye hear marvels of the hoard, the which twelve huge wains, packed full, were just able to bear away from the hill in four days and nights and each must make the trip three times a day. There was naught else but gems and gold, and had men paid therewith the wage of all the world, not a mark less had it been in worth. Forsooth Hagen did not crave it so without good cause. The greatest prize of all was a wishing-rod (3) of gold. He who knew its nature, might well be master over any man in all the world.

Many of Alberich's kinsmen journeyed with Gernot hence. When they stored away the hoard in Gunther's land and the queen took charge of everything, chambers and towers were filled therewith. Never did men hear tales told of such wondrous store of goods. And had it been a thousand times as much, if the Lord Siegfried were but alive again, Kriemhild would fain have stood empty-handed at his side. No more faithful wife did hero ever win. Now that she had the hoard, she brought many unknown warriors to the land. In truth the lady's hand gave in such wise that men have never seen such bounty more.

She used great courtesie; men owned this of the queen. To the rich and the poor she began to give so greatly that Hagen said, should she live yet a while, she would gain so many a man for her service that they would fare full ill.

Then spake King Gunther: "Her life and her goods be hers. How shall I hinder that she do with them as she will? Forsooth I hardly compassed it, that she became thus much my friend. Let us not reck to whom she deal out her silver and her gold."

Spake Hagen to the king: "No doughty man should leave to any wife aught of the heard. With her gifts she'll bring about the day when it well may rue the brave Burgundians sore."

Then spake King Gunther: "I swore an oath, that nevermore would I do her harm, and will keep it further, for she is my sister."

Spake then Hagen: "Let me be the guilty one."

Few of their oaths were kept. From the widow they took the mighty store and Hagen made him master of all the keys. This vexed her brother Gernot, when he heard the tale aright. Lord Giselher spake: "Hagen hath done my sister much of harm; I should prevent it. It would cost him his life, were he not my kin."

Siegfried's wife shed tears anew. Then spake the Lord Gernot: "Or ever we be imperiled by the gold, we should have it sunk entirely in the Rhine, that it belong to none."

Full pitifully she went before her brother Giselher. She spake: "Dear brother, thou shouldst think of me and be the guardian of both my life and goods."

Quoth he then to the lady: "That shall be done when we return again, for now we think to ride."

The king and his kindred voided then the land, the very best among them that one might find. Only Hagen alone remained at home, through the hatred he bare to Kriemhild, and did so willingly. Before the king was come again, Hagen had taken the treasure quite and sunk it all at Loche, (4) in the Rhine. He weened to use it, but that might not be. The lordings came again and with them many men. With her maids and ladies Kriemhild gan bewail her passing loss, for sore it grieved them. Gladly would Giselher have helped in all good faith. All spake alike: "He hath done wrong."

Hagen avoided the princes' wrath, until he gained their favor. They did him naught, but Kriemhild might never have borne him greater hate. Before

Hagen of Troneg thus hid the treasure, they had sworn with mighty oaths that it should lie concealed as long as any one of them might live. Later they could not give it to themselves or any other.

Kriemhild's mind was heavy with fresh sorrow over her husband's end, and because they had taken from her all her wealth. Her plaints ceased not in all her life, down to her latest day. After Siegfried's death, and this is true, she dwelt with many a grief full thirteen years, that she could not forget the warrior's death. She was true to him, as most folk owned.

ENDNOTES:
(1) "Marriage morning gift" was the gift which it was customary
    for the bridegroom to give the bride on the morning after
    the bridal night. On this custom see Weinhold, "Deutsche
    Frauen im Mittelalter", i, p. 402.
(2) "A1berich", see Adventure III, note 8. It is characteristic
    of the poem that even this dwarf is turned into a knight.
(3) "Wishing-rod", a magic device for discovering buried
    treasure. Cf. Grimm, "Deutsche Mythologie," ii, 813.
(4) "Loche", according to Piper, is the modern "Locheim" in the
    Rhine province.

ADVENTURE XX

How King Etzel (1) Sent To Burgundy For Kriemhild

That was in a time when Lady Helca (2) died and the king Etzel sought another wife, that his friends advised his marriage to a proud widow in the Burgundian land, hight Lady Kriemhild. Since fair Helca was dead, they spake: "Would ye gain a noble wife, the highest and the best king ever won, then take this same lady; the stalwart Siegfried was her husband."

Then spake the mighty king: "How might that chance, sith I am heathen and be christened not a whit, whereas the lady is a Christian and therefore would not plight her troth? It would be a marvel, and that ever happed."

The doughty warriors answered: "What if she do it, perchance, for the sake of your high name and your mickle goods? One should at least make a trial for the noble dame. Well may ye love the stately fair."

The noble king then spake: "Which of you be acquaint with the people and the land by the Rhine?"

Up spake then the good knight Rudeger of Bechelaren: (3) "I have known from a child the three noble and lordly kings, Gunther and Gernot, the noble knights and good; the third hight Giselher. Each of them doth use the highest honors and courtesie, as their forebears, too, have always done."

Then answered Etzel: "Friend, I prithee, tell me whether she should wear the crown in this my land. An' she be so fair, as hath been told me, it shall never rue my dearest kin."

"She compareth well in beauty with my Lady Helca, the royal queen. Certes, there might not be in all this world a king's bride more fair. He may well be of good cheer to whom she plight her troth."

He spake: "So bring it to pass, Rudeger, as I be dear to thee; and if ever I do lie at Kriemhild's side, I will requite thee for it as best I may. Then hast thou done my will in fullest wise. From my treasure chambers I will bid thee be given such store of horses, of clothes and all thou wilt, that thou and thy fellowship may live full merrily. I'll bid full plenty of these things be made ready against thine errand."

To this the lordly margrave Rudeger replied: "Craved I thy goods, that were not worthy of praise. With mine own goods, which I have from thy hands, will I gladly be thy envoy to the Rhine."

Then spake the mighty king: "Now when wilt thou ride for the fair? May God keep thee and my lady in all worship on the journey. May fortune help me, that she look with favor on my suit."

Rudeger made answer: "Ere we void the land, we must first make ready arms and trappings, that we may stand with honor before princes. I will lead to the Rhine five hundred stately men, that wherever in Burgundy I and mine be seen, all may say of thee: `Never did any king send afar so many men in better wise than thou hast done to the Rhine.' If thou, O mighty king, wilt not turn back on this account, I'll tell thee that her noble love was subject unto Siegfried, Siegmund's son. Him thou hast seen here. (4) Men could in right truth ascribe to him great worship."

Then spake King Etzel: "Tho' she was the warrior's wife, yet was the noble prince so peerless that I should not disdain the queen. She liketh me well for her passing beauty."

The margrave answered: "Then I will tell thee that we will start hence in four and twenty days. I'll send word to Gotelind, my dear lady, that I myself will be the messenger to Kriemhild."

Rudeger sent word to Bechelaren, at which the margravine grew both sorrowful and proud. He told her he should woo for the king a wife. Lovingly she thought on Helca, the fair. When the margravine heard the message, a deal she rued it; weeping beseemed her at the thought whether she should gain a lady as afore. When she thought on Helca, it grieved her heart full sore.

Rudeger should ride in seven days from Hungary; lusty and merry King Etzel was at this. There in the town of Vienna men prepared their weeds. Then might he no longer delay his journey. At Bechelaren Gotelind awaited him; the young margravine, too, Rudeger's child, gladly saw her father and his men. Many fair maids awaited them with joy. Ere the noble Rudeger rode from the city of Vienna to Bechelaren, all their clothes were placed upon the sumpters. They journeyed in such wise that not a whit was taken from them.

When they were come to tho town of Bechelaren, the host full lovingly bade lodge his fellowship and ease them well. The noble Gotelind saw the host come gladly, as likewise his dear daughter did, the young margravine. To her his coming could not be liefer. How fain she was to see the heroes from the Hunnish land! With smiling mien the noble maiden spake: "Now be my father and his men full welcome here."

Then great thanks were given to the young margravine by many a doughty knight in courteous wise. Well wot Gotelind Sir Rudeger's mood. When at night she lay close by his side, what kindly questions the margravine put, whither the king of the Huns had sent him. He spake: "My Lady Gotelind, I'll gladly make this known to thee. I must woo another lady for my lord, sith that the fair Helca hath died. I will ride for Kriemhild to the Rhine; she shall become a mighty queen here among the Huns."

"Would to God," spake Gotelind, "an' that might hap, sith we do hear such speech of her many honors, that she might perchance replace our lady for us in our old age, and that we might be fain to let her wear the crown in Hungary."

Then spake the margrave: "My love, ye must offer to those who are to ride with me to the Rhine, your goods in loving wise. When heroes travel richly, then are they of lofty mood."

She spake: "There be none that taketh gladly from my hand, to whom I would not give what well beseemeth him, or ever ye and your men part hence."

Quoth the margrave: "That doth like me well."

Ho, what rich cloths of silk were borne from their treasure chambers! With enow of this the clothing of the noble warriors was busily lined from the neck down to their spurs. Rudeger had chosen only men that pleased him well.

On the seventh morning the host and his warriors rode forth from Bechelaren. Weapons and clothes a plenty they took with them through the Bavarian land. Seldom did men assail them on the highways for robbery's sake, and within twelve days they reached the Rhine. Then might the tidings not be hid; men told it to the king and to his liegemen, that stranger guests were come. The host gan say, if any knew them, he should tell him so. One saw their sumpters bear right heavy loads. 'Twas seen that they were passing rich.

Anon in the broad town men purveyed them quarters. When that the many strangers had been lodged, these same lords were gazed upon full oft. The people wondered from whence these warriors were come to the Rhine. The host now sent for Hagen, if perchance they might be known to him. Then spake the knight of Troneg: "None of them have I ever seen, but when we now gaze upon them, I can tell you well from whence they ride hither to this land. They must indeed be strangers, an' I know them not full soon." (5)

Lodgings were now taken for the guests. The envoy and his fellowship were come in passing costly vesture. To the court they rode wearing good garments, cut in full cunning wise. Then spake the doughty Hagen: "As well as I can tell, for I have not seen the lord long time, they ride as if 'twere Rudeger from the Hunnish land, a lordly knight and a brave."

"How can I believe," spake at once the king, "that the lord of Bechelaren be come to this land?"

When King Gunther had ended his speech, Hagen, the brave, espied the good knight Rudeger. He and his friends all ran to meet them. Then five hundred knights were seen dismounting from their steeds. Fair were the men from Hungary greeted; messengers had never worn such lordly clothes. Then Hagen of Troneg spake full loudly: "Now be these knights, the lord of Bechelaren and all his men, welcome in God's name."

With worship the speedy knights were greeted. The next of kin to the king went to where they stood. Ortwin of Metz spake to Rudeger: "Never have we seen guests so gladly here at any time. This I can truly say."

On all sides they thanked the warriors for their greeting. With all their fellowship they hied them to the hall, where they found the king and with him many a valiant man. The lords rose from their seats; through their great chivalry this was done. How right courteously he met the messengers! Gunther and Gernot greeted the stranger and his vassals warmly, as was his due. He took the good knight Rudeger by the hand and led him to the seat where he sat himself. Men bade pour out for the guests (full gladly this was done) passing good mead and the best of wine that one might find in the land along the Rhine. Giselher and Gere both were come; Dankwart and Folker, too, had heard about the strangers. Merry they were of mood and greeted before the king the noble knights and good.

Then spake Hagen of Troneg to his lord: "These thy knights should ever requite what the margrave for our sake hath done; for this should the husband of fair Gotelind receive reward."

King Gunther spake: "I cannot hold my peace; ye must tell me how fare Etzel and Helca of the Hunnish land."

To this the margrave now made answer: "I'll gladly let you know." He rose from his seat with all his men and spake to the king: "An' may that be that ye permit me, O prince, so will I not conceal the tidings that I bring, but will tell them willingly."

Quoth the king: "The tidings that have been sent us through you, these I'll let you tell without the rede of friends. Pray let me and my vassals hear them, for I begrudge you no honor that ye here may gain."

Then spake the worthy envoy: "My great master doth commend to you upon the Rhine his faithful service and to all the kinsmen ye may have. This message is sent in all good faith. The noble king bade complain to you his need. His folk is joyless; my lady, the royal Helca, my master's wife, is dead. Through her hath many a high-born maid been orphaned, daughters of noble princes, whom she hath trained. Therefore it standeth full piteously in his land; they have alas none that might befriend them faithfully. The king's grief, I ween, will abate but slowly."

"Now God reward him," spake Gunther, "that he so willingly commendeth his service to me and to my kin. Full gladly have I here heard his greeting, and this both my kindred and my men shall fain requite."

Then spake the warrior Gernot of Burgundy: "The world must ever rue fair Helca's death, for her many courtesies, which she well knew how to use."

With this speech Hagen, the passing stately knight, agreed.

Then answered Rudeger, the noble and lordly envoy: "Sith ye permit me, O king, I shall tell you more, the which my dear lord hath hither sent you, sith he doth live so right sorrowfully in longing after Helca. Men told my lord that Kriemhild be without a husband, that Sir Siegfried be dead. If this be so, then shall she wear a crown before Etzel's knights, would ye but permit her. This my sovran bade me say."

Then spake the mighty king, full courteous was his mood: "And she care to do this, she shall hear my pleasure. This will I make known to you in these three days. Why should I refuse King Etzel before I've learned her wish?"

Meanwhile men bade purvey good easement for the guests. They were served so well that Rudeger owned he had good friends there among Gunthers men. Hagen served him gladly, as Rudeger had done to him of yore. Till the third day Rudeger thus remained. The king sent for his counsel (full wisely he acted) to see whether his kinsmen would think it well that Kriemhild take King Etzel to husband. All together they advised it, save Hagen alone. He spake to Gunther, the knight: "Have ye but the right wit, ye will take good care that ye never do this, tho' she were fain to follow."

"Why," spake then Gunther, "should I not consent? Whatever pleasure happen to the queen, I should surely grant her this; she is my sister. We ourselves should bring it to pass, if perchance it might bring her honor."

Then answered Hagen: "Give over this speech. Had ye knowledge of Etzel as have I, and should she harry him, as I hear you say, then first hath danger happed to you by right."

"Why?" quoth Gunther. "I'll take good care that I come not so near him that I must suffer aught of hatred on his part, an' she become his wife."

Said Hagen: "Never will I give you this advice."

For Gernot and Giselher men bade send to learn whether the two lords would think it well that Kriemhild should take the mighty and noble king. Hagen still gainsaid, but no one other. Then spake the knight Giselher of Burgundy: "Friend Hagen, ye may still show your fealty. Make her to forget the wrongs that ye have done her. Whatever good fortune she may have, this ye should not oppose. Ye have in truth done my sister so many an ill," continued Giselher, the full lusty knight, "that she hath good cause, if she be angry with you. Never hath one bereft a lady of greater joys."

Quoth Hagen: "I'll do you to wit what well I know. If she take Etzel and live long enow, she'll do us still much harm in whatever way she can. Forsooth full many a stately vassal will own her service."

To this brave Gernot answered: "It may not happen, that we ever ride to Etzel's land before they both be dead. Let us serve her faithfully, that maketh for our honor."

Again Hagen spake: "None can gainsay me, an' the noble Kriemhild wear the crown of Helca, she will do us harm as best she may. Ye should give it over, 'twould beseem you knights far better."

Wrathfully then spake Giselher, fair Uta's son: "Let us not all act as traitors. We should be glad of whatever honors may be done her. Whatever ye may say, Hagen, I shall serve her by my troth."

Gloomy of mood grew Hagen when he heard these words. Gernot and Giselher, the proud knights and good, and Gunther, the mighty, spake at last, if Kriemhild wished it, they would let it hap without all hate.

Then spake Prince Gere: "I will tell the lady that she look with favor upon King Etzel, to whom so many knights owe dread obedience. He can well requite her of all the wrongs that have been done her."

Then the doughty warrior hied him to where he saw Kriemhild. Kindly she received him. How quickly then he spake: "Ye may well greet me gladly and give me a messenger's meed. Fortune is about to part you from all your woes. For the sake of your love, my lady, one of the very best that ever gained a kingdom with great honors, or should wear a crown, hath sent envoys hither. Noble knights be wooing; this my brother bade me tell you."

109

Then spake the sorrow-laden dame: "God should forbid you and all my kinsmen that ye make a mock of me, poor woman. What could I be to a man who had ever gained heartfelt love from a faithful wife?"

Sorely she gainsaid it, but then came Gernot, her brother, and Giselher, the youth, and lovingly bade her ease her heart. It would do her good in truth, could she but take the king.

None might persuade the lady that she should marry any man. Then the knights begged: "If ye do naught else, pray let it hap that ye deign to see the messengers."

"I'll not deny," spake the noble dame, "but that I should gladly see the Margrave Rudeger for his passing courtesie. Were he not sent hither, whoever else might be the messenger, never should he become acquainted with me. Pray bid him come to-morrow to my bower. I'll let him hear my will in full and tell it him myself." At this her great laments brake forth anew.

The noble Rudeger now craved naught else but that he might see the high-born queen. He wist himself to be so wise that she could not but let the knight persuade her, if it should ever be. Early on the morrow when mass was sung, the noble envoys came. A great press arose; of those who should go to court with Rudeger, many a lordly man was seen arrayed. Full sad of mood, the high-born Kriemhild bided the noble envoy and good. He found her in the weeds she wore each day, whereas her handmaids wore rich clothes enow. She went to meet him to the door and greeted full kindly Etzel's liegeman. Only as one of twelve he went to meet her. Men offered him great worship, for never were come more lofty envoys. They bade the lording and his vassals seat them. Before her were seen to stand the two Margraves Eckewart and Gere, the noble knights and good. None they saw merry of mood, for the sake of the lady of the house. Many fair women were seen to sit before her, but Kriemhild only nursed her grief; her dress upon her breast was wot with scalding tears. This the noble margrave noted well on Kriemhild.

Then spake the high-born messenger: "Most noble princess, I pray you, permit me and my comrades that are come with me, to stand before you and tell you the tidings for the sake of which we have ridden hither."

"Now may ye speak whatso ye list," spake the queen. "I am minded to hear it gladly; ye be a worthy messenger."

The others noted well her unwilling mood.

Then spake Prince Rudeger of Bechelaren: "Etzel, a high-born king, hath in good faith sent you a friendly greeting, my lady, by messengers hither to this land. Many good knights hath he sent hither for your love. Great joy without grief he doth offer you most truly. He is ready to give you constant friendship, as he did afore to Lady Helca, who lay within his heart. Certes, through longing for her virtues he hath full often joyless days."

Then spake the queen: "Margrave Rudeger, were there any who knew my bitter sorrow, he would not bid me marry any man. Of a truth I lost the best of husbands that ever lady won."

"What may comfort grief," the bold knight replied, "but married joy. When that any gan gain this and chooseth one who doth beseem him, naught availeth so greatly for woe of heart. And ye care to love my noble master, ye shall have power over twelve mighty crowns. Thereto my lord will give you the lands of thirty princes, all of which his doughty hand hath overcome. Ye shall become the mistress over many worthy liegemen, who were subject to my Lady Helca, and over many dames of high and princely race, who owned her sway." Thus spake the brave knight and bold. "Thereto my lord will give you (this he bade me say), if ye would deign to wear with him the crown, the very highest power which Helca ever won; this shall ye rule before all Etzel's men."

Then spake the queen: "How might it ever list me to become a hero's bride? Death hath given me in the one such dole that I must ever live joyless unto mine end."

To this the Huns replied: "O mighty queen, your life at Etzel's court will be so worshipful that it will ever give you joy, an' it come to pass, for the mighty king hath many a stately knight. Helca's damosels and your maids shall together form one retinue, at sight of which warriors may well be blithe of mood. Be advised, my lady, ye will fare well in truth."

With courtesie she spake: "Now let be this speech until the morrow early, when ye shall come here again. Then will I give you answer to what ye have in mind."

The bold knights and good must needs obey.

When all were now come to their lodgings, the noble dame bade send for Giselher and for her mother, too. To the twain she said, that weeping did beseem her and naught else better.

Then spake her brother Giselher: "Sister, it hath been told me, and I can well believe it, that King Etzel would make all thy sorrows vanish, and thou takest him to be thy husband. Whatever others may advise, this thinketh me well done. He is well able to turn thy grief to joy," spake Giselher again; "from the

111

Rhone to the Rhine, from the Elbe down to the sea, there be no other king as mighty as he. Thou mayst well rejoice, an' he make thee his wife."

She spake: "My dear brother, why dost thou advise me this? Weeping and wailing beseem me better far. How should I go to court before his knights? Had I ever beauty, of this I am now bereft."

To her dear daughter the Lady Uta spake: "Whatever thy brothers counsel thee, dear child, that do. Obey thy kindred and it will go well with thee. I have seen thee now too long in thy great grief."

Then she prayed God full oft to grant her such store of goods that she might have gold, silver, and clothes to give, as at her husband's side of yore, when that he was still alive and well. Else would she never have again such happy hours. She thought within her mind: "And shall I give my body to a paynim (6) (I am a Christian wife), forever in the world must I bear shame. An' he gave me all the kingdoms in the world still 1 would not do it."

Thus she let the matter rest. All night until the break of day the lady lay upon her bed in thought. Her bright eyes never grew dry, till on the morn she went to matins. Just at the time for mass the kings were come and took their sister again in hand. In truth they urged her to wed the king of the Hunnish land; little did any of them find the lady merry. Then they bade fetch hither Etzel's men, who now would fain have taken their leave, whatever the end might be, whether they gained or lost their suit. Rudeger came now to court; his heroes urged him to learn aright the noble prince's mind. To all it seemed well that this be done betimes, for long was the way back into their land. Men brought Rudeger to where Kriemhild was found. Winningly the knight gan beg the noble queen to let him hear what message she would send to Etzel's land. I ween, he heard from her naught else than no, that she nevermore would wed a man. The margrave spake: "That were ill done. Why would ye let such beauty wither? Still with honor may ye become the bride of a worthy man."

Naught booted that they urged, till Rudeger told the noble queen in secret that he would make amends for all that ever happed to her. At this her great sorrow grew a deal more mild. To the queen he spake: "Let be your weeping. If ye had none among the Huns but me and my faithful kin and liegemen, sore must he repent it who had ever done you aught."

At this the lady's mood grew gentler. She spake: "Then swear me an oath, that whatever any do to me that ye will be the first to amend my wrongs."

Quoth the margrave: "For this, my lady, I am ready."

Rudeger with all his vassals swore that he would ever serve her faithfully and pledged his hand, that the noble knights from Etzel's land would ne'er refuse her aught.

Then the faithful lady thought: "Sith I, wretched wife, have won so many friends, I'll let the people say whatso they choose. What if my dear husband's death might still be avenged?" She thought: "Sith Etzel hath so many men-at-arms, I can do whatso I will, an' I command them. He is likewise so rich that I shall have wherewith to give; the baleful Hagen hath bereft me of my goods."

To Rudeger she spake: "Had I not heard that he were a paynim, gladly would I go whithersoever he listed and would take him to my husband."

Then spake the margrave: "Lady, give over this speech. He hath so many knights of Christian faith, that ye'll ever be joyful at his court. What if ye bring it to pass, that he should let himself be christened? Therefore may ye fain become King Etzel's wife."

Then her brothers spake again: "Now pledge your troth, dear sister. Ye should now give over your sadness."

They begged her till she sadly vowed before the heroes to become King Etzel's bride. She spake: "I will obey you, I poor queen, and fare to the Huns as soon as ever that may be, whenever I have friends who will take me to his land."

Of this fair Kriemhild pledged her hand before the knights.

Then spake the margrave: "If ye have two liegemen, I have still more. 'Twill be the best, that with worship we escort you across the Rhine. No longer, lady, shall ye tarry here in Burgundy. I have five hundred vassals and kinsmen, too; they shall serve you, lady, and do whatso ye bid, both here and there at home. I'll do by you the same whenever ye do mind me of the tale and never feel ashamed. Now bid the housings for your horses be made ready (Rudeger's counsel will never irk you) and tell it to your maids, whom ye would take along, for many a chosen knight will meet us on the road."

She still had harness with which they rode afore in Siegfried's time, so that she might take with her many maidens now with worship, whenever she would hence. Ho, what good saddles they fetched for the comely dames! Albeit they had aye worn costly robes, many more were now made ready, for much had been told them of the king. They opened up the chests, which stood afore well locked. For four and one half days they were aught but idle; from the presses they brought forth the stores that lay therein. Kriemhild now began to open up her treasure rooms, she fain would make all Rudeger's liegemen rich. Of the gold from the Nibelung land she still had such store that a hundred horses might not bear it; she weened her hand should deal it out among the Huns.

113

This tale Hagen heard told of Kriemhild. He spake: "Sith Kriemhild will not become my friend, so Siegfried's gold must stay behind. For why should I give to my foes such great store of goods? Well I wot what Kriemhild will do with this hoard. I can well believe, an' she take it with her, that it will be doled out to call forth hate against me. Nor have they steeds enow to bear it hence. Hagen doth intend to keep it, pray tell Kriemhild that."

When that she heard this tale, it irked her sore. It was likewise told to all three kings. Fain would they have changed it, but as this did not hap, the noble Rudeger spake full blithely: "Mighty queen, why mourn ye for the gold? King Etzel doth bear you such great love, that when his eyes do light upon you, such store he'll give you that ye can never spend it all; this will I swear to you, my lady."

Then spake the queen: "Most noble Rudeger, never hath king's daughter gained such wealth as that, of which Hagen hath bereft me."

Then came her brother Gernot to the treasure chamber. By leave of the king in the door he thrust the key. Kriemhild's gold was handed forth, a thousand marks or more. He bade the strangers take it; much this pleased King Gunther.

Then spake Gotelind's knight from Bechelaren: "And had my Lady Kriemhild all the hoard that was brought from the Nibelung land, little of it would mine or the queen's hand touch. Now bid them keep it, for I will none of it. Forsooth I brought from home such store of mine that we can lightly do without this on the road, for we be furnished for the journey in full lordly wise."

Aforr this her maids had filled twelve chests at leisure with the very best of gold that anywhere might be. This they took with them and great store of women's trinkets, which they should wear upon the road. Her thought too great the might of Hagen. Of her gold for offerings (7) she had still a thousand marks. For her dear husband's soul she dealt it out. This Rudeger thought was done in faithful love. Then spake the mournful lady: "Where be now my friends who for my sake would live in exile? Let those who would ride with me to the Hunnish land, take now my treasure and purchase horses and trappings."

Then spake the margrave Eckewart to the queen: "Since the day I first became your vassal, I have served you faithfully," spake the knight, "and aye will do the same by you until mine end. I will take with me also five hundred of my men and place them in your service right loyally. Naught shall ever part us, save death alone."

For this speech Kriemhild bowed her thanks; forsooth she had full need.

114

Men now led forth the palfreys; for they would ride away. Then many tears were shed by kinsfolk. Royal Uta and many a comely maiden showed that they were sad at Kriemhild's loss. A hundred high-born maids she took with her hence, who were arrayed as well befit them. Then from bright eyes the tears fell down, but soon at Etzel's court they lived to see much joy. Then came Lord Giselher and Gernot, too, with their fellowship, as their courtesie demanded. Fain would they escort their dear sister hence; of their knights they took with them full a thousand stately men. Then came Orwin and the doughty Gere; Rumolt, the master of the kitchen, must needs be with them, too. They purveyed them night quarters as far as the Danube's shore, but Gunther rode no further than a little from the town. Ere they fared hence from the Rhine, they had sent their messengers swiftly on ahead to the Hunnish land, who should tell the king that Rudeger had gained for him to wife the noble high-born queen.

ENDNOTES:
(1) "Etzel", see Adventure I, note 7.
(2) "Helca" (M.H.G. "Helche") or "Herka", Etzel's wife, is the daughter of king "Oserich" or "Osantrix", as the "Thidreksaga" calls him. In the latter work (chap. 73-80) we read how Rudeger (Rodingeir) took her by force from her father and brought her to Etzel to be the latter's bride. On her identity with the historical "Kerka" of Priscus, see Bleyer, PB. "Beit." xxxi, 542.
(3) "Rudeger of Bechelaren", or, as the name reads in the "Thidreksaga", "Rodingeir of Bakalar", is probably not an historical personage, but the hero of a separate legend. Evidence of this is seen in the fact that he calls himself an exile, though he is Etzel's mightiest vassal, with castles and lands in fief. He may have been introduced, as Wilmanns ("Anz." xviii 101) thinks, to play a role originally assigned to Dietrich, who is also an exile. Mullenhoff considered him to have been a mythical person. Bechelaren, or Pechlarn, lies at the junction of the Erlach with the Danube.
(4) "hast seen here". "Biterolf", 9471, relates that Dietrich had carried Siegfried, when young, by force to Etzel's court.
(5) "full soon". See Adventure III, note 4.
(6) "Paynim" (O F. "paienime", late Latin "paganismus"), 'heathen'.
(7) "gold for offerings". This was the gold to be used as offering when masses were sung for Siegfried's soul.

ADVENTURE XXI

How Kriemhild Journeyed To The Huns

Let now the messengers ride. We will do you to wit, how the queen journeyed through the lands and where Giselher and Gernot parted from her. They had served her as their fealty bade them. Down to Vergen (1) on the Danube they rode; here they gan crave leave of the queen, for they would ride again to the Rhine. Without tears these faithful kinsmen might not part. Doughty Giselher spake then to his sister: "Whenever, lady, thou shouldst need me, when aught doth trouble thee, let me but know, and I will ride in thy service to Etzel's land."

Those who were her kin she kissed upon the mouth. Lovingly they took their leave of Margrave Rudeger's men. The queen had with her many a fair-fashioned maid, full a hundred and four, that wore costly robes of rich, gay-colored silks. Many broad shields were borne close by the ladies on the road, but many a lordly warrior turned then from her.

They journeyed soon from thence down through Bavarian land. Here the tale was told that many unknown strangers had gathered there, where still a cloister standeth and where the Inn floweth into the Danube. In the town of Passau, where lived a bishop, lodgings were soon emptied and the prince's court as well, as they hurried forth to meet the strangers in the Bavarian land, where the Bishop Pilgrim (2) found fair Kriemhild. The knights of the land were little loth, when in her train they saw so many comely maids; with their eyes they courted the daughters of noble knights. Later good lodgings were given the noble guests.

With his niece the bishop rode toward Passau. When it was told the burghers of the town that Kriemhild was come, their prince's sister's child, well was she greeted by the merchants. The bishop had the hope that they would stay. Then spake Sir Eckewart: "That may not be. We must fare further down to Rudeger's land. Many knights await us, for all wot well the news."

Well wist fair Gotelind the tale. She tired her and her noble child with care. Rudeger had sent her word that it thought him good that she should cheer the mind of the queen by riding forth, with his vassals to the Enns (3) for to meet her. When this message had been given, one saw on every side the roads alive; on foot and horse they hastened to meet their guests. Now was the queen come to Efferding. (4) Enow there were from the Bavarian land who might perchance have done the guests much harm, had they robbed upon the roads,

116

as was their wont. That had been forestalled by the lordly margrave: he led a thousand knights or more.

Now Gotelind, the wife of Rudeger, was come; with her there rode many a noble knight in lordly vise. When they were come across the Traun, (5) upon the plain by Enns, one saw erected huts and tents, where the guests should have their lodgings for the night. Rudeger gave the vitaille to his guests. Fair Gotelind left her lodgings far behind her; along the road there trotted many a shapely palfrey with jingling bridle. Fair was the welcome; right well was Rudeger pleased. Among those who rode to meet them on the way, on either side, in praiseworthy wise, was many a knight. They practised chivalry, the which full many a maiden saw. Nor did the service of the knights mislike the queen. When that Rudeger's liegemen met the guests, many truncheons (6) were seen to fly on high from the warriors' hands in knightly custom. As though for a prize they rode before the ladies there. This they soon gave over and many warriors greeted each other in friendly wise. Then they escorted fair Gotelind from thence to where she saw Kriemhild. Scant leisure had they who wot how to serve the ladies.

The lord of Bechelaren rode now to his wife. Little it irked the noble margravine that he was come so well and sound from the Rhine. In part her cares had given way to joy. When she had welcomed him, he bade her dismount with the ladies of her train upon the sward. Many a noble knight bestirred him and served the ladies with eager zeal. Then Kriemhild spied the margravine standing with her meiny. No nearer she drew, but checked the palfrey with the bridle and bade them lift her quickly from the saddle. Men saw the bishop with Eckewart lead his sister's child to Gotelind. All stood aside at once. Then the exiled queen kissed Gotelind upon the mouth. Full lovingly spake Rudeger's wife: "Now well is me, dear lady, that I have ever seen with mine own eyes your charming self in these our lands. Naught liefer might hap to me in all these times."

"Now God requite you," quoth Kriemhild, "most noble Gotelind. Shall I and Botelung's (7) son remain alive and well, it may be lief to you that ye have seen me here."

Neither knew what must needs later hap. Many maidens went to meet each other in courtly wise. The warriors, too, were full ready with their service. After the greeting they sat them down upon the clover. With many they became acquaint, who were full strange to them aforetime. As it was now high noon, men bade pour out wine for the ladies. The noble meiny no longer tarried, but rode to where they found many broad pavilions; there ample service stood ready for the guests.

That night they had repose till early on the morn. Those from Bechelaren made ready for to lodge the worthy guests. So well had Rudeger planned, that

117

little enow they lacked. The embrasures in the walls stood open, the castle at Bechelaren was opened wide. In rode the guests whom men were fain to see; the noble host bade purvey them proper easement. Most lovingly Rudeger's daughter with her meiny went to welcome the queen. There, too, stood her mother, the margrave's wife; many a high-born maid was greeted with delight. They took each other by the hand and hied them hence to a broad hall, fashioned full fair, under which the Danube flowed along. Towards the breeze they sate and held great pastime. What more they did I cannot tell, save that Kriemhild's men-at-arms were heard to grumble that they fared so slowly on their way, for much it irked them. Ho, what good knights rode with them hence from Bechelaren!

Rudeger offered them much loving service. The queen gave Gotelind's daughter twelve ruddy armlets, and raiment too, as good as any that she brought to Etzel's land. Although the Nibelung gold was taken from her, yet she did win the hearts of all that saw her with the little she still might have. Great gifts were given to the courtiers of the host. In turn the Lady Gotelind offered the guests from the Rhine worship in such friendly wise, that men found passing few of the strangers that did not wear her jewels or her lordly robes.

When they had eaten and should depart, faithful service was proffered by the lady of the house to Etzel's bride. The fair young margravine, too, was much caressed. To the queen she spake: "Whenso it thinketh you good, I know well that my dear father will gladly send me to you to the Hunnish land." How well Kriemhild marked that the maiden loved her truly.

The steeds were harnessed and led before the castle of Bechelaren and the noble queen took leave of Rudeger's wife and daughter. With a greeting many a fair maid parted too. Full seldom did they see each other since these days. From Medelick (8) the folk bare in their hands many a rich cup of gold, in which they offered wine to the strangers on the highway. Thus they made them welcome. A host dwelt there, hight Astolt, (9) who showed them the road to the Austrian land, towards Mautern (10) down the Danube. There the noble queen was later served full well. From his niece the bishop parted lovingly. How he counseled her that she should bear her well and that she should purchase honor for herself, as Helca, too, had done! Ho, what great worship she later gained among the Huns!

To the Traisem (11) they escorted hence the guests. Rudeger's men purveyed them zealously, until the Huns came riding across the land. Then the queen became acquaint with mickle honor. Near the Traisem the king of the Hunnish land did have a mighty castle, hight Zeisenmauer, (12) known far and wide. Lady Helca dwelt there aforetime and used such great virtues that it might not lightly ever hap again, unless it be through Kriemhild. She wist so how to give, that after all her sorrow she had the joy that Etzel's liegemen gave her great worship, of which she later won great store among the heroes. Etzel's rule was known far and wide, so that all time one found at his court the boldest warriors of whom men ever heard, among Christian or among paynim. They were all come with him. All time there were at his court, what may not so lightly hap again, Christian customs and also heathen faith. In whatsoever wise each lived, the bounty of the king bestowed on all enow.

ENDNOTES:
(1) "Vergen" is the modern Pforing, below Ingolstadt. A ferry across the river existed here from ancient times.
(2) "Pilgrim", or "Pilgerin", as he is variously called, is an historical personage. He was bishop of Passau from 971 to 991. Without doubt he is a late introduction, according to Boer between 1181 and 1185. See Boer, ii, 204, and E.L. Dummler, "Pilgrim von Passau", Leipzig, 1854.
(3) "Enns" (M.H.G. "Ens") is one of the tributaries of the Danube, flowing into it about eleven miles southeast of Linz.
(4) "Efferding" (M.H.G. "Everdingen") is a town on the Danube, about thirteen miles west of Linz.
(5) "Traun" (M.H.G. "Trune") is a river of Upper Austria, forty-four miles southeast of Linz.
(6) "Truncheons", see Adventure II, note 8.
(7) "Botelung's son" is Attila, who is so called in our poem, in the "Klage", and in "Biterolf". In the earlier Norse version "Atli" is the son of "Budli". (On this point see Mullenhoff, "Zur Geschichte der Nibelungensage", p. 106, and Zsfd A., x, 161, and Bleyer, PB. Beit. xxxi, 459, where the names are shown to be identical.
(8) "Medelick" is the modern Molk, or Melk, a town on the Danube near the influx of the Bilach. It lies at the foot of a granite cliff on which stands a famous Benedictine abbey.
(9) "Astolt" appears only in this passage; nothing else is known of him.
(10) "Mantern" is situated at the influx of the Flanitz, opposite Stein in Lower Austria.
(11) "Traisem", Traisen, is a tributary of the Danube in Lower Austria, emptying near Traismauer.
(12) "Zeisenmauer" (M.H.G. "Zeizenmure"). All the MSS. but C and D have this reading. The latter have "Treysenmoure" and "treisem moure", which corresponds better to the modern name, as Zeiselmauer lies between Tulln and Vienna. It is possible, however, that the town on the Traisem was originally called Zeiselmauer, as the road leading from Traismauer to Tulln still bears the name of Zeiselstrasse. See Laehmann, "Anmerkungen", 1272, 3, and Piper, ii, 289, note to str. 1333.

ADVENTURE XXII

How Etzel Made Kriemhild His Bride

Until the fourth day she stayed at Zeisenmauer. The while the dust upon the highway never came to rest, but rose on every side, as if it were burning, where King Etzel's liegemen rode through Austria. Then the king was told aright how royally Kriemhild fared through the lands; at thought of this his sorrows vanished. He hasted to where he found the lovely Kriemhild. Men saw ride before King Etzel on the road many bold knights of many tongues and many mighty troops of Christians and of paynims. When they met the lady, they rode along in lordly wise. Of the Russians and the Greeks there rode there many a man. The right good steeds of the Poles and Wallachians were seen to gallop swiftly, as they rode with might and main. Each did show the customs of his land. From the land of Kiev (1) there rode many a warrior and the savage Petschenegers. (2) With the bow they often shot at the birds which flew there; to the very head they drew the arrows on the bows.

By the Danube there lieth in the Austrian land a town that men call Tulna. (3) There she became acquaint with many a foreign custom, the which size had never seen afore. She greeted there enow who later came through her to grief. Before Etzel there rode a retinue, merry and noble, courtly and lusty, full four and twenty princes, mighty and of lofty birth. They would fain behold their lady and craved naught more. Duke Ramung (4) of Wallachia, with seven hundred vassals, galloped up before her; like flying birds men saw them ride. Then came Prince Gibeek with lordly bands. The doughty Hornbog, (5) with full a thousand men, wheeled from the king away towards the queen. Loudly they shouted after the custom of their land. Madly too rode the kinsmen of the Huns. Then came brave Hawart (6) of Denmark and the doughty Iring, (7) free of guile was he, and Irnfried (8) of Thuringia, a stately man. With twelve hundred vassals, whom they had in their band, they greeted Kriemhild, so that she had therefrom great worship. Then came Sir Bloedel, (9) King Etzel's brother, from the Hunnish land, with three thousand men. In lordly wise he rode to where he found the queen. Then King Etzel came and Sir Dietrich, too, with all his fellowship. There stood many worshipful knights, noble, worthy, and good. At this Dame Kriemhild's spirits rose.

Then Sir Rudeger spake to the queen: "Lady, here will I receive the high-born king; whomso I bid you kiss, that must ye do. Forsooth ye may not greet alike King Etzel's men."

From the palfrey they helped the royal queen alight. Etzel, the mighty, bode no more, but dismounted from his steed with many a valiant man. Joyfully men saw them go towards Kriemhild. Two mighty princes, as we are told, walked by the lady and bore her train, when King Etzel went to meet her, where she greeted the noble lording with a kiss in gracious wise. She raised her veil and from out the gold beamed forth her rosy hue. Many a man stood there who vowed that Lady Helca could not have been more fair than she. Close by stood also Bloedel, the brother of the king. Him Rudeger, the mighty margrave, bade her kiss and King Gibeek, too. There also stood Sir Dietrich. Twelve of the warriors the king's bride kissed. She greeted many knights in other ways.

All the while that Etzel stood at Kriemhild's side, the youthful warriors did as people still are wont to do. One saw them riding many a royal joust. This Christian champions did and paynim, too, according to their custom. In what right knightly wise the men of Dietrich made truncheons from the shafts fly through the air, high above the shields, from the hands of doughty knights! Many a buckler's edge was pierced through and through by the German strangers. Great crashing of breaking shafts was heard. All the warriors from the land were come and the king's guests, too, many a noble man.

Then the mighty king betook him hence with Lady Kriemhild. Hard by them a royal tent was seen to stand; around about the plain was filled with booths, where they should rest them after their toils. Many a comely maid was shown to her place thereunder by the knights, where she then sate with the queen on richly covered chairs. The margrave had so well purveyed the seats for Kriemhild, that all found them passing good; at this King Etzel grew blithe of mood. What the king there spake, I know not. In his right lay her snow-white hand; thus they sate in lover's wise, since Rudeger would not let the king make love to Kriemhild secretly.

Then one bade the tourney cease on every side; in courtly wise the great rout ended. Etzel's men betook them to the booths; men gave them lodgings stretching far away on every side. The day had now an end; they lay at ease, till the bright morn was seen to dawn again, then many a man betook him to the steeds. Ho, what pastimes they gan ply in honor of the king! Etzel bade the Huns purvey all with fitting honors. Then they rode from Tulna to the town of Vienna, where they found many a dame adorned. With great worship these greeted King Etzel's bride. There was ready for them in great plenty whatever they should have. Many a lusty hero rejoiced at prospect of the rout.

The king's wedding feast commenced in merry wise. They began to lodge the guests, but quarters could not be found for all within the town. Rudeger therefore begged those that were not guests to take lodgings in the country round about. I ween men found all time by Lady Kriemhild, Sir Dietrich and many another knight. Their rest they had given over for toil, that they might purvey the guests good cheer. Rudeger and his friends had pastime good. The wedding feast fell on a Whitsuntide, when King Etzel lay by Kriemhild in the town of Vienna. With her first husband, I trow, she did not win so many men for service. Through presents she made her known to those who had never seen her. Full many among them spake to the guests: "We weened that Lady Kriemhild had naught of goods, now hath she wrought many wonders with her gifts."

The feasting lasted seventeen days. I trow men can no longer tell of any king whose wedding feast was greater. If so be, 'tis hidden from us. All that were present wore brand-new garments. I ween, she never dwelt before in Netherland with such retinue of knights. Though Siegfried was rich in goods, I trow, he never won so many noble men-at-arms, as she saw stand 'fore Etzel. Nor hath any ever given at his own wedding feast so many costly mantles, long and wide, nor such good clothes, of which all had here great store, given for Kriemhild's sake. Her friends and the strangers, too, were minded to spare no kind of goods. Whatever any craved, this they willingly gave, so that many of the knights through bounty stood bereft of clothes. Kriemhild thought of how she dwelt with her noble husband by the Rhine; her eyes grew moist, but she hid it full well, that none might see it. Great worship had been done her after many a grief. Whatever bounty any used, 'twas but a wind to that of Dietrich. What Botelung's son had given him, was squandered quite. Rudeger's lavish hand did also many wonders. Prince Bleedel of Hungary bade empty many traveling chests of their silver and their gold; all this was given away. The king's champions were seen to live right merrily. Werbel and Swemmel, (10) the minstrels of the king, each gained at the wedding feast, I ween, full thousand marks, or even better, when fair Kriemhild sate crowned at Etzel's side.

On the eighteenth morning they rode forth from Vienna. Many shields were pierced in tilting by spears, which the warriors bare in hand. Thus King Etzel came down to the Hunnish land. They spent the night at ancient Heimburg. (11) No one might know the press of folk, or with what force they rode across the land. Ho, what fair women they found in Etzel's native land! At mighty Misenburg (12) they boarded ship. The water which men saw flowing there was covered with steeds and men, as if it were solid earth. The wayworn ladies had their ease and rest. Many good ships were lashed together, that neither waves nor flood might do them harm. Upon them many a goodly tent was spread, as if they still had both land and plain.

From thence tidings came to Etzelburg, (13) at which both men and wives therein were glad. Helca's meiny, that aforetime waited on their mistress, passed many a happy day thereafter at Kriemhild's side. There many a noble maid stood waiting, who had great grief through Helca's death. Kriemhild found still seven royal princesses there, through whom all Etzel's land was graced. For the meiny the high-born maiden Herrat (14) cared, the daughter of Helca's sister, beseen with many courtly virtues, the betrothed of Dietrich, a royal child, King Nentwin's (15) daughter; much worship she later had. Blithe of heart she was at the coming of the guests; for this, too, mighty treasures were prepared. Who might tell the tale of how the king held court? Never had men lived better among the Huns with any queen.

When that the king with his wife rode from the shore, the noble Kriemhild was told full well who each one was; she greeted them the better. Ho, how royally she ruled in Helca's stead! She became acquaint with much loyal service. Then the queen dealt out gold and vesture, silk and precious stones. Whatever she brought with her across the Rhine to Hungary must needs be given all away. All the king's kinsmen and all his liegemen then owned her service, so that Lady Helca never ruled so mightily as she, whom they now must serve till Kriemhild's death. The court and all the land lived in such high honors, that all time men found the pastimes which each heart desired, through the favor of the king and his good queen.

ENDNOTES:
(1) "Kiev" (M.H.G. "Kiew") is now a government in the southwestern part of Russia. Its capital of the same name, situated on the Dnieper, is the oldest of the better known cities of Russia, and in the latter Middle Ages was an important station of the Hanseatic league.
(2) "Petschenegers", a Turkish tribe originally dwelling to the north of the Caspian. By conquest they acquired a kingdom extending from the Don to Transylvania. They were feared for their ferociousness and because they continually invaded the surrounding countries, especially Kiev.
(3) "Tulna" (M.H.G. "Tulne") is the modern Tulln, a walled town of Lower Austria, seventeen milos northwest of Vienna on the Danube.
(4) "Ramung and Gibeck" (M.H.G. "Gibeche") appear only in our poem, nothing else is known of them.
(5) "Hornbog" is frequently mentioned in the "Thidreksaga", but nothing otherwise is known of him.
(6) "Hawart" is perhaps identical with the Saxon duke Hadugot, who is reputed to have played an important part in the conquest of Thuringia. He evidently comes from the Low German version.
(7) "Iring" is considered by Wilmanns to have been originally an ancient deity, as the Milky Way is called "Iringe straze" or "Iringi". He occurs in a legend of the fall of the Thuringian kingdom, where he played such a prominent role that the Milky Way was named after him. See W. Grimm, "Heldensage", p. 394, who thinks, however, that the connection of Iring with the Milky Way is the result of a confusion.
(8) "Irnfried" is considered to be Hermanfrid of Thuringia, who was overthrown and killed in A.D. 535 by Theuderich with the

123

aid of the Saxons. See Felix Dahn, "Urgeschichte", iii, 73-79. He, too, comes from the Low German tradition.

(9) "Bloedel" is Bleda, the brother of Attila, with whom he reigned conjointly from A.D. 433 to 445. In our poem the name appears frequently with the diminutive ending, as "Bloedelin".

(10) "Werbel and Swemmel", who doubtless owe their introduction to some minstrel, enjoy special favor and are intrusted with the important mission of inviting the Burgundians to Etzel's court, an honor that would hardly be accorded to persons of their rank. Swemmel appears mostly in the diminutive form "Swemmelin".

(11) "Heimburg" lies on the Danube near the Hungarian border.

(12) "Misenburg" is the modern Wieselburg on the Danube, twenty-one miles southeast of Pressburg.

(13) "Etzelburg" was later identified with the old part of Budapest, called in German "Ofen", through the influence of Hungarish legends, but, as G. Heinrich has shown, had no definite localization in the older M.H.G. epics. See Bleyer, PB. Belt. xxxi 433 and 506. The name occurs in documents as late as the fifteenth century.

(14) "Herrat", the daughter of King "Nentwin" is frequently mentioned in the "Thidreksaga" as Dietrich's betrothed. She is spoken of as the exiled maid.

(15) "Nentwin" is not found in any other saga, and nothing else is known of him. See W. Grimm, "Heldensage", 103.

ADVENTURE XXIII

How Kriemhild Thought To Avenge Her Wrongs

With great worship of a truth they lived together until the seventh year. In this time the queen was delivered of a son, at which King Etzel could not have been more joyful. She would not turn back, until she brought it to pass that Etzel's child was christened after the Christian rite. Men named it Ortlieb; (1) at this great joy arose over all of Etzel's lands. Whatever courtly breeding Lady Helca had possessed, Dame Kriemhild practiced this full many a day. Herrat, the exiled maid, who in secret grieved full sore for Helca, taught her the customs. Well was she known to the strangers and the home-folk. They vowed that never had a kingdom had a better or more bounteous queen. This they held for true. She bare this praise among the Huns until the thirteenth year. Now wot she well, that none would thwart her, as royal men-at-arms still do to a prince's wife, and that all time she saw twelve kings stand before her. Over many a wrong she brooded, that had happed to her at home. She thought likewise on the many honors in the Nibelung land, which she had there enjoyed and of which Hagen's hand had quite bereft her at Siegfried's death, and if perchance she might not make him suffer for his deed. "That would hap, if I might but bring him to this land." She dreamed that Giselher, her brother, walked often with her hand in hand. Alway she kissed him in her gentle slumber; later suffering came to both. I ween, the foul fiend did counsel Kriemhild this, that she withdrew her friendship from Giselher, whom for forgiveness' sake she had kissed in the Burgundian land. At this hot tears again gan soil her robe. Early and late it lay within her heart, how without fault of hers they had made her wed a heathen man. Hagen and Gunther had brought her to this pass. This wish she seldom gave over in her heart. She thought: "I am so mighty and have such great wealth, that I can do my foes an injury yet. Full ready would I be for this towards Hagen of Troneg. My heart doth often yearn for my faithful kin. Might I be with those who did me wrong, my lover's death would be well avenged. Scarce can I abide this," spake Etzel's wife.

All the king's men, Kriemhild's warriors, bare her love in duty bound. Of the chamber Eckewart had charge, which won him friends. None might gainsay Dame Kriemhild's will. All time she thought: "I will beg the king, that he in kindly wise may grant me to bring my kinsmen to the Hunnish land." None marked the evil purpose of the queen. One night when she lay by the king, and he did hold her in his arms, as he was wont to love the noble dame, who was dear to him as life, the high-born lady thought her of her foes. To the king she spake: "Dear my lord, I would fain beseech you, by your grace, that ye would show me that ye did love my kinsfolk, if I have earned the favor."

Then spake the king (true was his heart): "I'll give you to know however well the knights may fare, I may well have joy of this, for never have I won better kin through woman's love."

Again the queen spake: "It hath been well told you, that I have high-born kin; therefore do I grieve that they so seldom reck to see me here. I hear the folk aver that I be banished."

Then spake king Etzel: "Dear lady mine, and it think you not too far, I'll bid hither to my lands, from across the Rhine, whomso ye be fain to see."

The lady joyed her when she heard his will. She spake: "Would ye show me your faith, my lord, then send envoys to Worms across the Rhine, through whom I may tell my kinsfolk what I have in mind. Thus there will come hither to our land many a noble knight and a good."

He answered: "It shall hap whenso ye bid. Ye might not be more glad to see your kin than I to see the sons of the noble Uta. It doth irk me sore, that they have been strangers to us so long a time. If it please you, dear lady mine, I would fain send my minstrels for your kinsmen to the Burgundian land."

He bade the good minstrels be fetched straightway. Quickly they hasted to where the king sate by the queen. He told the twain they should be envoys to the Burgundian land and bade full lordly weeds be made ready for them. Clothing was prepared for four and twenty warriors, and the message was told them by the king, how they should bid Gunther and his liegemen hither. Kriemhild, the queen, talked with them apart. Then spake the mighty king: "I'll tell you what to say. I offer to my kin my love and service, that it may please them to ride hither to my land. But few such welcome guests have I known, and if they perchance will fulfill my wish, tell Kriemhild's kinsmen that they must not fail to come this summer to my feast, for much of my joy doth lie upon the kinsmen of my wife."

Then spake the minstrel, the proud Swemmel: "When shall your feasting be in these lands, that I may tell it yonder to your kin?"

King Etzel answered: "On next midsummer's day."

"We'll do as ye command," spake then Werbel.

The queen bade them be brought secretly unto her bower, where she then talked with the envoys. From this but little joy happed to many a knight. To

126

the two messengers she spake: "Now earn ye mickle goods, in that ye do my pleasure full willingly and give the message which I send to my native land. I'll make you rich in goods and give you the lordly robes. And if ye see any of my kin at Worms upon the Rhine, ye must not tell them that ye ever saw me sad of heart. Tender my service to the heroes brave and good. Beg that they do as the king doth bid and thus part me from all my grief. The Huns ween, I be without kith and kin. Were I a knight, I'd visit them myself at times. And say to Gernot, too, the noble brother of mine, that none in the world doth love him more. Beg him to bring with him to this land our best of friends, that it may be to our honor. Say also to Giselher, that he remember well, I never gained grief through fault of his. Therefore would mine eyes fain sue him. For his great loyalty I would gladly have him here. Tell my mother also of the honors which I have, and if Hagen of Troneg be minded to stay at home, who then should lead them through the lands? From a child he knoweth the roads to Hungary." (2)

The envoys wist not, why it was done, that they should not let Hagen of Troneg stay upon the Rhine. Later it repented them full sore. With him many a knight was doomed to a savage death. Letters and messages had now been given them. They rode forth rich in goods, and well could lead a sumptuous life. Of Etzel and his fair wife they took their leave, their persons adorned full well with goodly weeds.

ENDNOTES:
(1) "Ortlieb" is not historical, and in the "Thidreksaga"
    Etzel's son is called Aldrian. Bleyer, "Die germanischen
    Elemente der ungarischen, Hunnensage", PB. Beit. xxxi, 570,
    attempt to prove the identity of the names by means of a
    form "Arda", giving on the one hand Hungarian "Aladar",
    "Aldrian", on the other German "Arte", "Orte".
(2) "Hungary". According to the account in "Waltharius", Hagen
    spent his youth as a hostage at Etzel's court.

127

ADVENTURE XXIV
How Werbel And Swemmel Brought The Message

When that Etzel had sent his envoys to the Rhine, these tidings flew from land to land. Through full speedy messengers he begged and bade to his high feasting. From this many a one met there his death. The envoys rode away from the Hunnish land to Burgundy. They were sent thither for three noble kings and for their men, that these should come to Etzel; therefore all gan haste. To Bechelaren they came a-riding, where served them gladly. Rudeger and Gotelind and the child of them twain delayed not to send their service through the envoys to the Rhine. Nor did they let them part hence without gifts, that Etzel's men might fare the better. To Uta and her sons Rudeger sent word that they had no more loyal margrave than he. To Brunhild, also, they tendered service and good wishes, constant fealty and a loving mind. When they heard the speech that the envoys would ride, the margravine begged God in heaven to keep them well.

Before the messengers were quite come through Bavarian land, the doughty Werbel sought out the good Bishop Pilgrim. What word he sent to his kin upon the Rhine, that I know not, but naught but ruddy gold he gave the messengers for love and let them ride.

Then spake the bishop: "And might I see them here, my sister's sons, I should be blithe of mood, for full seldom can I come to them upon the Rhine."

What roads they traveled to the Rhine, I cannot tell. None robbed them of their silver and their weeds; men feared their master's wrath. Certes the noble high-born king was a mighty lord.

Within a twelfth night Werbel and Swemmel came to the Rhine, to the land of Worms. To the kings and their liegemen tidings were told that there came strange messengers. Gunther, the lord of the Rhineland, gan ask: "Who will do us to wit, from whence these strangers ride into our land?"

This none wist, till Hagen of Troneg saw them, who then spake to Gunther: "New tidings be come to us, as I will vouch, for I have seen King Etzel's minstrels here. Them your sister hath sent to the Rhine; for their master's sake we must give them a kindly welcome."

Already they were riding up before the palace; never did a prince's minstrels journey in more lordly wise. Straightway the king's meiny bade them welcome. Men gave them lodgings and bade take in charge their trappings. Their traveling clothes were rich and so well fashioned that with honor they might come before the king, but they would not wear them longer there at court, and asked if there were any that desired them. At the selfsame moment folk were found who fain would take them, and to these they were sent. Then the strangers donned far better weeds, such as well befitted king's messengers for to wear.

Then Etzel's retainers went by leave to where the king was sitting; men saw this gladly. Hagen sprang courteously towards the messengers and greeted them in loving wise. For this the squires did say him thanks. That he might know their tidings, he gan ask how Etzel fared and all his men. Then spake the minstrel: "Never did the land stand better, nor were the folk more merry; now know that of a truth."

To the host they went; the hall was full. There men received the guests, as one must do by right, when kindly greetings be sent to the lands of other kings. Werbel found full many warriors there at Gunther's side. In courteous wise the king gan greet them: "Ye minstrels of the Huns and all your fellowship, be ye welcome. Hath the mighty Etzel sent you hither to the Burgundian land?"

To the king they bowed; then spake Werbel: "My dear lord, and also Kriemhild, your sister, do send you loyal service to this land. They have sent us to you knights in all good faith."

Spake the mighty prince: "Merry am I at this tale. How fareth Etzel," so asked the knight, "and Kriemhild, my sister, of the Hunnish land?"

Quoth the minstrel: "This tale I'll tell you; ye should know that never have folk fared better than the twain and all their followers, their kinsmen and their vassals. They joyed them of the journey, as we departed hence."

"Gramercy for his greetings which he hath sent me, and for those of my sister, sith it standeth so that the king and his men live thus in happiness, for I did ask the news in fear and trembling."

The two young princes were now also come, for they had but just heard the tale. For the sake of his sister Giselher, the youth, was fain to see the envoys. He spake to them in loving wise: "Ye messengers, be very welcome to us. An' ye would ride more often hither to the Rhine, ye would find friends here whom ye would be glad to see. Little of harm shall hap you in this land."

"We trust you in all honor," spake then Swemmel. "I could not convey to you with all my wits, how lovingly king Etzel and your noble sister, who live in such great worship, have sent their greetings. The queen doth mind you of your love and fealty, and that your heart and mind did ever hold her dear. But first and foremost we be sent to the king, that ye may deign to ride to Etzel's land. The mighty Etzel enjoined us strictly to beg you this and sent the message to you all, that if ye would not let your sister see you, he fain would know what he had done you that ye be so strange to him and to his lands. An' ye had never known the queen, yet would he fain bring it to pass that consent to come and see him. It would please him well if that might hap."

Then spake King Gunther: "In a sennight I will tell you the tale of what I have bethought me with my friends. Meanwhile hie you to your lodgings and rest you well."

Quoth Werbel again: "And could that be that we might see my lady, the royal Uta, afore we take our easement?"

The noble Giselher spake then full courteously: "None shall hinder that. An' ye would go before her, ye will do in full my mother's wish, for she will gladly see you for my sister's sake, the Lady Kriemhild; she will make you welcome."

Giselher led them to where they found the queen. Gladly she gazed upon the envoys from the Hunnish land. Through her courtesie she gave them gentle greeting. The good and courtly messengers then told their tale. "My lady offereth you of a truth," so spake Swemmel, "her love and duty. Might that be that she could see you oft, ye may well believe she had no better joy in all the world."

Then spake the queen: "That may not be. However gladly I would often see the dear daughter of mine, yet doth the wife of the noble king live, alas, too far from me. May she and Etzel be ever blessed. Pray let me know before ye leave, when ye would hence again; not in a long time have I seen messengers so gladly as I have you." The squires vowed that this should hap.

Those from the Hunnish land now rode to their lodgings. Meanwhile the mighty king had sent to fetch his friends. The noble Gunther asked his liegemen how they liked the speech. Many a one gan say that the king well might ride to Etzel's land. The very best among them advised him this, save Hagen alone; him misliked it sore. Privily he spake to the king: "Ye fight against yourself; ye know full well what we have done. We may well be ever on our guard with Kriemhild, for with mine own hand I slew her husband to death. How durst we ride to Etzel's land?"

Then spake the mighty king: "My sister gave over her wrath; with a kiss she lovingly forgave what we had done her, or ever she rode away. Unless be that the feud doth stand against you alone."

130

Quoth Hagen: "Now let the messengers from the Huns beguile you not, whatsoever they say. Would ye visit Kriemhild, easily may ye lose there both life and honor. Full long of vengeance is King Etzel's wife."

Then spake Prince Gernot to the council: "Why should we give it over, because ye rightly fear death in the Hunnish lands? It were an ill deed not to go to see our sister."

Then spake Prince Giselher to the knight: "Sith ye know you to be guilty, friend Hagen, ye should stay at home and guard you well, and let those who dare ride with us to my sister."

At this the knight of Troneg grew wroth of mood. "I will not that ye take any with you on the way, who durst better ride to court than I. Sith ye will not turn you, I will well show you that."

Then spake the master of the kitchen, Rumolt, the knight: "Ye can well have the strangers and the home-folk cared for here, after your own desire, for ye have full store of goods. I ween, Hagen hath never given you for a hostage; (1) but if ye will not follow him, Rumolt adviseth you, for I be bound to you in fealty and duty, that for my sake ye abide here and leave King Etzel there with Kriemhild. How might it fare more gently with you in all the world? Ye be well able to stand before your foes; so deck your body out with brave attire, drink the best of wine, and pay court to stately ladies. Thereto ye be served with the best of food that ever king did gain in the world. And were this not so, yet should ye tarry here for your fair wife's sake, before ye risk your life so childishly. Wherefore I do counsel you to stay at home. Your lands be rich, and one can redeem his pledges better at home than among the Huns. Who knoweth how it standeth there? Ye should stay at home, Sire, that is Rumolt's counsel."

"We will not stay," quoth Gernot. "Sith my sister and the mighty Etzel have bidden us in such friendly wise, why should we not accept? He that liketh not to go may stay at home."

To This Hagen answered: "Take not my speech amiss, however ye may fare. In all truth I counsel you, would ye guard your lives, then ride to the Huns well armed. Sith ye will not turn you, send for your men-at-arms, the best ye have or can find in any part; from among them all I'll choose a thousand doughty knights. Then Kriemhild's evil mood can bring you naught of harm."

"This rede I'll gladly follow," spake straightway the king. He then bade messengers ride far and wide throughout his lands. Three thousand champions or more they fetched. Little they weened to gain such grievous woe. Full merrily they rode to Gunther's court. Men bade give all that were to ride forth from Burgundy both steeds and trappings. The king gained full

131

many a one with willing mood. Then Hagen of Troneg bade his brother Dankwart lead eighty of their warriors to the Rhine. In knightly guise they came; these doughty men took with them harness and trappings into Gunther's land. Then came bold Folker, a noble minstrel he, with thirty of his men for the journey to Kriemhild's court. They had clothing such as a king might wear. Gunther bade make known, he would to the Hunnish land. I'll do you now to wit who Folker was. He was a noble lord, the liege of many doughty knights in Burgundy. A minstrel he was called, for that he wist how to fiddle. Hagen chose a thousand whom he well knew; oft had he seen what their hands had wrought in press of battle, or in whatever else they did. None might aver aught else of them than doughtiness.

The tarrying irked Kriemhild's envoys sore, for great was their fear of their lord. Daily they craved leave to go; this Hagen would not grant through craftiness. To his master he spake: "We should well guard against letting them ride away, until we ourselves fare forth a sennight later to Etzel's land. If any beareth us ill will, the better shall we wot it. Nor may Lady Kriemhild then make ready that through any plan of hers, men do us harm. An' this be her will, she'll fare full ill, for many a chosen liegeman had we hence."

Shields and saddles, and all the garments that they would take with them to Etzel's land, were now full ready for many a brave man-at-arms. Now men bade Kriemhild's messengers go before King Gunther. When they were come, Gernot spake: "The king will do as Etzel asked us, we will gladly come to his high feast to see our sister; be no more in doubt of that."

Then King Gunther spake: "Wist ye how to tell us, when this feast shall be, or in what time we should go thither?"

Swemmel replied: "Of a truth it shall be on next midsummer's day."

The king gave them leave (this had not happed as yet), if they would fain see Lady Brunhild, to go before her with his free will. This Folker hindered, which pleased her much. "Forsooth, my Lady Brunhild is not so well of mood, that ye may see her," spake the good knight. "Bide the morrow, and men will let you see her." When they weened to gaze upon her, it might not hap.

Then the mighty prince, who liked the envoys well, through his own courtesie, bade his gold be carried forth on the broad shields of which he had great store. Rich gifts were also given them by his kinsmen Giselher and Gernot, Gere and Ortwin. Well they showed, that they were generous, too. They offered the messengers such rich gifts, that for fear of their lord they durst not take them.

Now spake the envoy Werbel to the king: "Sir King, let your gifts stay here at home. We may carry none away; our lord forbade that we take aught of gifts. Then too, there is but little need."

132

Then the ruler of the Rhine waxed wroth, that they should thus refuse the gifts of so mighty a king. At last they were forced to take his gold and weeds, the which they later bare to Etzel's land. They would fain see the Lady Uta, or ever they departed hence, so the doughty Giselher brought the minstrels before his mother Uta. The lady sent the message, that whatever honors her daughter had, this gave her joy. Then the queen bade give the minstrels of her edgings and her gold, for the sake of King Etzel and Kriemhild whom she loved. Gladly they took the gifts; in good faith 'twas done.

The messengers had now taken their leave from thence, from wives and men. Merrily they rode away to Swabia. Thither Gernot bade his knights escort them, that none might do them harm. When they parted from those who should have them in their care, Etzel's power did guard them on all their ways, so that none bereft them of either horse or trappings. With great speed they hasted towards Etzel's land. To all the friends they wot of, they made known that in a short time the Burgundians would come hither from the Rhine to the Hunnish land. To the Bishop Pilgrim too, the tale was told. As they rode adown the highway before Bechelaren, men delayed not to tell Rudeger and Gotelind, the margrave's wife. Merry she grew that she should see them. Men saw the minstrels hasting with the tidings. They found King Etzel in the town of Gran. (2) Greeting after greeting they gave the king, of which full many had been sent him. He blushed for very joy.

Happy of mood was the queen, when she heard the tale aright that her brothers should come into the land. She gave the minstrels great gifts as meed. This was done for honor's sake. She spake: "Now tell me, both of you, Werbel and Swemmel, which of my kin are minded to be at the feast? Will the best of those we bade come hither to this land? Pray tell me what Hagen said when he heard the tale."

The minstrel answered: "He came on a morning early to the council, and but little of fair speech he spake thereby. When they pledged the journey hither to the Hunnish lands, that was as words of death to the wrathful Hagen. Your brothers, the three kings, will come in lordly mood. Whoever else may come, this tale I know not of a surety. The brave minstrel Folker vowed to ride along."

"Little do I reck," spake the queen, "whether I ever see Folker here. Of Hagen I be fond, he is a doughty hero. My spirits stand high that we may see him here."

Then the queen went to where she saw the king. How lovingly Dame Kriemhild spake: "How like you these tales, dear my lord? What I have ever craved, shall now be brought to pass."

"Thy wish is my joy," spake then the king. "Never have I been so blithe of mine own kin, when they should come hither to my lands. Through the kindness of thy kinsmen my care hath fled away."

King Etzel's officers bade everywhere palace and hall be purveyed with benches for the guests which were to come. Thereafter the king heard from them mickle weeping.

ENDNOTES:
(1) "Hostage", i.e., he has never betrayed you to your enemies.
(2) "Gran", royal free city of Hungary, on the right bank of the Danube opposite the influx of the Gran, twenty-four miles northwest of Budapest.

ADVENTURE XXV

How The Lords All Journeyed To The Huns

Now let us leave the tale of how they lived at Etzel's court. More high-mettled warriors never rode in such lordly wise to the land of any king; they had whatever they listed, both of weapons and of weeds. The ruler of the Rhineland clad his men, a thousand and sixty knights, (1) as I have heard, and nine thousand footmen, for the courtly feast. Those they left at home bewailed it in after time. The trappings were now borne across the court at Worms; then spake an aged bishop from Speyer to fair Uta: "Our friends would journey to the feasting. May God preserve their honor there."

The noble Lady Uta then spake to her sons: "Pray tarry here, good knights. Me-dreamed last night of direst woe, how all the fowls in this land lay dead."

"Who recketh aught of dreams," quoth Hagen, "he wotteth not how to say the proper words, when 'twould bring him great store of honors. I wish that my lord go to court to take his leave. We must gladly ride to Etzel's land. The arms of doughty heroes may serve kings there full well, where we shall behold Kriemhild's feast."

Hagen counseled the journey, but later it rued him sore. He would have advised against it, but that Gernot encountered him with such rude words. Of Siegfried, Lady Kriemhild's husband, he minded him; he spake: "Because of him Hagen will not make the journey to the court."

At this Hagen of Troneg spake: "I do it not from fear. Heroes, when it please you, begin the work. Certes I will gladly ride with you to Etzel's land." Later he carved to pieces many a helm and shield.

The skiffs were now made ready; many a knight stood there. Thither men bare whatever clothes they had. Busy they were until the even tide, then full merrily they set forth from home. Tents and pavilions were raised upon the green beyond the Rhine. When this had happed, the king bade his fair wife tarry with him. That night she still embraced her stately knight. Trumpeting and fluting rose early on the morn, as sign that they should ride. Then to the work they went. Whoso held in his arms his love caressed the fair. Later King Etzel's wife parted them with woe.

Fair Uta's sons, they had a liegeman, brave and true. When they would hence, he spake to the king in secret wise his mind. Quoth he: "I must bewail that ye make this journey to the court." He was hight Rumolt and was a hero of his hands. He spake: "To whom will ye leave your folk and lands? O that none can turn you warriors from your mind! These tidings from Kriemhild have never thought me good."

"Be the land and my little child, too, commended to thy care; serve well the ladies, that is my wish. Comfort any thou dost see in tears. Certes King Etzel's bride will never do us harm."

The steeds were now ready for the kings and their men. Many a one who lived there high of spirit, parted thence with loving kisses. This many a stately dame must later needs bewail. When the doughty knights were seen go toward the steeds, men spied full many ladies standing sadly there. Their hearts did tell them that this long parting boded them great harm. This doth never ease the heart.

The doughty Burgundians started on their way. Then in the land a mighty turmoil rose; on either side of the mountains there wept both men and wives. But however the folk might bear them, the knights jogged merrily along. With them rode the men of Nibelung, a thousand hauberks strong, who had left many comely dames at home whom they never saw again. Siegfried's wounds gave Kriemhild pain.

Gunther's liegemen now wended their way towards the river Main, up through Eastern Frankland. (2) Thither Hagen led them, for well he wot the way. Dankwart was their marshal, the hero from Burgundian land. As they rode away from the Eastern Frankland towards Swanfield, (3) men could tell the princes and their kin, the worshipful knights, by their lordly bearing. On the twelfth morning the king came to the Danube. Hagen of Troneg rode foremost of them all, giving to the Nibelungs helpful cheer. On the sandy shore the bold knight dismounted and bound his steed full soon to a tree. The river was swollen, the skiffs hidden away. Great fear the Nibelungs had, as to how they might come across, for the stream was much too broad. Full many a lusty knight alighted on the ground.

"Ill may it lightly hap with thee here," quoth Hagen, "O ruler of the Rhine. Now mayst thou thyself see the river is swollen, its flood is mighty. Certes, I ween, we shall lose here many a worthy knight to-day."

"Why dost thou rebuke me, Hagen?" spake the lordly king. "For thine own prowess' sake discomfit me no more, but seek us the ford across to the other bank, that we may take hence both steeds and trappings."

"Forsooth," quoth Hagen, "I be not so weary of life, that I would drown me in these broad waves. Sooner shall men die by my hands in Etzel's lands. That will I well. Stay by the water's side, ye proud knights and good, and I will seek the ferryman myself along the stream, who shall ferry us across to Gelfrat's (4) land."

Then the stalwart Hagen seized his good shield. Well was he armed. The shield he bare along, his helmet bound upon his head, bright enow it was. Above his breastplate he bare a sword so broad that most fiercely it cut on either edge. To and fro he sought the ferryman. He heard the splash of water and began to listen. In a fair spring wise women (5) were bathing for to cool them off. Now Hagen spied them and crept toward them stealthily. When they grew ware of this, they hurried fast to escape him; glad enow they were of this. The hero took their clothes, but did them naught else of harm.

Then spake one of the mermaids (Hadburg she was called): "Sir Knight Hagen, we'll do you here to wit, an' ye give us our weeds again, bold knight, how ye will fare upon this journey to the Hunnish court."

Like birds they floated before him on the flood. Therefore him-thought their senses strong and good; he believed the more what they would tell him. Well they answered what he craved of them. Hadburg spake again: "Ye may safely ride to Etzel's land. I'll stake my troth at once as pledge, that heroes never rode better to any realm for such great honors. Now believe that in truth."

In his heart Hagen was joyous at this rede. He gave them back their clothes and no longer tarried. As they donned their strange attire, they told him rightly of the journey to Etzel's land. The other mermaid spake (Siegelind she hight): "I will warn thee, Hagen, son of Aldrian. (6) For the sake of her weeds mine aunt hath lied to thee. An' thou comest to the Huns, thou wilt be sore deceived. Time is, that thou shouldst turn again, for ye heroes be bidden, that ye may die in Etzel's land. Whose rideth hither, hath taken death by the hand."

Answered Hagen: "Ye deceive us needlessly. How might it come to pass that we should all die there, through anybody's hate?"

Then gan they tell him the tale still more knowingly. The same one spake again: "It must needs be that none of you shall live, save the king's chaplain; this we know full well. He will come again safe and sound to Gunther's land."

Then spake bold Hagen, fierce of mood: "It were not well to tell my lords that we should all lose our lives among the Huns. Now show us over the stream, thou wisest of all wives."

She answered: "Sith ye will not turn you from the journey, up yonder where an inn doth stand, by the waterside, there is a ferryman and elsewhere none."

137

At once he ceased to ask for further tidings. After the angry warrior she called: "Pray bide a time, Sir Hagen! Forsooth ye are too much in haste. List further to the tale of how ye may cross to the other bank. The lord of these marches beareth the name of Else. (7) His brother is hight Knight Gelfrat, a lord in the Bavarian land. 'Twill go hard with you, an' ye will cross his land. Ye must guard you well and deal full wisely with the ferryman. So grim of mood is he that he'll not let you live, unless be that ye have your wits about you with the knight. An' ye will that he guide you, then give him his meed. He guardeth this land and is liegeman unto Gelfrat. And cometh he not betimes, so call across the flood and say, ye hight Amelrich. (8) He was a doughty here that; because of a feud did void this land. The ferryman will come when he heareth this name."

Haughty Hagen bowed then to the dames; he spake no more, but held his peace. Then by the river he hied him higher up upon the sandy shore, to where he found an inn upon the other bank. Loudly he began to call across the flood: "Now come and fetch me, ferryman," quoth the good knight, "and I will give thee as meed an arm ring of ruddy gold. Know, that of this passage I have great need in truth."

So noble was the ferryman that it behooved him not to serve, therefore he full seldom took wage of any wight. His squires, too, were full lofty of mood. All this time Hagen still stood alone, this side of the flood. He called with might and main, that all the water rang, for mickle and great was the hero's strength. "Now fetch me. I am Amelrich, Else's liegeman, that because of a great feud did void these lands."

High upon his spear (9) he offered him an arm band, bright and fair it was, of ruddy gold, that one should ferry him over to Gelfrat's land. The haughty ferryman, the which was newly wed himself, did take the oar in hand. As he would earn Hagen's gold so red, therefore he died the sword-grim death at the hands of the knight. The greed for great goods (10) doth give an evil end. Speedily the boatman rowed across to the sandy bank. When he found no trace of him whose name he heard, wroth he grew in earnest. When he spied Hagen, with fierce rage he spake to the hero: "Ye may perchance hight Amelrich, but ye are not like him whom I weened here. By father and by mother he was my brother. Sith ye have bewrayed me, ye may stay on this hither shore."

"No, by the mighty God," spake then Hagen, "I am a stranger knight and have warriors in my care. Now take ye kindly my meed to-day and ferry me over. I am in truth your friend."

The ferryman replied: "This may not be. My dear lords have foes, wherefore I never ferry strangers to this land. If ye love your life, step out quickly on the sand."

138

"Now do it not," spake Hagen; "sad is my mind. Take this good gold from me as a token of my love and ferry us across: a thousand horse and just as many men."

The grim boatman answered: "'Twill ne'er be done." He raised a mighty rudder oar, mickle and broad, and struck at Hagen (full wroth he grew at this), so that he fell upon his knees in the boat. The lord of Troneg had never met so fierce a ferryman. Still more the boatman would vex the haughty stranger. He smote with an oar, so that it quite to-broke (11) over Hagen's head (a man of might was he); from this the ferryman of Else took great harm. Hagen, fierce of mood, seized straightway his sheath, wherein he found his sword. His head he struck off and cast it on the ground. Eftsoon these tidings were made known to the proud Burgundians. At the very moment that he slew the boatman, the skiff gan drifting down the stream. Enow that irked him. Weary he grew before he brought it back. King Gunther's liegeman pulled with might and main. With passing swift strokes the stranger turned it, until the sturdy oar snapped in his hand. He would hence to the knights out upon the shore. None other oar he had. Ho, how quickly he bound it with a shield strap, a narrow band! Towards a wood he floated down the stream, where he found his sovran standing by the shore.

Many a stately man went down to meet him. The doughty knights and good received him with a kindly greeting. When they beheld in the skiff the blood reeking from a gaping wound which he had dealt the ferryman, Hagen was plied enow with questions by the knights. When that King Gunther spied the hot blood swirling in the skiff, how quickly he spake: "Wherefore tell ye me not, Hagen, whither the ferryman be come? I ween your prowess hath bereft him of his life."

At this he answered craftily: "When I found the skiff hard by a willow tree, I loosed it with my hand. I have seen no ferryman here to-day, nor hath harm happed to any one through fault of mine."

Then spake Sir Gernot of Burgundy: "I must needs fear the death of dear friends to-day. Sith we have no boatmen here at hand, how shall we come over? Therefore I must perforce stand sad."

Loudly then called Hagen: "Ye footmen, lay the trappings down upon the grass. I bethink me that once I was the very best of boatmen that one might find along the Rhine. I trow to bring you all safe across to Gelfrat's land."

They struck the horses, that these might the sooner come across the flood; passing well they swam, for the mighty waves bereft them of not a one. Some few drifted far adown the stream, as did befit their weariness. Then the knights bare to the skiff their gold and weeds, sith there was no help for the crossing. Hagen played the steersman, and so he ferried full many mighty warriors over to the sandy shore, into the unknown land. First he took across a thousand noble knights, then his own men-at-arms. Still there were more to come. Nine thousand footmen he ferried over to the land. Aught but idle was Hagen's hand that day. When he had carried them all safe across the flood, the doughty knight and good bethought him of the strange tales which the wild mermaids had told him afore. For this cause the king's chaplain near lost his life. He found the priest close by the chapel luggage, leaning with his hand upon the relics. Little might that boot him. When Hagen spied him, ill fared it with the hapless priest; he threw him from the skiff in haste. Enow of them called out: "Hold on, Sir Hagen, hold!"

Giselher, the youth, gan rage, but Hagen let none come between. Then spake Sir Gernot of Burgundy: "What availeth you now, Hagen, the chaplain's death? Had another done the deed, 'twould have irked you sore. For what cause have ye sworn enmity to the priest?"

The clerk (12) now tried to swim with might and main, for he would fain save his life, if perchance any there would help him. That might not be, for the stalwart Hagen was wroth of mood. He thrust him to the bottom, the which thought no one good. When the poor priest saw naught of help, he turned him back again. Sore was he discomfited, but though he could not swim, yet did God's hand help him, so that he came safe and sound to the land again. There the poor clerk stood and shook his robe. Hagen marked thereby that naught might avail against the tidings which the wild mermaids told him. Himthought: "These knights must lose their lives."

When the liegemen of the three kings unloaded the skiff and had borne all away which they had upon it, Hagen brake it to pieces and threw it in the flood, at which the bold knights and good did marvel much.

"Wherefore do ye that, brother," quoth Dankwart, "how shall we come over, when we ride homeward from the Huns, back to the Rhine?"

Later Hagen told him that might not be. The hero of Troneg spake: "I do it in the hope that if we have a coward on this journey, who through faintheartedness would run away, that in this stream he may die a shameful death."

They had with them from Burgundy land a hero of his hands, the which was named Folker. Wisely he spake all his mind. Whatever Hagen did, it thought the fiddler good. Their steeds were now ready, the sumpters laden well. On the journey they had taken no harm that irked them, save the king's chaplain alone. He must needs wander back on foot to the Rhine again.

ENDNOTES:
(1) "a thousand and sixty". This does not agree with the

140

account in Adventure XXIV, witere we read of a thousand of Hagen's men, eighty of Dankwart's, and thirty of Folker's. The nine thousand foot soldiers mentioned here are a later interpolation, as the "Thidreksaga" speaks of only a thousand all told.

(2) "Eastern Frankland", or East Franconia, is the ancient province of "Franconia Orientalis", the region to the east of the Spessart forest, including the towns of Fulda, Wurzburg and Barnberg. In "Biterolf" Dietlich journeys through Eastern Frankland to the Danube.

(3) "Swanfield" (M.H.G. "Swanevelde") is the ancient province of "Sualafeld" between the Rezat and the Danube.

(4) "Gelfrat" is a Bavarian lord and the brother of "Else", mentioned below. Their father's name was also Else.

(5) "Wise women", a generic name for all supernatural women of German mythology. While it is not specifically mentioned, it is probable that the wise women, or mermaids, as they are also called here, were 'swan maidens', which play an important role in many legends and are endowed with the gift of prophecy. They appear in the form of swans, and the strange attire of the wise women mentioned here refers to the so-called swan clothes which they wore and which enabled Hagen to recognize them as supernatural beings. On bathing they lay aside this garment, and he who obtains possession of it has them in his power. This explains their eagerness to give Hagen information, if he will return their garments to them. For an account of them see Grimm's "Mythologie", 355.

(6) "Aldrian" is not an historical personage; the name is merely a derivative of "aldiro", 'the elder', and signifies 'ancestor', just as Uta means 'ancestress'. In the "Thidreksaga" Aldrian is the king of the Nibelung land and the father of Gunther, Giselher, and Gernot, whereas Hagen is the son of an elf by the same mother.

(7) Else appears also in "Biterolf"; in the "Thidreksaga" he is called "Elsung", the younger, as his father bore the same name. See Adventure XXV, note 4.

(8) "Amelrich" is the ferryman's brother.

(9) "Spear". It was the custom to offer presents on a spear point, perhaps to prevent the recipient from treacherously using his sword. Compare the similar description in the "Hildebrandslied", 37, where we are told that gifts should be received with the spear.

(10) "Goods". In the "Thidreksaga" the ferryman desires the ring for his young wife, which explains better the allusion to marriage and the desire for wealth.

(11) "To-broke", see Adventure II, note 9.

(12) "Clerk", 'priest'.

ADVENTURE XXVI (1)

How Gelfrat Was Slain By Dankwart

Now when all were come upon the shore, the king gan ask: "Who will show us the right roads through this land, that we go not astray?"

Then the sturdy Folker spake: "For this I alone will have a care."

"Now hold," quoth Hagen, "both knight and squire. Certes, me-thinketh right that we should heed our friends. With full monstrous tales I'll make you acquaint: we shall never come again to the Burgundian land. Two mermaids told me early in the morning that we should not come back again. I will now counsel you what ye do: ye must arm you, ye heroes, for we have mighty foes. Ye must guard you well and ride in warlike guise. I thought to catch these mermaids in a lie. They swore that none of us would come home safe and sound, save the chaplain alone. Therefore would I fain have drowned him to-day."

These tidings flew from band to band and valiant heroes grew pale from woe, as they began to fear a grewsome death on this journey to Etzel's court. Forsooth they had great need. When they had crossed at Moering, (2) where Else's ferryman had lost his life, Hagen spake again: "Sith I have gained me foes upon the way, we shall surely be encountered. I slew this same ferryman early on the morn to-day. Well they wot the tale. Now lay on boldly, so that it may go hard with Gelfrat and Else, should they match our fellowship here to-day. I know them to be so bold that 'twill not be left undone. Let the steeds jog on more gently, that none ween we be a-fleeing on the road."

"This counsel I will gladly follow," quoth Giselher, the knight; "but who shall guide the fellowship across the land?"

They answered: "This let Felker do; the valiant minstrel knoweth both road and path."

Ere the wish was fully spoken, men saw the doughty fiddler standing there well armed. On his head he bound his helmet, of lordly color was his fighting gear. On his spear shaft he tied a token, the which was red. Later with the kings he fell into direst need.

Trustworthy tidings of the ferryman's death were now come to Gelfrat's ears. The mighty Else had also heard the tale. Loth it was to both; they sent to fetch their heroes, who soon stood ready. In a passing short time, as I'll let you hear, one saw riding towards them those who had wrought scathe and monstrous wounds in mighty battles. Full seven hundred or more were come to Gelfret. When they began to ride after their savage foes, their lords did lead them, of a truth. A deal too strong they hasted after the valiant strangers; they would avenge their wrath. Therefore many of the lordings' friends were later lost.

Hagen of Troneg had well planned it (how might a hero ever guard his kinsmen better), that he had in charge the rear guard, with his liegemen and his brother Dankwart. This was wisely done.

The day had passed away; the night was come. For his friends he feared both harm and woe, as beneath their shields they rode through the Bavarian land. A short time thereafter the heroes were assailed. On either side of the highway and in the rear hard by they heard the beat of hoofs. Their foes pressed on too hard. Then spake hold Dankwart: "They purpose to attack us here, so hind on your helmets, for that be well to do."

They stayed their journey, as though it must needs he; in the gloom they spied the gleam of shining shields. Hagen would no longer keep his peace; he called: "Who chaseth us upon the highway?"

To this Gelfrat must needs give answer. Quoth the margrave of Bavaria: "We seek our foes and have galloped on behind you. I know not who slew my ferryman to-day, but it doth rue me enow, for he was a hero of his hands."

Then spake Hagen of Troneg: "And was then the ferryman thine? The fault was mine, he would not ferry us over, so I slew the knight. Forsooth I had great need, for I had sheer gained at his hands my death. As meed I offered him gold and trappings, that he ferry me across to thy land, Sir Knight. This angered him so greatly that he smote me with a mighty oar. At this I waxed grim enow. I seized my sword and fended him his anger with a grievous wound. Thus the hero met his death. I'll make amends, as doth think thee best."

"Well I wist," spake Gelfrat, "when Gunther and his fellowship rode hither, that Hagen of Troneg would do us harm. Now he shall not live; the knight must stand for the ferryman's life."

Over the bucklers Gelfrat and Hagen couched their spears for the thrust; each would charge the other. Else and Dankwart rode full gloriously; they tested who they were, fierce was the fight. How might heroes ever prove each other better? From a mighty thrust Hagen was unhorsed by Gelfrat's hand. His martingale snapped, he learnt what it was to fall. The crash of shafts

143

resounded from their fellowship. Hagen, who from the thrust afore had come to earth, down on the grass, sprang up again. I trow, he was not gentle of mood towards Gelfrat then. Who held their steeds, I know not; both Hagen and Gelfrat had alighted on the sand and rushed together. Their fellowship helped thereby and became acquaint with strife. Albeit Hagen sprang at Gelfrat fiercely, the noble margrave smote from his shield a mickle piece, so that the sparks flew wide. Full nigh did Gunther's liegeman die therefrom. He began to call to Dankwart: "O help, dear brother! Certes, a hero of his hands hath matched me, he will not spare my life."

At this hold Dankwart spake: "I'll play the umpire here."

The hero then sprang nearer and with a sharp sword smote Gelfrat such a blow that he fell down dead. Else then would fain avenge the knight, but he and his fellowship parted from the fray with scathe. His brother had been slain, he himself was wounded; full eighty of his knights remained with grim death behind upon the field. Their lord must needs turn in flight from Gunther's men.

When those from the Bavarian land gave way and fled, one heard the savage blows resound behind them. Those of Troneg chased their foes; they were in passing haste, who had not weened to make amends. Then spake Dankwart, the knight, in their pursuit: "Let us turn soon on this road and let them ride, for they be wot with blood. Haste we to our friends, this I advise you of a truth."

When they were come again, where the scathe had happed, Hagen of Troneg spake: "Heroes, prove now what doth fail us here, or whom we have lost in the strife through Gelfrat's wrath."

Four they had lost whom they must needs bewail. But they had been paid for dearly; for them a hundred or better from the Bavarian land were slain. From their blood the shields of the men of Troneg were dimmed and wet. Through the clouds there partly broke the gleam of the shining moon, as Hagen spake again: "Let none make known to my dear lords what we have wrought here to-day. Let them rest without care until the morn."

When those who just had fought were now come again, the fellowship was full weary from the way. "How long must we still ride?" asked many a man.

Then spake the bold Dankwart: "We may not find lodgings here, ye must all ride until the day be come."

The doughty Folker, who had charge of the fellowship, bade ask the marshal: "Where may we find a place to-night, where our steeds may rest and our dear

144

lords as well?"

Bold Dankwart answered: "I cannot tell you that, we may not rest till it begin to dawn. Wherever then we find a chance, we'll lay us down upon the grass."

How loth it was to some when they heard this tale! They remained unmarked with their stains of warm red blood, until the sun shot his gleaming light against the morn across the hills. Then the king beheld that they had fought. Wrathfully the hero spake: "How now, friend Hagen? I ween, ye scorned to have me with you when your rings grew wet with blood? Who hath done this?"

Quoth he: "This Else did, who encountered us by night. We were attacked because of his ferryman. Then my brother's hand smote Gelfrat down. Else soon escaped us, constrained thereto by mickle need. A hundred of them and but four of ours lay dead in the strife."

We cannot tell you where they laid them down to rest. All of the folk of the land learned soon that the sons of the noble Uta rode to court. Later they were well received at Passau. The uncle of the noble king, the Bishop Pilgrim, was blithe of mood, as his nephews came to his land with so many knights. That he bare them good will, they learned full soon. Well were they greeted, too, by friends along the way, sith men could not lodge them all at Passau. They had to cross the stream to where they found a field on which they set up pavilions and costly tents. All one day they must needs stay there, and a full night too. What good cheer men gave them! After that they had to ride to Rudeger's land, to whom the tidings were brought full soon. When the way-worn warriors had rested them and came nearer to the Hunnish land, they found a man asleep upon the border, from whom Hagen of Troneg won a sturdy sword. The same good knight hight Eckewart (3) in truth; sad of mood he grew, that he lost his weapon through the journey of the knights. They found Rudeger's marches guarded ill.

"Woe is me of this shame," spake Eckewart. "Certes this journey of the Burgundians rueth me full sore. My joy hath fled, sith I lost Knight Siegfried. Alas, Sir Rudeger, how I have acted toward thee!"

When Hagen heard the noble warrior's plight, he gave him back his sword and six red arm bands. "These keep, Sir Knight, as a token that thou art my friend. A bold knight thou art, though thou standest alone upon the marches."

"God repay you for your arm bands," Eckewart replied. "Yet your journey to the Huns doth rue me sore. Because ye slew Siegfried, men hate you here. I counsel you in truth, that ye guard you well."

145

"Now may God protect us," answered Hagen. "These knights, the kings and their liegemen, have forsooth no other care, save for their lodgement, where we may find quarters in this land to-night. Our steeds be spent by the distant way and our food run out," quoth Hagen, the knight. "We find naught anywhere for sale, and have need of a host, who through his courtesie would give us of his bread to-night."

Then Eckewart made answer: "I'll show you a host so good that full seldom have ye been lodged so well in any land, as here may hap you, an' ye will seek out Rudeger, ye doughty knights. He dwelleth by the highway and is the best host that ever owned a house. His heart giveth birth to courtesie, as the sweet May doth to grass and flowers. He is aye merry of mood, when he can serve good knights."

At this King Gunther spake: "Will ye be my messenger and ask whether my dear friend Rudeger will for my sake keep us, my kinsmen and our men? I will repay thee this, as best I ever can."

"Gladly will I be the messenger," Eckewart replied. With a right good will he gat him on the road and told Rudeger the message he had heard, to whom none such pleasing news had come in many a day.

At Bechelaren men saw a knight pricking fast. Rudeger himself descried him; he spake: "Upon the road yonder hasteth Eckewart, a liegeman of Kriemhild."

He weened the foes had done him scathe. Before the gate he went to meet the messenger, who ungirt his sword and laid it from his hand. The tales he brought were not hidden from the host and his friends, but were straightway told them. To the margrave he spake: "Gunther, the lord of the Burgundian land, and Giselher, his brother, and Gernot, too, have sent me hither to you. Each of the warriors tendered you his service. Hagen and Folker, too, eagerly did the same in truth. Still more I'll tell you, that the king's marshal sendeth you by me the message, that the good knights have passing need of your lodgement."

Rudeger answered with a smile: "Now well is me of these tales, that the high-born kings do reck of my service. It shall not be denied them. Merry and blithe will I be, an' they come unto my house."

"Dankwart, the marshal, bade let you know whom ye should lodge in your house with them: sixty doughty champions, a thousand good knights, and nine thousand men-at-arms."

Merry of mood grew Rudeger; he spake: "Now well is me of these guests, that these noble warriors be coming to my house, whom I have served as yet full

146

seldom. Now ride ye forth for to meet them, my kinsmen and my men."

Knights and squires now hied them to their horses; it thought them right,

which their lord did bid. All the more they hasted with their service. As yet
Lady Gotelind wist it not, who sate within her bower.

ENDNOTES:
(1) "Adventure XXVI". This adventure is a late interpolation,
    as it is not found in the "Thidreksaga". Originally the
    river must be thought of as separating them from Etzel's
    kingdom.
(2) "Moering" (M.H.G. "Moeringen") lies between Pforing and
    Ingolstadt. In the "Thidreksaga" we are told that the
    mermaids were bathing in a body of water called "Moere",
    whereas in our poem they bathe in a spring. This may be the
    original form of the account and the form here contaminated.
    See Boer, i, 134.
(3) "Eckewart", see Adventure I, note 15. It will be remembered
    that he accompanied Kriemhild first to the Netherlands, then
    stayed with her at Worms after Siegfried's death, and
    finally journeyed with her to Etzel's court. Originally he
    must be thought of as guarding the boundary of Etzel's land.
    Without doubt he originally warned the Burgundians, as in
    the early Norse versions, where Kriemhild fights on the side
    of her brothers, but since this duty was given to Dietrich,
    he has nothing to do but to announce their arrival to
    Rudeger. His sleeping here may, however, be thought to
    indicate that it was too late to warn Gunther and his men.

ADVENTURE XXVII

How They Came To Bechelaren

Then the margrave went to where he found the ladies, his wife with his daughter, and told them straightway the pleasing tidings he had heard, that the brothers of their lady were coming thither to their house. "My dearest love," quoth Rudeger, "ye must receive full well the noble high-born kings, when they come here to court with their fellowship. Ye must give fair greeting, too, to Hagen, Gunther's man. With them there cometh one also, hight Dankwart; the other is named Folker, well beseen with courtesie. Ye and my daughter must kiss these and abide by the knights with gentle breeding." This the ladies vowed; quite ready they were to do it. From the chests they hunted out the lordly robes in which they would go to meet the warriors. Fair dames were passing busy on that day. Men saw but little of false colors on the ladies' cheeks; upon their heads they wore bright bands of gold. Rich chaplets (1) these were, that the winds might not dishevel their comely hair, and this is true i' faith.

Let us now leave the ladies with these tasks. Much hasting over the plain was done by Rudeger's friends, to where one found the lordings, whom men then received well into the margrave's land. When the margrave, the doughty Rudeger, saw them coming toward him, how joyfully he spake: "Be ye welcome, fair sirs, and your liegemen, too. I be fain to see you in my land." Low obeisance the knights then made, in good faith, without all hate. That he bare them all good will, he showed full well. Hagen he gave a special greeting, for him had he known of yore. (2) To Folker from Burgundy land he did the same. Dankwart he welcomed, too. The bold knight spake: "Sith ye will purvey us knights, who shall have a care for our men-at-arms whom we have brought?"

Quoth the margrave: "A good night shall ye have and all your fellowship. I'll purvey such guard for whatever ye have brought with you, of steeds and trappings, that naught shall be lost, that might bring you harm, not even a single spur. Ye footmen pitch the tents upon the plain. What ye lose I'll pay in full. Take off the bridles, let the horses run."

Seldom had host done this for them afore. Therefore the guests made merry. When that was done, the lordlings rode away and the footmen laid them everywhere upon the grass. Good ease they had; I ween, they never fared so gently on the way. The noble margravine with her fair daughter was come out before the castle. One saw stand by her side the lovely ladies and many a

148

comely maid. Great store of armlets and princely robes they wore. The precious stones gleamed afar from out their passing costly weeds. Fair indeed were they fashioned.

Then came the guests and alighted there straightway. Ho, what great courtesie one found among the Burgundian men! Six and thirty maids and many other dames, whose persons were wrought as fair as heart could wish, went forth to meet them with many a valiant man. Fair greetings were given there by noble dames. The young margravine kissed all three kings, as did her mother, too. Close at hand stood Hagen. Her father bade her kiss him, but when she gazed upon him, he seemed so fearful that she had fain left it undone. Yet she must needs perform what the host now bade her do. Her color changed first pale then red. Dankwart, too, she kissed, and then the minstrel. For his great prowess was this greeting given. The young margravine took by the hand Knight Giselher of the Burgundian land. The same her mother did to Gunther, the valiant man. Full merrily they went hence with the heroes. The host walked at Gernot's side into a broad hall, where the knights and ladies sate them down. Soon they bade pour out for the guests good wine. Certes, heroes might never be better purveyed than they. Rudeger's daughter was gazed upon with loving glances, so fair she was. Forsooth many a good knight caressed her in his mind. And well did she deserve this, so high she was of mood. The knights thought what they would, but it might not come to pass. Back and forth shot the glances at maids and dames. Of them sate there enow. The noble fiddler bare the host good will.

Then they parted after the custom, knights and ladies going to different sides. In the broad hall they set up the tables and served the strangers in lordly wise. For the sake of the guests the noble margravine went to table, but let her daughter stay with the maidens, where she sate by right. The guests saw naught of her, which irked them sore, in truth.

When they had eaten and drunk on every side, men brought the fair again into the hall; nor were merry speeches left unsaid. Many such spake Folker, this brave and lusty knight. Before them all the noble minstrel spake: "Mighty margrave, God hath dealt full graciously with you, for he hath given you a passing comely wife and thereto a life of joy. An' I were a prince," quoth the minstrel, "and should wear a crown, I would fain have to wife your comely daughter. This my heart doth wish. She is lovely for to see, thereto noble and good."

Then answered the margrave: "How might that be, that king should ever crave the dear daughter of mine? My wife and I are exiles; what booteth in such ease the maiden's passing comeliness?"

To this Gernot, the well-bred man, made answer: "An' I might have a love after mine own desire, I should be ever glad of such a wife."

Hagen, too, replied in full kindly wise: "My lord Giselher must take a wife. The margravine is of such high kin that I and all his liegemen would gladly serve her, should she wear a crown in Burgundy land."

This speech thought Rudeger passing good, and Gotelind too, indeed it joyed their mood. Then the heroes brought to pass that the noble Giselher took her to wife, as did well befit a king. Who may part what shall be joined together? Men prayed the margravine to go to court, and swore to give him the winsome maid. He, too, vowed to wed the lovely fair. For the maiden they set castles and land aside, and this the hand of the noble king did pledge with an oath, and Lord Gernot, too, that this should hap.

Then spake the margrave: "Sith I have naught of castles, I will ever serve you with my troth. As much silver and gold will I give my daughter, as an hundred sumpters may barely carry, that it may please the hero's kin in honor."

After the custom men bade them stand in a ring. Over against her many a youth stood, blithe of mood. In their minds they harbored thoughts, as young folk still are wont to do. Men then gan ask the winsome maid whether she would have the knight or no. Loth in part she was, and yet she thought to take the stately man. She shamed her of the question, as many another maid hath done. Her father Rudeger counseled her to answer yes, and gladly take him. In a trice young Giselher was at her side, and clasped her in his white hands, albeit but little time she might enjoy him.

Then Spake the margrave: "Ye noble and mighty kings, when ye now ride again (that is the custom) home to Burgundy, I will give you my child, that ye may take her with you."

This then they vowed. Now men must needs give over all the noisy joy. They bade the maiden hie her to her bower, and bade the guests to sleep and rest them against the day. Meanwhile men made ready the food; the host purveyed them well.

When now they had eaten, they would ride hence to the Hunnish lands. "I'll guard against that well," spake the noble host. "Ye must tarry still, for full seldom have I gained such welcome guests."

To this Dankwart replied: "Forsooth this may not be. Where would ye find the food, the bread and wine, that ye must have for so many warriors another night?"

When the host heard this, he spake: "Give o'er this speech. My dear lords, ye must not say me nay. Forsooth I'd give you vittaile for a fortnight, with all your fellowship that is come hither with you. King Etzel hath taken from me as yet full little of my goods."

However much they demurred, still they must needs tarry there until the fourth morning, when such deeds were done by the bounty of the host that it was told after. He gave his guests both mounts and robes. No longer might they stay, they must fare forth. Through his bounty bold Rudeger wot how to save but little. Naught was denied that any craved, it could not but please them all. Their noble meiny now brought saddled before the gate the many steeds, and to them came forth thee stranger knights. In their hands they bare their shields, for they would ride to Etzel's land. Before the noble guests come forth from the hall, the host had proffered everywhere his gifts. He wist how to live bountifully, in mickle honors. To Giselher he had given his comely daughter; to Gunther, the worshipful knight, who seldom took a gift, he gave a coat of mail, which the noble and mighty king wore well with honor. Gunther bowed low over noble Rudeger's hand. Then to Gernot he gave a weapon good enow, the which he later bare full gloriously in strife. Little did the margrave's wife begrudge him the gift, but through it good Rudeger was forced to lose his life. Gotelind offered Hagen a loving gift, as well befit her. He took it, sith the king had taken one, that he should not fare forth from her to the feasting, without her present. Later he gainsayed it. "Of all that I have ever seen," quoth Hagen, "I crave to bear naught else save that shield on yonder wall; fain would I take that with me into Etzel's land."

When the margravine heard Hagen's speech, it minded her of her grief—tears became her well. She thought full dearly on Nudung's (3) death, whom Wittich had slain; from this she felt the stress of sorrow. To the knight she spake: "I'll give you the shield. Would to God in heaven, that he still lived who bare it once in hand. He met his death in battle; for him must I ever weep, which giveth me, poor wife, dire woe."

The noble margravine rose from her seat and with her white hands she seized the shield. To Hagen the lady bare it, who took it in his hand. This gift was worthily bestowed upon the knight. A cover of shining silk concealed its colors, for it was set with precious stones. In sooth the daylight never shone on better shield. Had any wished to buy it at its cost, 'twere well worth a thousand marks. (4) Hagen bade the shield be borne away.

Then Dankwart came to court. To him the margrave's daughter gave great store of rich apparel, the which he later wore among the Huns in passing lordly wise. However many gifts were taken by them, naught would have come into the hands of any, save through the kindness of the host, who proffered them so fair. Later they became such foes that they were forced to strike him dead.

Now the doughty Folker went courteously with his fiddle and stood before

Gotelind. He played sweet tunes and sang to her his songs. Thus he took his leave and parted from Bechelaren. The margravine bade fetch a chest. Now hear the tale of friendly gifts! Twelve rings she took out and placed them on his hand. "These ye must bear hence to Etzel's land and wear them at court for my sake, whithersoever ye turn, that men may tell me how ye have served me yonder at the feast." What the lady craved, he later carried out full well.

Then spake the host to his guests: "Ye shall journey all the gentlier, for I myself will guide you and bid guard you well, that none may harm you on the road."

Then his sumpters were laden soon. The host was well beseen with five hundred men with steeds and vesture. These he took with him full merrily hence to the feasting. Not one of them later ever came alive to Bechlaren. With a loving kiss the host parted hence; the same did Giselher, as his gentle breeding counseled him. In their arms they clasped fair wives. This many a high-born maid must needs bewail in later times. On every side they opened the casements, for the host with his liegemen would now mount their steeds. I ween their hearts did tell them of the bitter woes to come. Then wept many a dame and many a comely maid. They pined for their dear kinsmen, whom nevermore they saw in Bechelaren. Yet these rode merrily across the sand, down along the Danube to the Hunnish land.

Then noble Rudeger, the full lusty knight, spake to the Burgundians: "Certes, the tidings that we be coming to the Huns must not be left unsaid, for king Etzel hath never heard aught that pleased him more."

So down through Austria the envoy sped, and to the folk on every side 'twas told that the heroes were coming from Worms beyond the Rhine. Naught could have been liefer to the courtiers of the king. On before the envoys hasted with the tidings, that the Nibelungs were already in the Hunnish land.

"Thou must greet them well, Kriemhild, lady mine. Thy dear brothers be coming in great state to visit thee."

Within a casement window Lady Kriemhild stood and looked out to see her kin, as friend doth for friend. Many a man she spied from her fatherland. The king, too, learned the tale and laughed for very pleasure. "Now well is me of my joys," quoth Kriemhild, "my kinsmen bring with them many a brand-new shield and white coat of mail. He who would have gold, let him bethink him of my sorrows, and I'll ever be his friend."

ENDNOTES:
(1) "Chaplets", see Adventure 10, note 1.
(2) "Of yore", see Adventure 23, note 2.
(3) "Nudung" was slain, according to the "Thidreksaga", chap.

335, by "Vidg"a (here Wittich, M.H.G. "Witege", the son of Wielant, the smith, in the battle of Gronsport. There, chap. 369, he is Gotelind's brother, but in "Biterolf" and the "Rosengarten" he is her son.

(4) "Marks", see Adventure V, note 5.

ADVENTURE XXVIII

How The Burgundians Came To Etzel's Castle

When the Burgundians were come to the land, old Hildebrand (1) of Berne did hear the tale, and sore it rued him. He told his lord, who bade him welcome well the lusty knights and brave. The doughty Wolfhart (2) bade fetch the steeds; then many a sturdy warrior rode with Dietrich, to where he thought to meet them on the plain where they had pitched full many a lordly tent. When Hagen of Troneg saw them riding from afar, to his lords he spake in courteous wise: "Now must ye doughty warriors rise from your seats and go to meet them, who would greet you here. Yonder cometh a fellowship I know full well, they be full speedy knights from the Amelung land, (3) whom the lord of Berne doth lead—high-mettled warriors they. Scorn not the service that they proffer."

Then with Dietrich there alighted from the steeds, as was mickle right, many a knight and squire. Towards the strangers they went, to where they found the heroes; in friendly wise they greeted those from the Burgundian land. Ye may now hear what Sir Dietrich said to the sons of Uta, as he saw them coming toward him. Their journey rued him sore; he weened that Rudeger wist it, and had told them the tale. "Be ye welcome, fair sirs, Gunther and Giselher, Gernot and Hagen, likewise Folker and the doughty Dankwart. Know ye not that Kriemhild still mourneth sorely for the hero of the Nibelung land?"

"Let her weep long time," quoth Hagen. "He hath lain these many years, done to death. Let her love now the Hunnish king. Siegfried cometh not again, he hath long been buried."

"Let us not talk of Siegfried's wounds, but if Kriemhild still live, scathe may hap again," so spake Sir Dietrich, the lord of Berne. "Hope of the Nibelungs, guard thee well against this."

"Why should I guard me?" spake the high-born king. "Etzel sent us envoys (why should I question more?) to say that we should ride to visit him, hither to this land. My sister Kriemhild sent us many a message, too."

"Let me counsel you," quoth Hagen, "to beg Sir Dietrich and his good knights to tell you the tidings further, and to let you know the Lady Kriemhild's mood."

154

Then the three mighty kings, Gunther and Gernot and Sir Dietrich, too, went and spake apart. "Pray tell us, good and noble knight of Berne, what ye do know of the queen's mood?"

Answered the lord of Berne: "What more shall I tell you? Every morning I hear King Etzel's wife wail and weep with piteous mind to the mighty God of heaven over the stalwart Siegfried's death."

"That which we have heard," spake bold Folker, the fiddler, "cannot be turned aside. We must ride to court and abide what may hap to us doughty knights among the Huns."

The brave Burgundians now rode to court. In lordly wise they came after the fashion of their land. Many a brave man among the Huns wondered what manner of man Hagen of Troneg be. It was enough that men told tales, that he had slain Kriemhild's husband the mightiest of all heroes. For that cause alone much questioning about Hagen was heard at court. The knight was fair of stature, that is full true; broad he was across the breast; his hair was mixed with gray; his legs were long, and fierce his glance; lordly gait he had.

Then one bade lodge the Burgundian men, but Gunther's fellowship was placed apart. This the queen advised, who bare him much hate, and therefore men later slew the footmen in their lodgings. Dankwart, Hagen's brother, he was marshal. The king earnestly commended to him his followers, that he purvey them well and give them enow to eat; The hero of Burgundy bare them all good will. Kriemhild, the fair, went with her maids-in-waiting to where, false of mood, she greeted the Nibelungs. Giselher alone she kissed and took by the hand. That Hagen of Troneg saw, and bound his helmet tighter. "After such a greeting," quoth Hagen, "doughty knights may well bethink them. One giveth kings a greeting different from their men. We have not made a good journey to this feast." (4)

She spake: "Be welcome to him that be fain to see you; I greet you not for your kinship. Pray tell me what ye do bring me from Worms beyond the Rhine, that ye should be so passing welcome to me here?"

"Had I known," quoth Hagen, "that knights should bring you gifts, I had bethought me better, for I be rich enow to bring you presents hither to this land."

"Now let me hear the tale of where ye have put the Nibelung hoard? It was mine own, as ye well know, and ye should have brought me that to Etzel's land."

"I' faith, my Lady Kriemhild, it is many a day sith I have had the care of the

155

Nibelung hoard. My lords bade sink it in the Rhine, and there it must verily lie till doomsday."

Then spake the queen: "I thought as much. Ye have brought full little of it hither to this land, albeit it was mine own, and I had it whilom in my care. Therefore have I all time so many a mournful day."

"The devil I'll bring you," answered Hagen. "I have enough to carry with my shield and breastplate; my helm is bright, the sword is in my hand, therefore I bring you naught."

Then the queen spake to the knights on every side: "One may not bring weapons to the hall. Sir Knights, give them to me, I'll have them taken in charge."

"I' faith," quoth Hagen, "never shall that be done. In sooth I crave not the honor, O bounteous princess, that ye should bear my shield and other arms to the lodgings; ye be a queen. This my father did not teach me, I myself will play the chamberlain."

"Alack for my sorrows," spake Lady Kriemhild. "Why will Hagen and my brother not let their shields be taken in charge? They be warned, and wist I, who hath done this, I'd ever plan his death."

To this Sir Dietrich answered in wrath: "'Tis I, that hath warned the noble and mighty princes and the bold Hagen, the Burgundian liegeman. Go to, thou she-devil, thou durst not make me suffer for the deed."

Sore abashed was King Etzel's wife, for bitterly she feared Sir Dietrich. At once she left him, not a word she spake, but gazed with furious glance upon her foes. Two warriors then grasped each other quickly by the hand, the one was Sir Dietrich, the other Hagen. With gentle breeding the lusty hero spake: "Forsooth I rue your coming to the Huns, because of what the queen hath said."

Quoth Hagen: "There will be help for that."

Thus the two brave men talked together. King Etzel saw this, and therefore he began to query: "Fain would I know," spake the mighty king, "who yonder warrior be, whom Sir Dietrich greeteth there in such friendly wise. He carrieth high his head; whoever be his father, he is sure a doughty knight."

A liegeman of Kriemhild made answer to the king: "By birth he is from Troneg, his father hight Aldrian; however blithe he bear him here, a grim man is he. I'll let you see full well that I have told no lie."

156

"How shall I know that he be so fierce?" replied the king. As yet he wist not the many evil tricks that the queen should later play upon her kin, so that she let none escape from the Huns alive.

"Well know I Aldrian, for he was my vassal (5) and here at my court gained mickle praise and honor. I dubbed him knight and gave hint of my gold. The faithful Helca loved him inly. Therefore I have since known Hagen every whit. Two stately youths became my hostages, he and Walther of Spain. (6) Here they grew to manhood; Hagen I sent home again, Walther ran away with Hildegund."

He bethought him of many tales that had happed of yore. He had spied aright his friend of Troneg, who in his youth had given him yeoman service. Later in his old age he did him many a dear friend to death.

ENDNOTES:
(1) "Hildebrand" is the teacher and armor bearer of Dietrich.
    He is the hero of the famous "Hildebrandslied".
(2) "Wolfhart" is Hildebrand's nephew. In the "Thidreksaga" he
    falls in the battle of Gronsport.
(3) "Amelung land" is the name under which Dietrich's land
    appears. Theodorich, the king of the East Goths, belonged
    to the race of the Amali.
(4) "Feast". That Kriemhild kissed only Giselher, who was
    innocent of Siegfried's death, aroused Hagen's suspicions.
(5) "Vassal". No other account speaks of Aldrian as being at
    Etzel's court. He is probably confused here with his son,
    for Hagen's stay with Etzel in various legends, as also in
    our poem a few lines further down.
(6) "Walther of Spain" is Walther of Aquitania, a legendary
    personage of whom the O.E. fragment "Waldere", the Latin
    epic "Waltharius", a M.H.G. epic, and the "Thidreksaga"
    tell. He flees with Hildegund, the daughter of the
    Burgundian King Herrich, from Etzel's court, as related
    here, but has to fight for his life against overpowering
    numbers, in the "Thidreksaga" against the pursuing Huns, in
    the other sources against the Burgundians. In both cases
    Hagen is among his foes, but takes no part in the fight at
    first, out of friendship for Walther.

How Hagen Would Not Rise For Kriemhild

Then the two worshipful warriors parted, Hagen of Troneg and Sir Dietrich. Over his shoulder Gunther's liegeman gazed for a comrade-at-arms, whom he then quickly won. Folker he saw, the cunning fiddler, stand by Giselher, and begged him to join him, for well he knew his savage mood. He was in all things a bold knight and a good. Still they let the lordings stand in the court, only these twain alone men saw walk hence far across the court before a spacious palace. These chosen warriors feared the hate of none. They sate them down upon a bench before the house over against a hall, the which belonged to Kriemhild. Upon their bodies shone their lordly weeds. Enow who gazed upon them would than have known the knights; as wild beasts the haughty heroes were stared upon by the Hunnish men. Etzel's wife, too, gazed upon them through a window, at which fair Kriemhild waxed sad again. Of her sorrows it minded her and she began to weep. Much it wondered Etzel's men what had so quickly saddened her mood. Quoth she: "That Hagen hath done, ye heroes brave and good."

To the lady they spake: "How hath that happed, for but newly we did see you joyful? None there be so bold, an' he hath done you aught, but it will cost him his life, if ye bid us venge you."

"Ever would I requite it, if any avenged my wrongs. I would give him all he craved. Behold me at your feet," spake he queen; "avenge me on Hagen, that he lose his life."

Then sixty bold men made them ready eftsoon for Kriemhild's sake. They would hence to slay the bold knight Hagen and the fiddler, too. With forethought this was done. When the queen beheld the band so small, grim of mood she spake to the knights: "What ye now would do, ye should give over. With so few durst ye never encounter Hagen. And however strong and bold Hagen of Troneg be, he who sitteth by his side, Folker, the fiddler, is stronger still by far. He is an evil man. Certes, ye may not so lightly match these knights."

When they heard this, four hundred doughty warriors more did make them ready. The noble queen craved sore to do them harm. Thereby the heroes later fell in mickle danger. When she saw her followers well armed, the queen spake to the doughty knights: "Now bide a while, ye must stand quite still in truth. Wearing my crown, I will go to meet my foes. List ye to the wrongs that Hagen of Troneg, Gunther's man, hath done me. I know him to be so haughty that he'll not deny a whit. Little I reek what hap to him on this account."

Then the fiddler, a bold minstrel, spied the noble queen walk down the flight of steps that led downward from a house. When bold Folker saw this, to his comrade-at-arms he spake: "Now behold, friend Hagen, how she walketh yonder, who hath faithlessly bidden us to this land. I have never seen with a queen so many men bearing sword in hand march in such warlike guise. Know ye, friend Hagen, whether she bear you hate? If so be, I counsel you to guard the better your life and honor. Certes, methinks this good. They be wroth of mood, as far as I can see, and some be so broad of chest that he who would guard himself should do so betimes. I ween there be those among them who wear bright breastplates. Whom they would attack, I cannot say."

Then, angry of mood, the brave knight Hagen spake: "Well I wot that all this be done against me, that they thus bear their gleaming swords in hand. For aught of them, I still may ride to the Burgundian land. Now tell me, friend Folker, whether ye will stand by me, if perchance Kriemhild's men would fight me? Pray let me hear that, if so be ye hold me dear. I'll aid you evermore with faithful service."

"I'll help you surely," spake the minstrel; "and should I see the king with all his warriors draw near us, not one foot will I yield from fear in aiding you, the while I live."

"Now may God in heaven requite you, noble Folker; though they strive against me, what need I more? Sith ye will help me, as I hear you say, let these warriors come on full-armed."

"Let us rise now from our seats," spake the minstrel. "Let us do her honor as she passeth by, she is a high-born dame, a queen. We shall thereby honor ourselves as well."

"For my sake, no," quoth Hagen. "Should I go hence, these knights would think 'twas through fear. Not for one of them will I ever rise from my seat. It beseemeth us both better, forsooth, to leave this undone, for why should I honor one who doth bear me hatred? Nor will I do this, the while I live; I reck not how King Etzel's wife doth hate me."

Haughty Hagen laid across his knees a gleaming sword from whose pommel a sparkling jasper, greener than grass, did shine. Its hilt was golden, its sheath an edging of red. That it was Siegfried's, Kriemhild knew full well. She must needs grow sad when that she knew the sword, for it minded her of her wrongs; she began to weep. I ween bold Hagen had done it for this cause. Folker, the bold, drew nearer to the bench a fiddle bow, strong, mickle, and long, like unto a broad, sharp sword, and there the two lusty knights sate

159

undaunted. These two brave men did think themselves so lordly, that they would not leave their seats through fear of any man. The noble queen walked therefore to their very feet and gave them hostile greeting. She spake: "Now tell me, Hagen, who hath sent for you, that ye durst ride hither to this land, sith ye know full well what ye have done me? Had ye good wits, ye should have left it undone, by rights."

"No one sent for me," quoth Hagen. "Men bade to this land three knights, who hight my lords. I am their liegeman, and full seldom have I stayed behind when they journeyed to any court."

Quoth she: "Now tell me further, why ye did this, through the which ye have earned my hate? Ye slew Siegfried, my dear husband, for which I have cause enow to weep until mine end."

Quoth he: "What booteth more, enow is already said. It is just I, Hagen, who slew Siegfried, a hero of his hands. How sorely did he atone that Lady Kriemhild railed at comely Brunhild. 'Tis not to be denied, O mighty queen, I alone am to blame for this scathful scathe. (1) Let him avenge it who will, be he wife or man. Unless be I should lie to you, I have dons you much of harm."

Quoth she: "Now hear, ye knights, how he denieth no whit of my wrongs. Men of Etzel, I care not what hap to him from this cause."

The proud warriors all gazed at one another. Had any began the fight, it would have come about that men must have given the honors to the two comrades, for they had oft wrought wonders in the fray. What the Huns had weened to do must now needs be left undone through fear.

Then spake one of the men-at-arms: "Why gaze ye thus at me? What I afore vowed, I will now give over. I will lose my life for no man's gift. Forsooth King Etzel's wife would fain lead us into wrong."

Quoth another hard by: "Of the selfsame mind am I. An' any give me towers of good red gold, I would not match this fiddler, for his fearful glances, the which I have seen him cast. Hagen, too, I have known from his youthful days, wherefore men can tell me little of this knight. I have seen him fight in two and twenty battles, through which woe of heart hath happed to many a dame. He and the knight from Spain trod many a war path, when here at Etzel's court they waged so many wars in honor of the king. Much this happed, wherefore one must justly honor Hagen. At that time the warrior was of his years a lad. How gray are they who then were young! Now is he come to wit and is a man full grim. Balmung, (2) too, he beareth, the which he won in evil wise."

160

Therewith the strife was parted, so that no one fought, which mightily rued the queen. The warriors turned them hence; in sooth they feared their death at the fiddler's hands, and surely they had need of this. Then spake the fiddler: "We have now well seen that we shall find foes here, as we heard tell afore. Let us go to court now to the kings, then dare none match our lords in fight. How oft a man doth leave a thing undone through fear, the which he would not do, when friend standeth by friend in friendly (3) wise, an' he have good wits. Scathe to many a man is lightly warded off by forethought."

Quoth Hagen: "Now will I follow you."

They went to where they found the dapper warriors standing in the court in a great press of welcoming knights.

Bold Folker gan speak loudly to his lords: "How long will ye stand and let yourselves be jostled? Ye must go to court and hear from the king of what mind he be."

Men then saw the brave heroes and good pair off. The prince of Berne took by the hand the mighty Gunther of Burgundian land. Irnfried (4) took the brave knight Gernot, while Rudeger was seen to go to court with Giselher. But however any paired, Folker and Hagen never parted, save in one fray, when their end was come, and this noble ladies must needs greatly bewail in after time. With the kings one saw go to court a thousand brave men of their fellowship, thereto sixty champions that were come with them, whom the bold Hagen had taken from his land. Hawart and Iring, (5) two chosen men, were seen to walk together near the kings. Men saw Dankwart and Wolfhart, a peerless knight, display their chivalry before all eyes.

When the lord of the Rhine had entered the hall, the mighty Etzel delayed no longer, but sprang from his throne when he saw him come. Never did so fair a greeting hap from any king. "Be welcome, Sir Gunther, and Sir Gernot, too, and your brother Giselher. I sent you truly my faithful service to Worms beyond the Rhine. All your fellowship, too, I welcome. Now be ye passing welcome, ye two knights, Folker, the brave, and Sir Hagen likewise, to me and to my lady, here in this our land. She sent you many a messenger to the Rhine."

Then spake Hagen of Troneg: "I heard much talk of that, and were I not come to the Huns for the sake of my lords, I should have ridden in your honor to this land."

The noble host then took his dear guests by the hand and led them to the settle where he sate himself. Busily they poured out for the guests in broad bowls of gold, mead, morat, (6) and wine and bade those far from home be welcome. Then spake King Etzel: "Let me tell you this; it might not liefer hap to me in all this world, than through you heroes, that ye be come to see me. Through this much sadness is also taken from the queen. Me-wondereth greatly what I have done you noble strangers, that ye never recked to come into my land. My sadness is turned to joy, since now I see you here."

To this Rudeger, a high-mettled knight, made answer: "Ye may be glad to see them. Good is the fealty which the kinsmen of my lady wot how to use so well. They bring also to your house many a stately knight."

Upon a midsummer's eve the lords were come to the court of the mighty Etzel. Seldom hath there been heard such lofty greeting as when he welcomed the heroes. When now the time to eat was come, the king went with them to the board. Never did host sit fairer with his guests. Men gave them meat and drink to the full. All that they craved stood ready for them, for mickle wonders had been told about these knights.

ENDNOTES:
(1) "Scathful scathe" here imitates the M.H.G. "scaden scedelich".
(2) "Balmung", see Adventure III, note 7.
(3) "friend... friendly". This repetition occurs in the original.
(4) "Irnfried", see Adventure XXII, note 8.
(5) "Hawart" and "Iring", Adventure XXII, notes 6 and 7.
(6) "Morat" (M.H.G. "moraz") from late Latin "moratum", mulberry wine, is a beverage composed of honey flavored with mulberry-juice.

162

ADVENTURE XXX

How They Kept The Watch

The day had now an end, and the night drew nigh. Care beset the wayworn travelers, as to when they should go to bed and rest them. This Hagen bespake with Etzel, and it was told them soon.

Gunther spake to the host: "God be with you, we would fain go to our sleep, pray give us leave. We will come early on the morrow, whensoever ye bid."

Etzel parted then full merrily from his guests. Men pressed the strangers on every side, at which brave Folker spake to the Huns: "How dare ye crowd before the warriors' feet? An' ye will not leave this, ye will fare full ill. I'll smite some man so heavy a fiddle blow, that if he have a faithful friend he may well bewail it. Why give ye not way before us knights? Methinks 'twere well. All pass for knights, but be not of equal mettle."

As the fiddler spake thus in wrath, Hagen, the brave, looked behind him. He spake: "The bold gleeman doth advise you right, ye men of Kriemhild, ye should hie you to your lodgings. I ween none of you will do what ye are minded, but would ye begin aught, come early on the morrow, and let us wanderers have peace to-night. Certes, I ween that it hath never happed with such good will on the part of heroes."

Then the guests were brought into a spacious hall, which they found purveyed on every side with costly beds, long and broad, for the warriors. Lady Kriemhild planned the very greatest wrongs against them. One saw there many a cunningly wrought quilt from Arras (1) of shining silken cloth and many a coverlet of Arabian silk, the best that might be had; upon this ran a border that shone in princely wise. Many bed covers of ermine and of black sable were seen, beneath which they should have their ease at night, until the dawn of day. Never hath king lain so lordly with his meiny.

"Alas for these night quarters," spake Giselher, the youth, "and alas for my friends, who be come with us. However kindly my sister greeted us, yet I do fear me that through her fault we must soon lie dead."

"Now give over your care," quoth Hagen, the knight. "I'll stand watch myself to-night. I trow to guard us well, until the day doth come. Therefore have no fear; after that, let him survive who may."

All bowed low and said him gramercy. Then went they to their beds. A short while after the stately men had laid them down, bold Hagen, the hero, began to arm him. Then the fiddler, Knight Folker, spake: "If it scorn you not, Hagen, I would fain hold the watch with you to-night, until the early morn."

The hero then thanked Folker in loving wise: "Now God of heaven requite you, dear Folker. In all my cares, I would crave none other than you alone, whenever I had need. I shall repay you well, and death hinder me not."

Both then donned their shining armor and either took his shield in hand, walked out of the house and stood before the door. Thus they cared for the guests in faithful wise. The doughty Folker leaned his good shield against the side of the hall, then turned him back and fetched his fiddle and served his friends as well befit the hero. Beneath the door of the house he sate him down upon a stone; bolder fiddler was there never. When the tones of the strings rang forth so sweetly, the proud wanderers gave Folker thanks. At first the strings twanged so that the whole house resounded; his strength and his skill were both passing great. Then sweeter and softer he began to play, and thus many a care-worn man he lulled to sleep. When he marked that all had fallen asleep, the knight took again his shield and left the room and took his stand before the tower, and there he guarded the wanderers against Kriemhild's men.

'Twas about the middle of the night (I know not but what it happed a little earlier), that bold Folker spied the glint of a helmet afar in the darkness. Kriemhild's men would fain have harmed the guests. Then the fiddler spake: "Sir Hagen, my friend, it behooveth us to bear these cares together. Before the house I see armed men stand, and err I not, I ween, they would encounter us!"

"Be silent," quoth Hagen, "let them draw nearer before they be ware of us. Then will helmets be dislodged by the swords in the hands of us twain. They will be sent back to Kriemhild in evil plight."

One of the Hunnish warriors (full soon that happed) marked that the door was guarded. How quickly then he spake: "That which we have in mind may not now come to pass. I see the fiddler stand on guard. On his head he weareth a glittering helmet, shining and hard, strong and whole. His armor rings flash out like fire. By him standeth Hagen; in sooth the guests be guarded well."

Straightway they turned again. When Folker saw this, wrathfully he spake to his comrade-at-arms: "Now let me go from the house to the warriors. I would fain put some questions to Lady Kriemhild's men."

"For my sake, no," quoth Hagen. "If ye leave the house, the doughty knights are like to bring you in such stress with their swords, that I must aid you even should it be the death of all my kin. As soon as we be come into the fray, twain

164

of them, or four, would in a short time run into the house and would bring such scathe upon the sleepers, that we might never cease to mourn."

Then Folker answered: "Let us bring it to pass that they note that I have seen them, so that Kriemhild's men may not deny that they would fain have acted faithlessly."

Straightway Folker then called out to them: "How go ye thus armed, ye doughty knights? Would ye ride to rob, ye men of Kriemhild? Then must ye have the help of me and my comrade-at-arms."

To this none made reply. Angry grew his mood. "Fy! Ye evil cowards," spake the good knight, "would ye have murdered us asleep? That hath been done full seldom to such good heroes."

Then the queen was told that her messengers had compassed naught. Rightly it did vex her, and with wrathful mood she made another plan. Through this brave heroes and good must needs thereafter perish.

ENDNOTES:
(1) "Arras", the capital of Artois in the French Netherlands.
     In older English "arras" is used also for tapestry.

ADVENTURE XXXI (1)

How They Went To Church

"My coat of mail groweth cold," said Folker. "I ween the night hath run its course. By the air I mark that day is near."

Then they waked the many knights who still lay sleeping. The light of dawn shone into the hall upon the strangers. On all sides Hagen gan wake the warriors, if perchance they would fain go to the minster for mass. Men now loudly rang the bells in Christian fashion. Heathens and Christians did not sing alike, so that it was seen full well that they were not as one. Gunther's liegemen now would go to church, and all alike had risen from their beds. The champions laced them into such goodly garments, that never did hero bring better clothes to the land of any king. This vexed Hagen. He spake: "Heroes, ye should wear here other clothes. Certes, ye know full well the tales. Instead of roses, bear weapons in your hands; instead of jeweled chaplets, your bright helms and good, sith ye know full well the wicked Kriemhild's mood. Let me tell you, we must fight to-day, so instead of silken shirts, wear hauberks, and instead of rich cloaks, good shields and broad, so that if any grow angry with you, ye be full armed. Dear my lords, and all my kin and liegemen, go willingly to church and make plaint to the mighty God of your fears and need, for know full sure that death draweth nigh us. Nor must ye forget to confess aught that ye have done and stand full zealously before your God. Of this I warn you, noble knights, unless God in heaven so will, ye'll never more hear mass."

So the princes and their liegemen went to the minster. In the holy churchyard bold Hagen bade them halt, that they might not be parted. He spake: "Of a truth none knoweth what will hap to us from the Huns. Place, my friends, your shields before your feet, and if any proffer you cold greeting, repay it with deep and mortal wounds. That is Hagen's counsel, that ye may so be found as doth befit your honor."

Folker and Hagen, the twain, then hied them to the spacious minster. This was done that the queen might press upon them in the crowd. Certes, she was passing grim. Then came the lord of the land and his fair wife, her body adorned with rich apparel; Doughty warriors, too, were seen to walk beside her. One saw the dust rise high from Kriemhild's band. When mighty Etzel spied the kings and their fellowship thus armed, how quick he spake: "Why do I see my friends thus go with helmets? Upon my troth, it grieveth me, and hath any done them aught, I shall gladly make amends, as doth think them

166

good. Hath any made heavy their hearts or mood, I'll show them well, that it doth irk me much. I am ready for whatever they command me."

To this Hagen answered: "None hath done us aught; it is the custom of my lordings that they go armed at all high feasts for full three days. We should tell Etzel, had aught been done us."

Kriemhild heard full well what Hagen spake. How right hostilely she gazed into his eyes! She would not tell the custom of their land, albeit she had known it long in Burgundy. However grim and strong the hate she bare them, yet had any told Etzel the truth, he would have surely hindered what later happed. Because of their great haughtiness they scorned to tell him. When the great crowd went past with the queen, these twain, Hagen and Folker, would not step back more than two hand-breadths, the which irked the Huns. Forsooth they had to jostle with the lusty heroes. This thought King Etzel's chamberlains not good. Certes, they would have fain angered the champions, but that they durst not before the noble king. So there was much jostling, but nothing more.

When they had worshiped God and would hence again, many a Hunnish warrior horsed him passing soon, At Kriemhild's side stood many a comely maid, and well seven thousand knights rode with the queen. Kriemhild with her ladies sate her down at the easements by the side of the mighty Etzel, which was him lief, for they would watch the lusty heroes joust. Ho, what stranger knights rode before them in the court! Then was come the marshal with the squires. Bold Dankwart had taken to him his lord's retainers from the Burgundian land; the steeds of the Nibelungs they found well saddled. When now the kings and their men were come to horse, stalwart Folker gan advise that they should ride a joust after the fashion of their land. At this the heroes rode in lordly wise; none it irked what the knight had counseled. The hurtling and the noise waxed loud, as the many men rode into the broad court. Etzel and Kriemhild themselves beheld the scene. To the jousts were come six hundred knights of Dietrich's men to match the strangers, for they would have pastime with the Burgundians. Fain would they have done it, had he given them leave. Ho, what good champions rode in their train! The tale was told to Sir Dietrich and he forbade the game with Gunther's men; he feared for his liegemen, and well he might.

When those of Berne had departed thence, there came the men of Rudeger from Bechelaren, five hundred strong, with shields, riding out before the hall. It would have been lief to the margrave, had they left it undone. Wisely he rode then to them through the press and said to his knights, that they were ware that Gunther's men were evil-minded toward them. If they would leave off the jousting, it would please him much. When now these lusty heroes parted from them, then came those of Thuringia, as we are told, and well a thousand brave men from Denmark. From the tilting one saw many truncheons (2) flying hence. Irnfried and Hawart now rode into the tourney. Proudly those from the Rhine awaited them and offered the men of Thuringia many a joust. Many a lordly shield was riddled by the thrusts. Thither came then Sir Bloedel with three thousand men. Well was he seen of Etzel and Kriemhild, for the knightly sports happed just before the twain. The queen saw it gladly, that the Burgundians might come to grief. Schrutan (3) and Gibecke, Ramung and Hornbog, (4) rode into the tourney in Hunnish wise. To the heroes from Burgundian land they addressed them. High above the roof of the royal hall the spear-shafts whirled. Whatever any there plied, 'twas but a friendly rout. Palace and hall were heard resounding loud through the clashing of the shields of Gunther's men. With great honor his meiny gained the meed. Their pastime was so mickle and so great, that from beneath the housings of the good steeds, which the heroes rode, there flowed the frothy sweat. In haughty wise they encountered with the Huns.

Then spake the fiddler, Folker the minstrel: "I ween these warriors dare not match us. I've aye heard the tale, that they bear us hate, and forsooth it might never fortune better for them than now." Again Folker spake: "Let our steeds be now led away to their lodgings and let us joust again toward eventide, and there be time. Perchance the queen may accord to the Burgundians the prize."

Then one was seen riding hither so proudly, that none of all the Huns could have done the like. Certes, he must have had a sweetheart on the battlements. As well attired he rode as the bride of any noble knight. At sight of him Folker spake again: "How could I give this over? This ladies' darling must have a buffet. None shall prevent me and it shall cost him dear. In truth I reck not, if it vex King Etzel's wife."

"For my sake, No," spake straightway King Gunther. "The people will blame us, if we encounter them. 'Twill befit us better far, an' we let the Huns begin the strife."

King Etzel was still sitting by the queen.

"I'll join you in the tourney," quoth Hagen then. "Let the ladies and the knights behold how we can ride. That will be well, for they'll give no meed to King Gunther's men."

The doughty Folker rode into the lists again, which soon gave many a dame great dole. His spear he thrust through the body of the dapper Hun; this both maid and wife were seen thereafter to bewail. Full hard and fast gan Hagen and his liegemen and sixty of his knights ride towards the fiddler, where the play was on. This Etzel and Kriemhild clearly saw. The three kings would not leave their minstrel without guard amidst the foe. Cunningly a thousand heroes rode; with haughty bearing they did whatso they would. When now the wealthy Hun was slain, men heard his kin cry out and wail. All the courtiers asked: "Who hath done this deed?"

"That the fiddler did, Folker, the valiant minstrel."

The margrave's kindred from the Hunnish land called straightway for their swords and shields, and would fain have done Folker to death. Fast the host gan hasten from the windows. Great rout arose from the folk on every side. The kings and their fellowship, the Burgundian men, alighted before the hall and drove their horses to the rear. Then King Etzel came to part the strife. From the hand of a kinsman of the Hun he wrenched a sturdy weapon and drove them all back again, for full great was his wrath. "Why should my courtesie to these knights go all for naught? Had ye slain this minstrel at my court," spake King Etzel, "'twere evil done. I saw full well how he rode, when he thrust through the Hun, that it happed through stumbling, without any fault of his. Ye must let my guests have peace."

Thus he became their safe-guard. To the stalls men led away the steeds; many a varlet they had, who served them well with zeal in every service. The host now hied him to his palace with his friends, nor would he let any man grow wroth again. Then men set up the tables and bare forth water for the guests. Forsooth the men from the Rhine had there enow of stalwart foes. 'Twas long before the lords were seated.

Meanwhile Kriemhild's fears did trouble her passing sore. She spake: "My lord of Berne, I seek thy counsel, help, and favor, for mine affairs do stand in anxious wise."

Then Hildebrand, a worshipful knight, made answer to her: "And any slay the Nibelungs for the sake of any hoard, he will do it without my aid. It may well repent him, for they be still unconquered, these doughty and lusty knights."

Then Spake Sir Dietrich in his courteous wise: "Let be this wish, O mighty queen. Thy kinsmen have done me naught of wrong, that I should crave to match these valiant knights in strife. Thy request honoreth thee little, most noble queen, that thou dost plot against the life of thy kinsfolk. They came in hope of friendship to this land. Siegfried will not be avenged by Dietrich's hand."

When she found no whit of faithlessness in the lord of Berne, quickly she promised Bloedel a broad estate, that Nudung (5) owned aforetime. Later he was slain by Hagen, so that he quite forgot the gift. She spake: "Thou must help me, Sir Bloedel, forsooth my foes be in this house, who slew Siegfried, my dear husband. Ever will I serve him, that helpeth me avenge this deed."

To this Bloedel replied: "My lady, now may ye know that because of Etzel I dare not, in sooth, advise to hatred against them, for he is fain to see thy kinsmen at his court. The king would ne'er forget it of me, and I did them aught of wrong."

"Not so, Sir Bloedel, for I shall ever be thy friend. Certes, I'll give thee silver and gold as guerdon and a comely maid, the wife of Nudung, whose lovely body thou mayst fain caress. I'll give thee his land and all his castles, too, so that thou mayst always live in joy, Sir knight, if thou dost now win the lands where Nudung dwelt. Faithfully will I keep, whatso I vow to thee to-day."

When Sir Bloedel heard the guerdon, and that the lady through her beauty would befit him well, he weened to serve the lovely queen in strife. Because of this the champion must needs lose his life. To the queen he spake: "Betake you again to the hall, and before any be aware, I'll begin a fray and Hagen must atone for what he hath done you. I'll deliver to you King Gunther's liegeman bound. Now arm you, my men," spake Bloedel. "We must hasten to the lodgings of the foes, for King Etzel's wife doth crave of me this service, wherefore we heroes must risk our lives."

When the queen left Bloedel in lust of battle, she went to table with King Etzel and his men. Evil counsels had she held against the guests. Since the strife could be started in no other wise (Kriemhild's ancient wrong still lay deep buried in her heart), she bade King Etzel's son be brought to table. How might a woman ever do more ghastly deed for vengeance' sake? Four of Etzel's men went hence anon and bare Ortlieb, (6) the young prince, to the lordings' table, where Hagen also sat. Because of this the child must needs die through Hagen's mortal hate.

When now the mighty king beheld his son, kindly he spake to the kinsmen of his wife: "Now see, my friends, this is the only son of me and of your sister. This may be of profit to you all, for if he take after his kinsmen, he'll become a valiant man, mighty and noble, strong and fashioned fair. Twelve lands will I give him, and I live yet a while. Thus may the hand of young Ortlieb serve you well. I do therefore beseech you, dear friends of mine, that when ye ride again to your lands upon the Rhine, ye take with you your sister's son and act full graciously toward the child, and bring him up in honor till he become a man. Hath any done you aught in all these lands, he'll help you to avenge it, when he groweth up."

This speech was also heard by Kriemhild, King Etzel's wife.

"These knights might well trust him," quoth Hagen, "if he grew to be a man, but the young prince doth seem so fey, (7) that I shall seldom be seen to ride to Ortlieb's court."

The king glanced at Hagen, for much the speech did irk him; and though the gentle prince said not a word, it grieved his heart and made him heavy of his mood. Nor was Hagen's mind now bent on pastime. But all the lordings and the king were hurt by what Hagen had spoken of the child; it vexed them sore, that they were forced to hear it. They wot not the things as yet, which should happen to them through this warrior.

ENDNOTES:
(1) "Adventure XXXI". This adventure is of late origin, being found only in our poem. See the introduction.
(2) "Truncheons", see Adventure II, note 8.
(3) "Schrutan". This name does not occur elsewhere. Piper suggests, that perhaps a Scotchman is meant, as "Skorottan" appears in the "Thidreksaga", chap. 28, as an ancient name of Scotland.
(4) "Gibecke", "Ramung" and "Hornbog", see Adventure XXII, notes 4 and 5.
(5) "Nudung", see Adventure XXVII, note 3.
(6) "Ortlieb". In the "Thidreksaga" Etzel's son is called Aldrian. There, however, he is killed because he strikes Hagen in the face, here in revenge for the killing of the Burgundian footmen.
(7) "Fey", see Adventure V, note 2.

ADVENTURE XXXII (1)

How Bloedel Was Slain

Full ready were now Bloedel's warriors. A thousand hauberks strong, they hied them to where Dankwart sate at table with the squires. Then the very greatest hate arose among the heroes. When Sir Bloedel drew near the tables, Dankwart, the marshal, greeted him in courteous wise. "Welcome, Sir Bloedel, in our house. In truth me-wondereth at thy coming. What doth it mean?"

"Forsooth, thou needst not greet me," so spake Bloedel; "for this coming of mine doth mean thine end. Because of Hagen, thy brother, by whom Siegfried was slain, thou and many other knights must suffer here among the Huns."

"Not so, Sir Bloedel," quoth Dankwart, "else this journey to your court might rue us sore. I was but a little child when Siegfried lost his life. I know not what blame King Etzel's wife could put on me."

"Of a truth, I wot not how to tell you of these tales; thy kinsmen, Gunther and Hagen, did the deed. Now ward you, ye wanderers, ye may not live. With your death must ye become Kriemhild's pledge."

"And ye will not turn you," quoth Dankwart, "then do my entreaties rue me; they had better far been spared."

The doughty knight and brave sprang up from the table; a sharp weapon, mickle and long, he drew and dealt Bloedel so fierce a sword-stroke that his head lay straightway at his feet. "Let that be thy marriage morning gift," (2) spake Dankwart, the knight, "for Nudung's bride, whom thou wouldst cherish with thy love. They call betroth her to another man upon the morn. Should he crave the dowry, 'twill be given to him eftsoon." A faithful Hun had told him that the queen did plan against them such grievous wrongs.

When Bloedel's men beheld their lord lie slain, no longer would they stand this from the guests. With uplifted swords they rushed, grim of mood, upon the youthful squires. Many a one did rue this later. Loudly Dankwart called to all the fellowship: "Ye see well, noble squires, how matters stand. Now ward you, wanderers! Forsooth we have great need, though Kriemhild asked us here in right friendly wise."

Those that had no sword reached down in front of the benches and lifted

172

many a long footstool by its legs. The Burgundian squires would now abide no longer, but with the heavy stools they dealt many bruises through the helmets. How fiercely the stranger youths did ward them! Out of the house they drove at last the men-at-arms, but five hundred of them, or better, stayed behind there dead. The fellowship was red and wot with blood.

These grievous tales were told now to Etzel's knights; grim was their sorrow, that Bloedel and his men were slain. This Hagen's brother and his squires had done. Before the king had learned it, full two thousand Huns or more armed them through hatred and hied them to the squires (this must needs be), and of the fellowship they left not one alive. The faithless Huns brought a mickle band before the house. Well the strangers stood their ground, but what booted their doughty prowess? Dead they all must lie. Then in a few short hours there rose a fearful dole. Now ye may hear wonders of a monstrous thing. Nine thousand yeomen lay there slain and thereto twelve good knights of Dankwart's men. One saw him stand alone still by the foe. The noise was hushed, the din had died away, when Dankwart, the hero, gazed over his shoulders. He spake: "Woe is me, for the friends whom I have lost! Now must I stand, alas, alone among my foes."

Upon his single person the sword-strokes fell thick and fast. The wife of many a hero must later mourn for this. Higher he raised his shield, the thong he lowered; the rings of many an armor he made to drip with blood. "Woe is me of all this sorrow," quoth Aldrian's son. (3) "Give way now, Hunnish warriors, and let me out into the breeze, that the air may cool me, fight-weary man."

Then men saw the warrior walk forth in full lordly wise. As the strife-weary man sprang from the house, how many added swords rang on his helmet! Those that had not seen what wonders his hand had wrought sprang towards the hero of the Burgundian land. "Now would to God," quoth Dankwart, "that I might find a messenger who could let my brother Hagen know I stand in such a plight before these knights. He would help me hence, or lie dead at my side."

Then spake the Hunnish champions: "Thou must be the messenger thyself, when we bear thee hence dead before thy brother. For the first time Gunther's vassal will then become acquaint with grief. Passing great scathe hast thou done King Etzel here."

Quoth he: "Now give over these threats and stand further back, or I'll wot the armor rings of some with blood. I'll tell the tale at court myself and make plaint to my lords of my great dole."

So sorely he dismayed King Etzel's men that they durst not withstand him with their swords, so they shot such great store of darts into his shield that he must needs lay it from his hand for very heaviness. Then they weened to overpower him, sith he no longer bare a shield. Ho, what deep wounds he struck them through their helmets! From this many a brave man was forced to reel before him, and bold Dankwart gained thereby great praise. From either side they sprang upon him, but in truth a many of them entered the fray too soon. Before his foes he walked, as doth a boar to the woods before the dogs. How might he be more brave? His path was ever wot with recking' blood. Certes, no single champion might ever fight better with his foes than he had done. Men now saw Hagen's brother go to court in lordly wise. Sewers (4) and cupbearers heard the ring of swords, and full many a one cast from his hand the drink and whatever food he bare to court. Enow strong foes met Dankwart at the stairs.

"How now, ye sewers," spake the weary knight. "Forsooth ye should serve well the guests and bear to the lords good cheer and let me bring the tidings to my dear masters."

Those that sprang towards him on the steps to show their prowess, he dealt so heavy a sword-stroke, that for fear they must needs stand further back. His mighty strength wrought mickle wonders.

ENDNOTES:
(1) Adventure XXXII. The details of the following scenes differ materially in the various sources. A comparative study of them will be found in the works of Wilmanns and Boer.
(2) "Marriage morning gift" (M.H.G. "morgengabe") was given by the bridegroom to the bride on the morning after the wedding. See Adventure XIX, note 1.
(3) "Aldrian's son", i.e., Dankwart.
(4) "Sewers" (O.F. "asseour", M.L. "adsessor" 'one who sets the table'; cf. F. "asseoir" 'to set', 'place', Lat. "ad sedere"), older English for an upper servant who brought on and removed the dishes from the table.

ADVENTURE XXXIII

How The Burgundians Fought The Huns

When brave Dankwart was come within the door, he bade King Etzel's meiny step aside. His garments dripped with blood and in his hand he bare unsheathed a mighty sword. Full loud he called out to the knight: "Brother Hagen, ye sit all too long, forsooth. To you and to God in heaven do I make plaint of our woe. Our knights and squires all lie dead within their lodgements."

He called in answer: "Who hath done this deed?"

"That Sir Bloedel hath done with his liegemen, but he hath paid for it dearly, as I can tell you, for with mine own hands I struck off his head."

"It is but little scathe," quoth Hagen, "if one can only say of a knight that he hath lost his life at a warrior's hands. Stately dames shall mourn him all the less. Now tell me, brother Dankwart, how comes it that ye be so red of hue? Ye suffer from wounds great dole, I ween. If there be any in the land that hath done you this, 'twill cost his life, and the foul fiend save him not."

"Ye see me safe and sound; my weeds alone are wet with blood. This hath happed from wounds of other men, of whom I have slain so many a one to-day that, had I to swear it, I could not tell the tale."

"Brother Dankwart," he spake, "guard us the door and let not a single Hun go forth. I will hold speech with the warriors, as our need constraineth us, for our meiny lieth dead before them, undeserved."

"If I must be chamberlain," quoth the valiant man, "I well wet how to serve such mighty kings and will guard the stairway, as doth become mine honors." Naught could have been more loth to Kriemhild's knights.

"Much it wondereth me," spake Hagen, "what the Hunnish knights be whispering in here. I ween, they'd gladly do without the one that standeth at the door, and who told the courtly tale to us Burgundians. Long since I have heard it said of Kriemhild, that she would not leave unavenged her dole of heart. Now let us drink to friendship (1) and pay for the royal wine. The young lord of the Huns shall be the first."

175

Then the good knight Hagen smote the child Ortlieb, so that the blood spurted up the sword towards his hand and the head fell into the lap of the queen. At this there began a murdering, grim and great, among the knights. Next he dealt the master who taught the child a fierce sword-stroke with both his hands, so that his head fell quickly beneath the table to the ground. A piteous meed it was, which he meted out to the master. Hagen then spied a gleeman sitting at King Etzel's board. In his wrath he hied him thither and struck off his right hand upon the fiddle. "Take this as message to the Burgundian land."

"Woe is me of my hand," spake the minstrel Werbel. "Sir Hagen of Troneg, what had I done to you? I came in good faith to your masters' land. How can I now thrum the tunes, sith I have lost my hand?"

Little recked Hagen, played he nevermore. In the hall he dealt out fierce deadly wounds to Etzel's warriors, passing many of whom he slew. Enow of folk in the house he did to death. The doughty Folker now sprang up from the board; loud rang in his hands his fiddle bow. Rudely did Gunther's minstrel play. Ho, what foes he made him among the valiant Huns! The three noble kings, too, sprang up from the table. Gladly would they have parted the fray, or ever greater scathe was done. With all their wit they could not hinder it, when Folker and Hagen gan rage so sore. When that the lord of the Rhine beheld the fray unparted, the prince dealt his foes many gaping wounds himself through the shining armor rings. That he was a hero of his hands, he gave great proof. Then the sturdy Gernot joined the strife. Certes, he did many a hero of the Huns to death with a sharp sword, the which Rudeger had given him. Mighty wounds he dealt King Etzel's warriors. Now the young son of Lady Uta rushed to the fray. Gloriously his sword rang on the helmets of Etzel's warriors from the Hunnish land. Full mickle wonders were wrought by bold Giselher's hand. But how so doughty they all were, the kings and their liegemen, yet Folker was seen to stand before them all against the foe; a good hero he. Many a one he made to fall in his blood through wounds. Etzel's men did fend them, too, full well, yet one saw the strangers go hewing with their gleaming swords through the royal hall and on every side was heard great sound of wail. Those without would now fain be with their friends within, but at the entrance towers they found small gain. Those within had gladly been without the hall, but Dankwart let none go either up or down the steps. Therefore there rose before the towers a mighty press, and helmets rang loudly from the sword-blows. Bold Dankwart came into great stress thereby; this his brother feared, as his loyalty did bid him.

Loudly then Hagen called to Folker: "See ye yonder, comrade, my brother stand before the Hunnish warriors amid a rain of blows? Friend, save my brother, or ever we lose the knight."

"That will I surely," quoth the minstrel, and through the palace he went a-fiddling, his stout sword ringing often in his hand. Great thanks were tendered by the warriors from the Rhine. Bold Folker spake to Dankwart: "Great discomfiture have ye suffered to-day, therefore your brother bade me hasten to your aid. Will ye stand without, so will I stand within."

Sturdy Dankwart stood without the door and guarded the staircase against whoever came, wherefore men heard the swords resound in the heroes' hands. Folker of Burgundy land performed the same within. Across the press the bold fiddler cried: "Friend Hagen, the hall is locked; forsooth King Etzel's door is bolted well. The hands of two heroes guard it, as with a thousand bars." When Hagen of Troneg beheld the door so well defended, the famous hero and good slung his shield upon his back and gan avenge the wrongs that had been done him there. His foes had now no sort of hope to live.

When now the lord of Berne, the king of the Amelungs, (2) beheld aright that the mighty Hagen broke so many a helm, upon a bench he sprang and spake: "Hagen poureth out the very worst of drinks."

The host, too, was sore adread, as behooved him now, for his life was hardly safe from these his foes. O how many dear friends were snatched away before his eyes! He sate full anxious; what booted it him that he was king? Haughty Kriemhild now cried aloud to Dietrich: "Pray help me hence alive, most noble knight, by the virtues of all the princes of the Amelung land. If Hagen reach me, I shall grasp death by the hand."

"How shall I help you, noble queen?" spake Sir Dietrich. "I fear for myself in sooth. These men of Gunther be so passing wroth that at this hour I cannot guard a soul."

"Nay, not so, Sir Dietrich, noble knight and good. Let thy chivalrous mood appear to-day and help me hence, or I shall die." Passing great cause had Kriemhild for this fear.

"I'll try to see if I may help you, for it is long since that I have soon so many good knights so bitterly enraged. Of a truth I see blood spurting through the helmets from the swords."

Loudly the chosen knight gan call, so that his voice rang forth as from a bison's horn, until the broad castle resounded with his force. Sir Dietrich's strength was passing great in truth.

When Gunther heard this man cry out in the heated strife, he began to heed. He spake: "Dietrich's voice hath reached mine ears, I ween our champions have bereft him of some friend to-day. I see him on the table, he doth beckon with his hand. Ye friends and kinsmen from Burgundian land, give over the

177

strife. Let's hear and see what here hath fortuned to the knight from my men-at-arms."

When Gunther thus begged and bade in the stress of the fray, they sheathed their swords. Passing great was his power, so that none struck a blow. Soon enow he asked the tidings of the knight of Berne. He spake: "Most noble Dietrich, what hath happed to you through these my friends? I am minded to do you remedy and to make amends. If any had done you aught, 'twould grieve me sore."

Then spake Sir Dietrich: "Naught hath happed to me, but I pray you, let me leave this hall and this fierce strife under your safe-guard, with my men. For this favor I will serve you ever."

"How entreat ye now so soon," quoth Wolfhart (3) then. "Forsooth the fiddler hath not barred the door so strong, but what we may open it enow to let us pass."

"Hold your tongue," spake Sir Dietrich; "the devil a whit have ye ever done."

Then: spake King Gunther: "I will grant your boon. Lead from the hall as few or as many as ye will, save my foes alone; they must remain within. Right ill have they treated me in the Hunnish land."

When Dietrich heard these words, he placed his arm around the high-born queen, whose fear was passing great. On his other side he led King Etzel with him hence; with Dietrich there also went six hundred stately men.

Then spake the noble Margrave Rudeger: "Shall any other who would gladly serve you come from this hall, let us hear the tale, and lasting peace shall well befit good friends."

To this Giselher of the Burgundian land replied: "Peace and friendship be granted you by us, sith ye are constant in your fealty. Ye and all your men, ye may go hence fearlessly with these your friends."

When Sir Rudeger voided the hall, there followed him, all told, five hundred men or more, kinsmen and vassals of the lord of Bechelaren, from whom King Gunther later gained great scathe. Then a Hunnish champion spied Etzel walking close by Dietrich. He, too, would take this chance, but the fiddler dealt him such a blow that his head fell soon before King Etzel's feet. When the lord of the land was come outside the house, he turned him about and gazed on Folker. "Woe is me of these guests. This is a direful need, that all my warriors should lie low in death before them. Alas for the feasting," quoth the noble king. "Like a savage boar there fighteth one within, hight Folker, who is

178

a gleeman. I thank my stars that I escaped this fiend. His glees have an evil sound, the strokes of his how draw blood; forsooth his measures fell many a hero dead. I wot not, with what this minstrel twitteth us, for I have never had such baleful guest."

They had permitted whom they would to leave the hall. Then there arose within a mighty uproar; sorely the guests avenged what there had happed them. Ho, what helmets bold Folker broke! The noble King Gunther turned him toward the sound. "Hear ye the measures, Hagen, which Folker yonder fiddleth with the Huns, when any draweth near the towers? 'Tis a blood-red stroke he useth with the bow."

"It rueth me beyond all measure," quoth Hagen, "that in this hall I sate me down to rest before the hero did. I was his comrade and he was mine; and come we ever home again, we shall still be so, in loyal wise. Now behold, most noble king, Folker is thy friend, he earneth gladly thy silver and thy gold. His fiddle bow doth cut through the hardest steel, on the helmets he breaketh the bright and shining gauds! (4) Never have I seen fiddler stand in such lordly wise as the good knight Folker hath stood to-day. His glees resound through shield and helmet. Certes he shall ride good steeds and wear lordly raiment."

Of all the kinsmen of the Huns within the hall, not one of these remained alive. Thus the clash of arms died out, since none strove with them longer. The lusty knights and bold now laid aside their swords.

ENDNOTES:
(1) "Friendship" translates the M.H.G. "minne trinken" 'to drink to the memory of a person', an old custom originating with the idea of pouring out a libation to the gods. Later it assumed the form of drinking to the honor of God, of a saint, or of an absent friend. See Grimm, "Mythologie", p. 48.
(2) "Amelungs", see Adventure XXVIII, note 3.
(3) "Wolfhart", see Adventure XXVIII, note 2.
(4) "Gauds", ornaments.

ADVENTURE XXXIV

How They Cast Out The Dead

The lordings sate them down for weariness. Folker and Hagen came forth from the hall; upon their shields the haughty warriors leaned. Wise words were spoken by the twain. Then Knight Giselher of Burgundy spake: "Forsooth, dear friends, ye may not ease you yet; ye must bear the dead from out the hall. I'll tell you, of a truth, we shall be attacked again. They must no longer lie here beneath our feet. Ere the Huns vanquish us by storm, we'll yet how wounds, which shall ease my heart. For this," quoth Giselher, "I have a steadfast mind."

"Well is me of such a lord," spake then Hagen. "This rede which my young master hath given us to-day would befit no one but a knight. At this, Burgundians, ye may all stand glad."

Then they followed the rede, and to the door they bare seven thousand dead, the which they cast outside. Down they fell before the stairway to the hall, and from their kinsmen rose a full piteous wall. Some there were with such slight wounds that, had they been more gently treated, they would have waxed well again; but from the lofty fall, they must needs lie dead. Their friends bewailed this, and forsooth they had good cause.

Then spake Folker, the fiddler, a lusty knight: "Now I mark the truth of this, as hath been told me. The Huns be cravens, like women they wail; they should rather nurse these sorely wounded men."

A margrave weened, he spake through kindness. Seeing one of his kinsmen lying in the blood, he clasped him in his arms and would have borne him hence, when the bold minstrel shot him above the dead to death. The flight began as the others saw this deed, and all fell to cursing this selfsame minstrel. He snatched javelin, sharp and hard, the which had been hurled at him by a Hun, and cast it with might across the court, far over the folk. Thus he forced Etzel's warriors to take lodgement further from the hall. On every side the people feared his mighty prowess.

Many thousand men now stood before the hall. Folker and Hagen gan speak to Etzel all their mind, wherefrom these heroes bold and good came thereafter into danger. Quoth Hagen: "'Twould well beseem the people's hope, if the lords would fight in the foremost ranks, as doth each of my lordings here. They hew through the helmets, so that the blood doth follow the sword."

Etzel was brave; he seized his shield. "Now fare warily," spake Lady Kriemhild, "and offer the warriors gold upon your shield. If Hagen doth but reach you there, ye'll be hand in hand with death."

The king was so bold he would not turn him back, the which doth now seldom hap from so mighty a lord. By his shield-thong they had to draw him hence. Once again grim Hagen began to mock him. "It is a distant kinship," quoth Hagen, the knight, "that bindeth Etzel and Siegfried. He loved Kriemhild, or ever she laid eyes on thee. Most evil king, why dost thou plot against me?"

Kriemhild, the wife of the noble king, heard this speech; angry she grew that he durst thus revile her before King Etzel's liegemen. Therefore she again began to plot against the strangers. She spake: "For him that slayeth me Hagen of Troneg and bringeth me his head, I will fill King Etzel's shield with ruddy gold, thereto will I give him as guerdon many goodly lands and castles."

"Now I know not for what they wait," spake the minstrel. "Never have I seen heroes stand so much like cowards, when one heard proffered such goodly wage. Forsooth King Etzel should never be their friend again. Many of those who so basely eat the lording's bread, and now desert him in the greatest need, do I see stand here as cravens, and yet would pass for brave. May shame ever be their lot!"

ADVENTURE XXXV

How Iring Was Slain

Then cried Margrave Iring of Denmark: "I have striven for honor now long time, and in the storm of battle have been among the best. Now bring me my harness, for in sooth I will encounter me with Hagen."

"I would not counsel that," spake Hagen, "but bid the Hunnish knights stand further back. If twain of you or three leap into the hall, I'll send them back sore wounded down the steps."

"Not for that will I give it over," quoth Iring again. "I've tried before such daring things; in truth with my good sword I will encounter thee alone. What availeth all thy boasting, which thou hast done in words?"

Then were soon arrayed the good Knight Iring and Irnfried of Thuringia, a daring youth, and the stalwart Hawart and full a thousand men. Whatever Iring ventured, they would all fain give him aid. Then the fiddler spied a mighty troop, that strode along well armed with Iring. Upon their heads they bare good helmets. At this bold Folker waxed a deal full wroth of mood. "See ye, friend Hagen, Iring striding yonder, who vowed to match you with his sword alone? How doth lying beseem a hero? Much that misliketh me. There walk with him full a thousand knights or more, well armed."

"Say not that I lie," spake Hawart's liegeman. "Gladly will I perform what I have vowed, nor will I desist therefrom through any fear. However frightful Hagen be, I will meet him single-handed."

On his knees Iring begged both kinsmen and vassals to let him match the knight alone. This they did unwillingly, for well they knew the haughty Hagen from the Burgundian land. But Iring begged so long that at last it happed. When the fellowship beheld his wish and that he strove for honor, they let him go. Then a fierce conflict rose between the twain. Iring of Denmark, the peerless high-born knight, bare high his spear and covered him with his shield. Swiftly he rushed on Hagen before the hall, while a great shout arose from all the knights around. With might and main they cast the spears with their hands through the sturdy shields upon their shining armor, so that the shafts whirled high in air. Then the two brave men and fierce reached for their swords. Bold Hagen's strength was mickle and great, but Iring smote him, that

182

the whole hall rang. Palace and towers resounded from their blows, but the knight could not achieve his wish.

Iring now left Hagen stand unharmed, and hied him to the fiddler. He weened to fell him by his mighty blows, but the stately knight wist how to guard bin, well. Then the fiddler struck a blow, that the plates of mail whirled high above the buckler's rim. An evil man he was, for to encounter, so Iring let him stand and rushed at Gunther of the Burgundian land. Here, too, either was strong enow in strife. The blows that Gunther and Iring dealt each other drew no blood from wounds. This the harness hindered, the which was both strong and good.

He now let Gunther be, and ran at Gernot, and gan hew sparks of fire from his armor rings. Then had stalwart Gernot of Burgundy nigh done brave Iring unto death, but that he sprang away from the prince (nimble enow he was), and slew eftsoon four noble henchmen of the Burgundians from Worms across the Rhine. At this Giselher might never have waxed more wroth. "God wot, Sir Iring," spake Giselher, the youth, "ye must pay me weregild (1) for those who have fallen dead this hour before you."

Then at him he rushed and smote the Dane, so that he could not stir a step, but sank before his hands down in the blood, so that all did ween the good knight would never deal a blow again in strife. But Iring lay unwounded here before Sir Giselher. From the crashing of the helmet and the ringing of the sword, his wits had grown so weak that the brave knight no longer thought of life. Stalwart Giselher had done this with his might. When now the ringing gan leave his head, the which he had suffered from the mighty stroke, he thought: "I am still alive and nowhere wounded. Now first wot I of Giselher's mighty strength." On either side he heard his foes. Wist they the tale, still more had happed him. Giselher, too, he marked hard by; he bethought him, how he might escape his foes. How madly he sprang up from the blood! Well might he thank his nimbleness for this. Out of the house he ran to where he again found Hagen, whom he dealt a furious blow with his powerful hand.

Hagen thought him: "Thou art doomed. Unless be that the foul fiend protect thee, thou canst not escape alive."

Yet Iring wounded Hagen through his crest. This the hero wrought with Waska, (2) a passing goodly sword. When Sir Hagen felt the wound, wildly he brandished his weapon in his hand. Soon Hawart's liegeman was forced to yield his ground, and Hagen gan pursue him down the stairs. Brave Iring swung his shield above his head, but had the staircase been the length of three, Hagen would not have let him strike a blow the while. Ho, what red sparks did play above his helmet!

Iring returned scatheless to his liegemen. Then the tidings were brought to

183

Kriemhild, of that which he had wrought in strife with Hagen of Troneg. For this the queen gan thank him highly. "Now God requite thee, Iring, thou peerless hero and good. Thou hast comforted well my heart and mind. I see that Hagen's weeds be wot with blood." For very joy Kriemhild herself relieved him of his shield.

"Be not too lavish of your thanks," spake Hagen. "'Twould well befit a knight to try again. A valiant man were he, if he then came back alive. Little shall the wound profit you, which I have at his bands; for that ye have seen the rings wot with blood from my wound doth urge me to the death of many a man. Now first am I enraged at Hawart's liegeman. Small scathe hath Knight Iring done me yet."

Meanwhile Iring of Denmark stood in the breeze; he cooled his harness and doffed his casque. All the folk then praised his prowess, at which the margrave was in passing lofty mood. Again Sir Iring spake: "My friends, this know; arm me now quickly, for I would fain try again, if perchance I may not conquer this overweening man."

His shield was hewn to pieces, a better one he gained; full soon the champion was armed again. Through hate he seized a passing heavy spear with which he would encounter Hagen yonder. Meantime the death-grim man awaited him in hostile wise. But Knight Hagen would not abide his coming. Hurling the javelin and brandishing his sword, he ran to meet him to the very bottom of the stairs. Forsooth his rage was great. Little booted Iring then his strength; through the shields they smote, so that the flames rose high in fiery blasts. Hagen sorely wounded Hawart's liegeman with his sword through shield and breastplate. Never waxed he well again. When now Knight Iring felt the wound, higher above his helmet bands he raised his shield. Great enow he thought the scathe he here received, but thereafter King Gunther's liegeman did him more of harm. Hagen found a spear lying now before his feet. With this he shot Iring, the Danish hero, so that the shaft stood forth from his head. Champion Hagen had given him a bitter end. Iring must needs retreat to those of Denmark. Or ever they unbound his helmet and drew the spear-shaft from his head, death had already drawn nigh him. At this his kinsmen wept, as forsooth they had great need.

Then the queen came and bent above him. She gan bewail the stalwart Iring and bewept his wounds, indeed her grief was passing sharp. At this the bold and lusty warrior spake before his kinsmen: "Let be this wail, most royal queen. What availeth your weeping now? Certes, I must lose my life from these wounds I have received. Death will no longer let me serve you and Etzel." To the men of Thuringia and to those of Denmark he spake: "None of you must take from the queen her shining ruddy gold as meed, for if ye encounter Hagen, ye must gaze on death."

Pale grew his hue; brave Iring bare the mark of death. Dole enow it gave them, for no longer might Hawart's liegeman live. Then the men of Denmark must needs renew the fray. Irnfried and Hawart with well a thousand champions leaped toward the hall. On every side one heard a monstrous uproar, mighty and strong. Ho, what sturdy javelins were cast at the Burgundian men! Bold Irnfried rushed at the minstrel, but gained great damage at his hands. Through his sturdy helmet the noble fiddler smote the landgrave. Certes, he was grim enow! Then Sir Irnfried dealt the valiant gleeman such a blow that his coat of mail burst open and his breastplate was enveloped with a bright red flame. Yet the landgrave fell dead at the minstrel's hands. Hawart and Hagen, too, had come together. Wonders would he have seen, who beheld the fight. The swords fell thick and fast in the heroes' hands. Through the knight from the Burgundian land Hawart needs must die. When the Thuringians and the Danes espied their lordings dead, there rose before the hall a fearful strife, before they gained the door with mighty hand. Many a helm and shield was hacked and cut thereby.

"Give way," spake Folker, "and let them in, for else what they have in mind will not be ended. They must die in here in full short time. With death they'll gain what the queen would give them."

When these overweening men were come into the hall, the head of many a one sank down so low that he needs must die from their furious strokes. Well fought the valiant Gernot, and the same did Giselher, the knight. A thousand and four were come into the hall and many a whizzing stroke of the swords was seen flash forth, but soon all the warriors lay slain therein. Mickle wonders might one tell of the Burgundian men. The hall grew still, as the uproar died away. On every side the dead men's blood poured through the openings down to the drain-pipes. This the men from the Rhine had wrought with their passing strength.

Those from the Burgundian land now sate them down to rest and laid aside their swords and shields. But still the valiant minstrel stood guard before the hall. He waited, if any would perchance draw near again in strife. Sorely the king made wail, as did the queen. Maids and ladies were distraught with grief. Death, I ween, had conspired against them, wherefore many of the warriors perished through the guests.

ENDNOTES:
(1) "Weregild" (O.E. "wer", 'a man', "gild", 'payment of money'), legal term for compensation paid for a man killed.
(2) "Waska". In "Biterolf" it is the name of the sword of Walther of Wasgenstein and is connected with the old German name, "Wasgenwald", for the Vosges.

185

"Now unbind your helmets," spake the good Knight Hagen. "I and my comrade will guard you well, and should Etzel's men be minded to try again, I'll warn my lords as soon as I ever can."

Then many a good knight bared his head. They sate them down upon the wounded, who had fallen in the blood, done to death at their hands. Evil looks were cast upon the noble strangers. Before the eventide the king and the queen brought it to pass that the Hunnish champions tried again. Men saw full twenty thousand warriors stand before them, who must perforce march to the fray. Straightway there rose a mighty storming towards the strangers. Dankwart, Hagen's brother, the doughty knight, sprang from his lordings' side to meet the foes without the door. All weened that he were dead, yet forth he stood again unscathed. The furious strife did last till nightfall brought it to a close. As befitted good knights, the strangers warded off King Etzel's liegemen the livelong summer day. Ho, how many a bold knight fell doomed before them! This great slaughter happed upon midsummer's day, when Lady Kriemhild avenged her sorrow of heart upon her nearest kin and upon many another man, so that King Etzel never again gained joy.

The day had passed away, but still they had good cause for fear. They thought, a short and speedy death were better for them, than to be longer racked with monstrous pain. A truce these proud and lusty knights now craved; they begged that men would bring the king to see them. Forth from the hall stepped the heroes, bloody of hue, and the three noble kings, stained from their armor. They wist not to whom they should make plaint of their mighty wounds. Thither both Etzel and Kriemhild went; the land was theirs and so their band waxed large. He spake to the strangers: "Pray tell me, what ye will of me? Ye ween to gain here peace, but that may hardly be. For damage as great as ye have done me, in my son and in my many kinsmen, whom ye have slain, peace and pardon shall be denied you quite; it shall not boot you aught, an' I remain alive."

To this King Gunther answered: "Dire need constrained us; all my men-at-arms lay dead before thy heroes in the hostel. How did I deserve such pay? I came to thee in trust, I weened thou wast my friend."

Young Giselher of Burgundy likewise spake: "Ye men of Etzel, who still do live, what do ye blame me with? What have I done to you, for I rode in friendly wise into this land of yours."

Quoth they: "From thy friendliness this castle is filled with grief and the land as well. We should not have taken it ill, in sooth, if thou hadst never come from Worms beyond the Rhine. Thou and thy brothers have filled this land with orphans."

Then spake Knight Giselher in angry mood: "And ye will lay aside this bitter hate and make your peace with us stranger knights, 'twere best for either side. We have not merited at all what Etzel here doth do us."

Then spake the host to his guests: "Unlike are my wrongs and yours. The mickle grievance from the loss and then the shame, which I have taken here, are such that none of you shall e'er go hence alive."

At this mighty Gernot spake to the king: "May God then bid you act in merciful wise. Slay, if ye will, us homeless knights, but let us first descend to you into the open court. That will make to you for honor. Let be done quickly whatever shall hap to us. Ye have still many men unscathed, who dare well encounter us and bereave us storm-weary men of life. How long must we warriors undergo these toils?"

King Etzel's champions had nigh granted this boon and let them leave the hall, but Kriemhild heard it and sorely it misliked her. Therefore the wanderers were speedily denied the truce. "Not so, ye Hunnish men. I counsel you in true fealty, that ye do not what ye have in mind, and let these murderers leave the hall, else must your kinsmen suffer a deadly fall. Did none of them still live, save Uta's sons, my noble brothers, and they came forth into the breeze and cooled their armor rings, ye would all be lost. Bolder heroes were never born into the world."

Then spake young Giselher: "Fair sister mine, full evil was my trust, when thou didst invite me from across the Rhine hither to this land, to this dire need. How have I merited death here from the Huns? I was aye true to thee; never did I do thee wrong, and in the hope that thou wast still my friend, dear sister mine, rode I hither to thy court. It cannot be but that thou grant us mercy."

"I will not grant you mercy, merciless is my mood. Hagen of Troneg hath done me such great wrongs that it may never be amended, the while I live. Ye must all suffer for this deed," so spake King Etzel's wife. "And ye will give me Hagen alone as hostage, I will not deny that I will let you live, for ye be my brothers and children of one mother, and will counsel peace with these heroes that be here."

187

"Now God in heaven forbid," spake Gernot; "were there here a thousand of us, the clansmen of thy kin, we'd rather all lie dead, than give thee a single man as hostage. Never shall this be done."

"We all must die," spake then Giselher, "but none shall hinder that we guard us in knightly wise. We be still here, if any list to fight us; for never have I failed a friend in fealty."

Then spake bold Dankwart (it had not beseemed him to have held his peace): "Forsooth my brother Hagen standeth not alone. It may yet rue those who here refuse the truce. I'll tell you of a truth, we'll make you ware of this."

Then spake the queen: "Ye full lusty heroes, now go nigher to the stairs and avenge my wrongs. For this I will ever serve you, as I should by right. I'll pay Hagen well for his overweening pride. Let none at all escape from the house, and I will bid the hall be set on fire at all four ends. Thus all my wrongs shall be well avenged."

Soon were King Etzel's champions ready still stood without into the hall with blows and shots. Mickle waxed the din, yet the lordings and their liegemen would not part. For very fealty they could not leave each other. Etzel's queen then bade the hall be set on fire, and thus they racked the bodies of the knights with fire and flame. Fanned by the breeze, the whole house burst into flames full soon. I ween, no folk did ever gain such great distress. Enow within cried out: "Alack this plight! We would much rather die in stress of battle. It might move God to pity, how we all are lost! The queen now wreaketh monstrously on us her wrath."

Quoth one of them within: "We must all lie dead. What avail us now the greetings which the king did send us? Thirst from this great heat giveth me such dole, that soon, I ween, my life must ebb away in anguish."

Then spake Hagen of Troneg: "Ye noble knights and good, let him whom pangs of thirst constrain, drink here this blood. In such great heat, 'tis better still than wine. We can purvey us at this time none better."

One of the warriors hied him then to where he found a corpse, and knelt him down beside the wound; then he unbound his helmet and began to drink the flowing blood. However little wont to such a drink, him thought it passing good: "Sir Hagen, now God requite you," spake the weary man, "that I have drunk so well at your advice; seldom hath better wine been proffered me. And I live yet a while, I shall ever be your friend."

When now the others heard this, it thought them good, and soon there were many more that drank the blood. From this the body of each gained much of

188

strength; but many a stately dame paid dear for this through the loss of loving kin. Into the hall the fire fell thick and fast upon them, but with their shields they turned it from them to the ground. Both the heat and the smoke did hurt them sore; in sooth, I ween, that nevermore will such anguish hap to heroes.

Again Hagen of Troneg spake: "Stand by the sides of the hall. Let not the firebrands fall upon your helmet bands, but stamp them with your feet down deeper in the blood. Forsooth it is an evil feast which the queen doth give us here."

In such dire woes the night did wear away at last, and still the brave minstrel and his comrade Hagen stood before the hall, a-leaning on their shields. More scathe they awaited from those of Etzel's band. Then spake the fiddler: "Now go we into the hall. Then the Huns will ween, that we all be dead from the torture that hath been done us here. They'll yet see us go to meet them in the strife."

Now spake Giselher of Burgundy, the youth: "I trow the day dawneth, a cooling wind doth blow. May God in heaven let us live to see a liefer time, for my sister Kriemhild hath given us here an evil feast."

Again one spake: "I see the day. Sith we cannot hope for better things, so arm you, heroes, think on your life. Certes, King Etzel's wife will come to meet us soon again."

The host weened well, that his guests were dead from their toil and the pangs of fire; but yet within the hall six hundred brave men, as good as any knight that king ever gained, were still alive. Those set to guard the strangers had well seen that the guests still lived, despite the damage and the dole that had been done both to the lordings and their men. In the hall one saw them stand full safe and sound. They then told Kriemhild that many were still alive, but the queen replied: "It could never be, that any should have lived through such stress of fire. Rather will I believe that all lie dead."

The lordings and their men would still fain have lived, had any listed to do them mercy, but they could find none among those of the Hunnish land. So with full willing hand they avenged their dying. On this same day, towards morning, men proffered them a fierce attack as greeting, which brought the champions in stress again. Many a stout spear was hurled upon them, but the bold and lordly warriors warded them in knightly wise. High rose the mood of Etzel's men at the thought that they should earn Queen Kriemhild's gold. Thereto they were minded to perform whatso the King did bid them. Many of them because of this must soon needs gaze on death. Of pledges and of gifts one might tell wonders. She bade the ruddy gold be carried forth on shields and gave it to whomsoever craved it and would take it. Certes, greater wage was nevermore given against foes. To the hall a mickle force of well-armed warriors marched.

Then cried bold Folker: "We're here again, ye see. Never saw I heroes more gladly come to fight than these that have taken the king's gold to do us scathe."

Then enow did call: "Nearer, heroes, nearer, that we may do betimes what we must bring to an end. Here dieth none that is not doomed to die."

Soon their shields were seen sticking full of darts that had been thrown. What more can I say? Full twelve hundred men tried hard to match them, surging back and forth. The strangers cooled well their mood with wounds. None might part the strife, and so blood was seen to flow from mortal wounds, many of which were dealt. Each one was heard to wail for friends. All the great king's doughty warriors died, and loving kinsmen mourned them passing sore.

ADVENTURE XXXVII

How Margrave Rudeger Was Slain

The strangers had done full well at dawn. Meanwhile Gotelind's husband came to court. Bitterly faithful Rudeger wept when he saw the grievous wounds on either side. "Woe is me," quoth the champion, "that I was ever born, sith none may stay this mickle grief! However fain I would make for peace, the king will not consent, for he seeth ever more and more the sufferings of his men."

Then the good Knight Rudeger sent to Dietrich, if perchance they might turn the fate of the high-born kings. The king of Berne sent answer: "Who might now forfend? King Etzel will let none part the strife."

Then a Hunnish warrior, that saw Rudeger stand with weeping eyes, and many tears had he shed, spake to the queen: "Now behold how he doth stand, that hath the greatest power at Etzel's court and whom both lands and people serve. Why have so many castles been given to Rudeger, of which he doth hold such store from the king in fief? Not one sturdy stroke hath he dealt in all this strife. Methinks, he recketh not how it fare here at court, sith he hath his will in full. Men say of him, he be bolder than any other wight. Little hath that been seen in these parlous (1) days."

Sad in heart the faithful vassal gazed at him whom he heard thus speak. Him-thought: "Thou shalt pay for this. Thou sayest, I be a craven, and hast told thy tale too loud at court."

His fist he clenched, then ran he at him and smote the Hunnish man so mightily that he lay dead at his feet full soon. Through this King Etzel's woe grew greater.

"Away, thou arrant coward," cried Rudeger, "forsooth I have enow of grief and pain, How dost thou taunt me, that I fight not here? Certes, I have good cause to hate the strangers, and would have done all in my power against them, had I not led the warriors hither. Of a truth I was their safeguard to my master's land. Therefore the hand of me, wretched man, may not strive against them."

Then spake Etzel, the noble king, to the margrave: "How have ye helped us, most noble Rudeger! We have so many fey (2) in the land, that we have no need of more. Full evil have ye done."

At this the noble knight made answer: "Forsooth he grieved my mood and twitted me with the honors and the goods, such store of which I have received from thy hand. This hath cost the liar dear."

The queen, too, was come and had seen what fortuned to the Huns through the hero's wrath. Passing sore she bewailed it; her eyes grew moist as she spake to Rudeger: "How have we deserved that ye should increase the sorrows of the king and me? Hitherto ye have told us, that for our sake ye would risk both life and honor. I heard full many warriors accord to you the palm. Let me mind you of your fealty and that ye swore, when that ye counseled me to Etzel, good knight and true, that ye would serve me till one of us should die. Never have I, poor woman, had such great need of this."

"There's no denying that I swore to you, my lady, for your sake I'd risk both life and honor, but I did not swear that I would lose my soul. 'Twas I that bade the high-born lordings to this feast."

Quoth she: "Bethink thee, Rudeger, of thy great fealty, of thy constancy, and of thine oaths, that thou wouldst ever avenge mine injuries and all my woes."

Said the margrave: "Seldom have I denied you aught."

Mighty Etzel, too, began implore; upon their knees they sank before the knight. Men saw the noble margrave stand full sad. Pitifully the faithful warrior spake: "Woe is me, most wretched man, that I have lived to see this day. I must give over all my honors, my fealty, and my courtesie, that God did bid me use. Alas, great God of heaven, that death will not turn this from me! I shall act basely and full evil, whatever I do or leave undone. But if I give over both, then will all people blame me. Now may he advise me, who hath given me life."

Still the king and the queen, too, begged unceasingly. Through this warriors must needs thereafter lose their lives at Rudeger's hands, when the hero also died. Ye may well hear it now, that he deported him full pitifully. He wist that it would bring him scathe and monstrous woe. Gladly would he have refused the king and queen. He feared full sore that if he slew but one of the strangers, the world would bear him hate.

Then the brave man addressed him to the king: "Sir King, take back again all that I have from you, my land with its castles, let not a whit remain to me. On foot will I wander into other lands."

At this King Etzel spake: "Who else should help me then? I'll give thee the land and all its castles, as thine own, that thou mayst avenge me on my foes. Thou shalt be a mighty king at Etzel's side."

Then answered Rudeger: "How shall I do this deed? I bade them to my house and home; in friendly wise I offered them both food and drink and gave them gifts. How may I counsel their death? People will lightly ween, that I be craven. No service of mine have I refused these noble lordings and their men. Now I rue the kinship I have gained with them. I gave my daughter to Giselher, the knight; to none in all the world could she have been better given, for courtesie and honor, for fealty and wealth. Never have I seen so young a prince of such right courteous mind."

Then Kriemhild spake again: "Most noble Rudeger, take pity on our griefs, on mine and on the king's. Bethink thee well, that king did never gain such baneful guests."

To the noble dame the margrave spake: "Rudeger's life must pay to-day for whatsoever favors ye and my lord have shown me. Therefore must I die; no longer may it be deferred. I know full well, that my castles and my lands will be voided for you to-day through the hand of one of these men. To your mercy I commend my wife and children and the strangers (3) who be at Bechelaren."

"Now God requite thee, Rudeger," spake the king, and both he and the queen grew glad. "Thy people shall be well commended to our care. For mine own weal I trust thou too shalt go unscathed."

Etzel's bride began to weep. Then body and soul he staked upon the venture. He spake: "I must perform what I have vowed. Alas for my friends, whom I am loth to fight."

Men saw him go sadly from the presence of the king. Close at hand he found his warriors standing. He spake: "Ye must arm you all, my men, for, alas, I must needs encounter the bold Burgundians."

They bade the squires run nimbly to where lay their arms. Whether it were helm or buckler, 'twas all brought forth to them by their meiny. Later the proud strangers heard told baleful tales. Rudeger was now armed, and with him five hundred men; thereto he gained twelve champions, who would fain win renown in the stress of battle. They wist not that death drew nigh them. Then Rudeger was seen to march with helmet donned. The margrave's men bare keen-edged swords, and their bright shields and broad upon their arms. This the fiddler saw; greatly he rued the sight. When young Giselher beheld his lady's father walk with his helm upon his head, how might he know what he meant thereby, save that it portended good? Therefore the noble prince waxed passing merry of mood.

"Now well is me of such kinsmen," spake Knight Giselher, "whom we have won upon this journey; from my wife we shall reap much profit here. Lief it is to me, that this betrothal hath taken place."

193

"I know not whence ye take your comfort," spake then the minstrel; "when have ye seen so many heroes walk with helmets donned and swords in hand, for the sake of peace? Rudeger doth think to win his castles and his lands in fight with us."

Or ever the fiddler had ended his speech, men saw the noble Rudeger before the house. At his feet he placed his trusty shield, and now both service and greeting he must needs refuse his friends. Into the hall the noble margrave called: "Ye doughty Nibelungs, now guard you well on every side. Ye were to profit by me, now I shall bring you scathe. Aforetime we were friends, but of this troth I now would fain be rid."

The hard-pressed men were startled at this tale, for none gained aught of joy, that he whom they did love would now fain fight them. From their foes they had already suffered mickle stress of war. "Now God of heaven forbid," spake Gunther, the knight, "that ye should give over your love of us and your great fealty, on which we counted of a truth. Better things I trow of you, than that ye should ever do this deed."

"Alas, I cannot give it over, but must fight you, for I have vowed it. Now ward you, brave heroes, and ye love your life. King Etzel's wife would not release me from mine oath."

"Ye declare this feud too late," spake the highborn king. "Now may God requite you, most noble Rudeger, for all the love and fealty that ye have shown us, if ye would only act more kindly at the end. I and my kinsmen, we ought ever to serve you for the noble gifts ye gave us, when ye brought us hither faithfully to Etzel's land. Now, noble Rudeger, think on this."

"How gladly would I grant you," spake Knight Rudeger, "that I might weigh out my gifts for you with full measure, as willingly as I had hoped, if I never should be blamed on that account."

"Turn back, noble Rudeger," spake then Gernot, "for host did never give his guests such loving cheer as ye did us. This shall profit you well, and we remain alive."

"Would to God," spake Rudeger, "most noble Gernot, that ye were on the Rhine and I were dead with passing honor, sith I must now encounter you! Never did friends act worse to heroes."

"Now God requite you, Sir Rudeger," answered Gernot, "for your passing rich gifts. Your death doth rue me, if such knightly virtues shall be lost with you. Here I bear your sword that ye gave me, good knight and true. It hath never failed me in all this need. Many a knight fell dead beneath its edges. It is bright and steady, glorious and good; nevermore, I ween, will warrior give so rich a gift. And will ye not turn back, but come to meet us, and slay aught of the friends I still have here, with your own sword will I take your life. Then will ye rue me, Rudeger, ye and your high-born wife."

"Would to God, Sir Gernot, that this might come to pass, that all your will might here be done, and that your kinsmen escaped unscathed! Then both my daughter and my wife may trust you well, forsooth."

Then of the Burgundians there spake fair Uta's son: "Why do ye so, Sir Rudeger? Those that be come with us, do all like you well. Ye encounter us in evil wise; ye wish to make your fair daughter a widow far too soon. If ye and your warriors match me now with strife, how right unkindly do ye let it appear, that I trust you well above all other men and therefore won me your daughter to wife."

"Think on your fealty, most noble and high-born king. And God let you escape," so spake Rudeger, "let the maiden suffer not for me. For your own virtue's sake, vouchsafe her mercy."

"That I should do by right," spake the youthful Giselher, "but if my noble kinsmen here within must die through you, then my steadfast friendship for you and for your daughter must be parted."

"Now may God have mercy on us," answered the valiant man. Then they raised their shields, as though they would hence to fight the guests in Kriemhild's hall, but Hagen cried full loud adown the steps. "Pray tarry awhile, most noble Rudeger," so spake Hagen; "I and my lords would fain have further parley, as doth befit our need. What can the death of us wanderers avail King Etzel? I stand here in a fearful plight; the shield that Lady Gotelind gave me to bear hath been cut to pieces by the Huns. I brought it with friendly purpose into Etzel's land. O that God in heaven would grant, that I might bear so good a shield as that thou hast in thy hand, most noble Rudeger! Then I should no longer need a hauberk in the fray."

"Gladly would I serve thee with my shield, durst I offer it before Kriemhild. Yet take it, Hagen, and bear it on thine arm. Ho, if thou couldst only wield it in the Burgundian land!"

When he so willingly offered to give the shield, enow of eyes grew red with scalding tears. 'T was the last gift that ever Rudeger of Bechelaren gave to any knight. However fierce Hagen, and however stern of mood, the gift did touch him, which the good hero, so near to death, had given. Many a noble knight gan mourn with him.

195

"Now God in heaven requite you, most noble Rudeger. Your like will nevermore be found, who giveth homeless warriors such lordly gifts. God grant that your courtesie may ever live." Again Hagen spake: "Woe is me of these tales, we had so many other griefs to bear. Let complaint be made to heaven, if we must fight with friends."

Quoth the margrave: "Inly doth this grieve me."

"Now God requite you, for the gift, most noble Rudeger. Howso these high-born warriors deport them toward you, my hand shall never touch you in the fight, and ye slew them all from the Burgundian land."

Courteously the good Sir Rudeger bowed him low. On every side they wept, that none might soothe this pain of heart. That was a mighty grief. In Rudeger would die the father of all knightly virtues.

Then Folker, the minstrel, spake from out the hall: "Sith my comrade Hagen hath made his peace with you, ye shall have it just as steadfastly from my hand, for well ye earned it, when we came into this land. Most noble margrave, ye shall be mine envoy, too. The margravine gave me these ruddy arm rings, that I should wear them here at the feasting. These ye may yourself behold, that ye may later be my witness."

"Now God of heaven grant," spake Rudeger, "that the margravine may give you more! I'll gladly tell these tales to my dear love, if I see her in health again. Of this ye shall not doubt."

When he had vowed him this, Rudeger raised high his shield. No longer he bided, but with raging mood, like a berserker, he rushed upon the guests. Many a furious blow the noble margrave struck. The twain, Folker and Hagen, stepped further back, as they had vowed to him afore. Still he found standing by the tower such valiant men, that Rudeger began the fight with anxious doubts. With murderous intent Gunther and Gernot let him in, good heroes they! Giselher stood further back, which irked him sore, in truth. He voided Rudeger, for still he had hope of life. Then the margrave's men rushed at their foes; in knightly wise one saw them follow their lord. In their hands they bare their keen-edged swords, the which cleft there many a helm and lordly shield. The tired warriors dealt the men of Bechelaren many a mighty blow, that cut smooth and deep through the shining mail, down to the very quick.

Rudeger's noble fellowship was now come quite within. Into the fight Folker and Hagen sprang anon. They gave no quarter, save to one man alone. Through the hands of the twain the blood streamed down from the helmets. How grimly rang the many swords within! The shield plates sprang from their fastenings, and the precious stones, cut from the shields, fell down into the gore. So grimly they fought, that men will never do the like again. The lord of

Bechelaren raged to and fro, as one who wotteth how to use great prowess in the fray. Passing like to a worshipful champion and a bold did Rudeger bear him on that day. Here stood the warriors, Gunther and Gernot, and smote many a hero dead in the fray. Giselher and Dankwart, the twain, recked so little, that they brought full many a knight to his last day of life. Full well did Rudeger make appear that he was strong enow, brave and well-armed. Ho, what knights he slew! This a Burgundian espied; perforce it angered him, and thus Sir Rudeger's death drew near.

The stalwart Gernot accosted the hero; to the margrave he spake: "It appeareth, ye will not leave my men alive, most noble Rudeger. That irketh me beyond all measure, no longer can I bear the sight. So may your present work you harm, sith ye have taken from me such store of friends. Pray address you unto me, most noble man and brave, your gift shall be paid for as best I can."

Or ever the margrave could reach his foe, bright armor rings must needs grow dull with blood. Then at each other sprang these honor-seeking men. Either gan guard him against mighty wounds. So sharp were their swords, that naught might avail against them. Then Rudeger, the knight, smote Gernot a buffet through his helmet, the which was as hard as flint, so that the blood gushed forth. But this the bold knight and good repaid eftsoon. High in his hand he now poised Rudeger's gift, and though wounded unto death, he smote him a stroke through his good and trusty shield down to his helmet band. And so fair Gotelind's husband was done to death. Certes, so rich a gift was never worse repaid. So fell alike both Gernot and Rudeger, slain in the fray, through each other's hand.

Then first waxed Hagen wroth, when he saw the monstrous scathe. Quoth the hero of Troneg: "Evil hath it fared with us. In these two men we have taken a loss so great that neither their land nor people will e'er recover from the blow. Rudeger's champions must answer to us homeless men."

"Alas for my brother, who hath here been done to death. What evil tales I hear all time! Noble Rudeger, too, must ever rue me. The loss and the grievous wounds are felt on either side."

When Lord Giselher saw his betrothed's father dead, those within the hall were forced to suffer need. Fiercely death sought his fellowship; not one of those of Bechelaren escaped with life. Gunther and Giselher and Hagen, too, Dankwart and Folker, the right good knights, went to where they found the two men lying. Then by these heroes tears of grief were shed.

"Death doth sorely rob us," spake Giselher, the youth. "Now give over your weeping and go we bite the breeze, that the mailed armor of us storm-weary men may cool. Certes, I ween, that God in heaven vouchsafeth us no more to live."

This champion was seen to sit and that to lean against the wall, but all again were idle. Rudeger's heroes lay still in death. The din had died away; the hush endured so long, it vexed King Etzel.

"Alack for such services," spake the queen. "They be not so true, that our foes must pay with their life at Rudeger's hands. I trow, he doth wish to lead them back to the Burgundian land. What booteth it, King Etzel, that we have given him whatso he would? The knight hath done amiss, he who should avenge us, doth make his peace."

To this Folker, the full dapper knight, made answer: "This is not true, alas, most noble queen. Durst I give the lie to such a high-born dame, then had ye most foully lied against Rudeger. He and his champions be cozened in this peace. So eagerly he did what the king commanded, that he and all his fellowship lie here in death. Now look around you, Kriemhild, to see whom ye may now command. The good Knight Rudeger hath served you to his end. And ye will not believe the tale, we'll let you see."

To their great grief 'twas done; they bare the slain hero to where the king might see him. Never had there happed to Etzel's men a grief so great. When they saw the margrave borne forth dead, no scribe might write or tell the frantic grief of men and women, which there gan show itself from dole of heart. King Etzel's sorrow waxed so great that the mighty king did voice his woe of heart, as with a lion's roar. Likewise did his queen. Beyond all measure they bewailed the good Knight Rudeger's death.

ENDNOTES:
(1) "Parlous", older English for 'perilous'.
(2) "Fey", 'doomed to death', here in the sense of 'already slain'. See Adventure V, note 2.
(3) "Strangers", i.e., those who are sojourning there far from home.

198

ADVENTURE XXXVIII

How All Sir Dietrich's Warriors Were Slain

On every side one heard a grief so great, that the palace and the towers rang with the wailing. Then a liegeman of Dietrich heard it, too. How quickly he gan haste him with the fearful tales! To the lording he spake: "Hear, my lord, Sir Dietrich, however much I've lived to see till now, yet heard I never such a monstrous wail, as now hath reached mine ears. I ween, King Etzel himself hath come to grief. How else might all be so distressed? One of the twain, the king or Kriemhild, hath sorely been laid low by the brave strangers in their wrath. Full many a dapper warrior weepeth passing sore."

Then spake the Knight of Borne: "My faithful men, now haste ye not too fast. Whatever the homeless warriors may have done, they be now in mickle need. Let it profit them, that I did offer them my peace."

At this brave Wolfhart spake: "I will hie me hence and ask for tidings of what they have done, and will tell you then, my most dear lord, just as I find it, what the wail may be."

Then spake Sir Dietrich: "Where one awaiteth wrath, and rude questions then are put, this doth lightly sadden the lofty mood of warriors. In truth, I will not, Wolfhart, that ye ask these questions of them."

Then he told Helfrich (1) to hasten thither speedily, and bade him find from Etzel's men or from the guests themselves, what there had fortuned, for men had never seen from folks so great a grief. The messenger gan ask: "What hath here been done?"

At this one among them spake: "Whatever of joy we had in the Hunnish land hath passed away. Here lieth Rudeger, slain by the Burgundians' hands; and of those who were come with him, not one hatch 'scaped alive."

Sir Helfrich could never have had a greater dole. Sorely weeping, the envoy went to Dietrich. Never was he so loth to tell a tale. "What have ye found for us?" quoth Dietrich. "Why weep ye so sore, Knight Helfrich?"

Then spake the noble champion: "I have good cause for wail. The Burgundians have slain the good Sir Rudeger."

199

At this the hero of Berne made answer: "Now God forbid. That were a fearful vengeance, over which the foul fiend would gloat. Wherewith hath Rudeger deserved this at their hands? I know full well, forsooth, he is the strangers' friend."

To this Wolfhart answered: "And have they done this deed, 'twill cost them all their lives. 'Twould be our shame, should we let this pass, for of a truth the hand of the good knight Rudeger hath served us much and oft."

The lord of the Amelungs bade learn it better. In bitter grief he sate him at a window and begged Hildebrand to hie him to the strangers, that he might find from them what had been done. The storm-brave warrior, Master Hildebrand, (2) bare neither shield nor weapon in his hand. In courtly wise he would hie him to the strangers; for this he was chided by his sister's son. Grim Wolfhart spake: "And ye will go thither so bare, ye will never fare without upbraiding; ye must return with shame. But if ye go there armed, each will guard against that well."

Then the wise man armed him, through the counsel of youth. Or ever he was ware, all Dietrich's warriors had donned their war-weeds and held in their hands their swords. Loth it was to the hero, and he would have gladly turned their mind. He asked whither they would go.

"We will hence with you. Perchance Hagen of Troneg then will dare the less to address him to you with scorn, which full well he knoweth how to use." When he heard this, the knight vouchsafed them for to go.

Soon brave Folker saw the champions of Berne, the liegemen of Dietrich, march along, well armed, begirt with swords, while in their hands they bare their shields. He told it to his lords from out the Burgundian land. The fiddler spake: "Yonder I see the men of Dietrich march along in right hostile wise, armed cap-a-pie. They would encounter us; I ween 'twill go full ill with us strangers."

Meanwhile Sir Hildebrand was come. Before his feet he placed his shield, and gan ask Gunther's men: "Alas, good heroes, what had Rudeger done you? My Lord Dietrich hath sent me hither to you to say, that if the hand of any among you hath slain the noble margrave, as we are told, we could never stand such mighty dole."

Then spake Hagen of Troneg: "The tale is true. How gladly could I wish, that the messenger had told you false, for Rudeger's sake, and that he still did live, for whom both man and wife may well ever weep."

When they heard aright that he was dead, the warriors made wail for him, as

200

their fealty bade them. Over the beards and chins of Dietrich's champions the tears were seen to run. Great grief had happened to them.

Siegstab, (3) the Duke of Berne, then spake: "Now hath come to an end the cheer, that Rudeger did give us after our days of dole. The joy of all wayfaring folk lieth slain by you, sir knights."

Then spake the Knight Wolfwin (4) of the Amelungs: "And I saw mine own father dead to-day, I should not make greater dole, than for his death. Alas, who shall now comfort the good margrave's wife?"

Angry of mood Knight Wolfhart spake: "Who shall now lead the warriors to so many a fight, as the margrave so oft hath done? Alas, most noble Rudeger, that we should lose thee thus!"

Wolfbrand (5) and Helfrich and Helmnot, too, with all their men bewailed his death. For sighing Hildebrand might no longer ask a whit. He spake: "Sir knights, now do what my lord hath sent you here to do. Give us the corse of Rudeger from out the hall, in whom our joy hath turned to grief, and let us repay to him the great fealty he hath shown to us and to many another man. We, too, be exiles, just as Rudeger, the knight. Why do ye let us wait thus? Let us bear him away, that we may yet requite the knight in death. More justly had we done it, when he was still alive."

Then spake King Gunther: "Never was there so good a service as that, which a friend doth do to a friend after his death. When any doeth that, I call it faithful friendship. Ye repay him but rightly, for much love hath he ever shown you."

"How long shall we still beseech?" spake Knight Wolfhart. "Sith our best hope hath been laid low in death by you, and we may no longer have him with us, let us bear him hence to where the warrior may be buried."

To this Folker made answer: "None will give him to you. Fetch ye him from the hall where the warrior lieth, fallen in the blood, with mortal wounds. 'Twill then be a perfect service, which ye render Rudeger."

Quoth brave Wolfhart: "God wot, sir minstrel, ye have given us great dole and should not rouse our ire. But that I durst not for fear of my lord, ye should all fare ill. We must perforce abstain, sith he forbade us strife."

Then spake the fiddler: "He hath a deal too much fear who doth abstain from all that one forbiddeth him. That I call not a real hero's mood." This speech of his war comrade thought Hagen good.

"Long not for that," answered Wolfhart, "or I'll play such havoc with your fiddle strings, that ye'll have cause to tell the tale, when ye ride homeward to the Rhine. I cannot brook in honor your overweening pride."

Quoth the fiddler: "If ye put out of tune my strings, then must the gleam of your helmet grow dim from this hand of mine, however I ride to the Burgundian land."

Then would he leap at him, but his uncle Hildebrand grasped him firmly. "I ween, thou wouldst rage in thy silly anger. Then hadst thou lost forever the favor of my lord."

"Let go the lion, master, he is so fierce of mood," quoth the good knight Folker. "Had he slain the whole world with his one hand, I'll smite him, and he come within my reach, so that he may never sing the answer to my song."

At this the men of Berne waxed passing wroth of mood. Wolfhart, a doughty knight and a good, snatched up his shield. Like a wild lion he ran to meet him, swiftly followed by all his friends. But howsoever great the strides he took towards the hall, yet did old Hildebrand overtake him at the steps. He would not let him reach the fray before him. At the hands of the homeless knights they later found the strife they sought. Master Hildebrand then sprang at Hagen. In the hands of both one heard the swords ring out. That both were angry, might be plainly seen; from the swords of the twain streamed forth a blast of fire-red sparks. Then they were parted in the stress of battle by the men of Berne, as their strength did bid them. At once Hildebrand turned him away from Hagen, but stout Wolfhart addressed him to Folker the bold. Such a blow he smote the fiddler upon his good helmet, that the sword's edge pierced to the very helmet bands. This the bold gleeman repaid with might; he smote Wolfhart, so that the sparks flew wide. Enow of fire they struck from the armor rings, for each bare hatred to the other. Then Knight Wolfwin of Berne did part them—an' he be not a hero, never was there one.

With willing hand Gunther, the champion, greeted the heroes of the Amelung land. Lord Giselher made many a gleaming helmet red and wot with blood. Dankwart, Hagen's brother, a fierce man was he; whatever he had done before to Etzel's warriors in strife was as a wind to the fury with which bold Aldrian's son now fought. Ritschart (6) and Gerbart, Helfrich and Wichart had spared themselves full seldom in many battle storms; this they now made Gunther's liegemen note full well. Wolfbrand, too, was seen in the strife bearing him in lordly wise. Old Hildebrand fought as though he raged. At Wolfhart's hands many good knights, struck by the sword, must needs fall dead down into the blood. Thus the bold champions and good avenged Knight Rudeger.

Then Lord Siegstab fought as his prowess bade him. Ho, what good helmets of his foes this son of Dietrich's sister clove in the strife! Nor might he ever do better in the fray. When sturdy Folker espied that bold Siegstab hewed a

202

bloody stream from the hard armor rings, wroth of mood the hero grew. He sprang to meet him, and Siegstab lost his life full soon at the fiddler's hands, for Folker gave him such a sample of his art, that he soon lay dead, slain by his sword. This old Hildebrand avenged, as his might did bid him.

"Alas for my dear lord," spake Master Hildebrand, "who lieth here dead at Folker's hands. Now shall the fiddler no longer live."

How might bold Hildebrand ever be fiercer? Folker he smote, so that on all sides the clasps flew to the walls of the hall from helmet and shield of the doughty gleeman. Thus stout Folker was done to death. At this the men of Dietrich pressed forward to the strife. They smote so that the armor rings whirled far and wide, and high through the air the sword-points wore seen to fly. From the helmets they drew the warm gushing stream of blood. When Hagen of Troneg saw Folker dead, that was the greatest sorrow, that he had gained at the feasting in kinsman or in liegeman. Alas, how fiercely Hagen gan venge the knight! "Now old Hildebrand shall not profit by this deed. My helpmate lieth slain by the hero's hand, the best war comrade that I did ever win." Higher he raised his helmet, and ran, slashing as he went.

Stout Helfrich slew Dankwart. Loth enow it was to Gunther and Giselher, when they saw him fall in cruel need, but with his own hands he himself had well avenged his death. Meanwhile Wolfhart raged back and forth, hewing alway King Gunther's men. For the third time he was come through the hall, and many a warrior fell, struck by his hands.

Then Lord Giselher cried out to Wolfhart: "Alas, that I have ever gained so grim a foe! Noble knight and brave, now address you unto me. I'll help to make an end; this may be no longer."

At this Wolfhart turned him in strife to Giselher, and each smote other many a gaping wound. He pressed so mightily toward the king, that the blood beneath his feet spurted high above his head. With grim and fearful blows the son of fair Uta then greeted the brave knight Wolfhart. However strong the warrior, he might not save his life. Never could so young a king have been more brave; Wolfhart he smote through his stout hauberk, that his blood streamed down from the wound. Unto death he wounded Dietrich's liegeman. None save a champion had done such deed. When brave Wolfhart felt the wound, he let fall his shield and lifted higher in his hand his mighty sword (sharp enow it was); through both helmet and armor rings the hero smote Giselher. Thus each did other fiercely unto death.

Now was none left of Dietrich's men. Old Hildebrand saw Wolfhart fall; never before his death, I ween, did such dole happen to him. The men of Gunther all lay dead, and those of Dietrich, too. Hildebrand hied him to where Wolfhart had fallen in the gore, and clasped in his arms the brave knight and good. He would fain bear him from the hall, but he was a deal too heavy, and so he must needs let him lie. Then the dying warrior looked upward from the blood in which he lay; well he saw, that his uncle would fain help him hence. Though wounded unto death, he spake: "Dear uncle mine, ye may not aid me now. 'Tis well, methinks, that ye should guard you against Hagen. A fierce mood he beareth in his heart. And if perchance my kinsmen would mourn me after I am dead; pray tell the nearest and the best, that they weep not for me; there is no need of that. At the hands of a king I have met a glorious death and have also avenged me, so that the wives of the good knights may well bewail it. If any ask you of this, ye may boldly say, that full a hundred lie slain by my hand alone."

Then Hagen, too, bethought him of the gleeman, whom bold Hildebrand had robbed of life. To the knight he spake: "Ye'll requite me now my sorrows. Through your hatred ye have bereft us of many a lusty knight."

He dealt Hildebrand such a blow, that men heard Balmung ring, the which bold Hagen had taken from Siegfried, when he slew the knight. Then the old man warded him; in sooth he was brave enow. Dietrich's champion struck with a broad sword, that cut full sore, at the hero of Troneg, but could not wound King Gunther's liegeman. Hagen, however, smote him through his well-wrought hauberk. When old Hildebrand felt the wound, he feared more scathe at Hagen's hand; his shield he slung across his back and thus Sir Dietrich's man escaped from Hagen, though sorely wounded.

Now of all the knights none was alive save the twain, Gunther and Hagen alone. Dripping with blood old Hildebrand went to where he found Dietrich, and told him the baleful tale. He saw him sitting sadly, but much more of dole the prince now gained. He spied Hildebrand in his blood-red hauberk, and asked him tidings, as his fears did prompt him.

"Now tell me, Master Hildebrand, how be ye so wot with your lifeblood? Pray who hath done you this? I ween, ye have fought with the strangers in the hall. I forbade it you so sorely, that ye should justly have avoided it."

Then said he to his lord: "'Twas Hagen that did it. He dealt me this wound in the hall, when I would fain have turned me from the knight. I scarce escaped the devil with my life."

Then spake the Lord of Berne: "Rightly hath it happed you, for that ye have broken the peace, which I had sworn them, sith ye did hear me vow friendship to the knights. Were it not mine everlasting shame, ye should lose your life."

"My Lord Dietrich, now be ye not so wroth; the damage to my friends and me is all too great. Fain would we have carried Rudeger's corse away, but King Gunther's liegemen would not grant it us."

204

"Woe is me of these sorrows! If Rudeger then be dead, 'twill bring me greater dole, than all my woe. Noble Gotelind is the child of my father's sister; alas for the poor orphans, that be now in Bechelaren."

Rudeger's death now minded him of ruth and dole. Mightily the hero gan weep; in sooth he had good cause. "Alas for this faithful comrade whom I have lost! In truth I shall ever mourn for King Etzel's liegeman. Can ye tell me, Master Hildebrand, true tidings, who be the knight, that hath slain him there?"

Quoth he: "That stout Gernot did, with might and main, but the hero, too, fell dead at Rudeger's hands."

Again he spake to Hildebrand: "Pray say to my men, that they arm them quickly, for I will hie me hither, and bid them make ready my shining battle weeds. I myself will question the heroes of the Burgundian land."

Then spake Master Hildebrand: "Who then shall join you? Whatso of living men ye have, ye see stand by you. 'Tis I alone; the others, they be dead."

He started at this tale; forsooth, he had good cause, for never in his life had he gained so great a grief. He spake: "And are my men all dead, then hath God forgotten me, poor Dietrich. Once I was a lordly king, mighty, high, and rich." Again Sir Dietrich spake: "How could it hap, that all the worshipful heroes died at the hands of the battle-weary, who were themselves hard pressed? Were it not for mine ill-luck, death were still a stranger to them. Sith then mine evil fortune would have it so, pray tell me, are any of the strangers still alive?"

Then spake Master Hildebrand: "God wet, none other save only Hagen and Gunther, the high-born king."

"Alas, dear Wolfhart, and I have lost thee too, then may it well rue me, that ever I was born. Siegstab and Wolfwin and Wolfbrand, too! Who then shall help me to the Amelung land? Bold Helfrich, hath he, too, been slain, and Gerbart and Wiehart? How shall I ever mourn for them in fitting wise? This day doth forever end my joys. Alas, that none may die for very grief!"

ENDNOTES:
(1) "Helfrich" appears also in the "Thidreksaga", chap. 330, where we are told that he was the bravest and courtliest of all knights.
(2) "Master Hildebrand", see Adventure XXVIII, note 1.
(3) "Siegstab" is Dietrich's nephew. He also appears in the "Thidreksaga", but in a different role.

(4) "Wolfwin" is mentioned in the "Klage", 1541, as Dietrich's nephew.

(5) "Wolfbrand" and "Helmnot" appear only here.

(6) "Ritschart". With the exception of Helfrich (see Above note 1), these names do not occur elsewhere, though one of the sons of Haimon was called Wichart.

ADVENTURE XXXIX

How Gunther And Hagen And Kriemhild Were Slain

Then Sir Dietrich fetched himself his coat of mail, and Master Hildebrand helped him arm. The mighty man made wail so sore, that the whole house resounded with his voice. But then he gained again a real hero's mood. The good knight was now armed and grim of mind; a stout shield he hung upon his arm. Thus he and Master Hildebrand went boldly hence.

Then spake Hagen of Troneg: "Yonder I see Sir Dietrich coming hither; he would fain encounter us, after the great sorrow, that hath here befallen him. To-day we shall see, to whom one must give the palm. However strong of body and grim of mood the lord of Berne thinketh him to be, right well dare I match him," so spake Hagen, "an' he will avenge on us that which hath been done him."

Dietrich and Hildebrand heard this speech, for Hagen came to where he found the champion stand before the house, leaning against the wall. Dietrich set his good shield upon the ground, and spake in grievous dole: "Gunther, mighty king, why have ye so acted against me, banished man? What have I done to you? I stand alone, bereft of all my comfort. Ye thought it not enow of bitter need, when ye did kill Knight Rudeger, our friend. Now ye have robbed me of all my men. Forsooth I never had wrought you heroes sorrow such as this. Think on yourselves and on your wrongs. Doth not the death of your kinsmen and all the hardship grieve the minds of you good knights? Alas, what great dole Rudeger's death doth give me! Never in all the world hath more of sorrow happed to any man. Ye thought but little on me and on your pain. Whatsoever joy I had, that lieth slain by you. Certes, I never can bewail my kin enow."

"Forsooth we be not so guilty," answered Hagen. "Your warriors came to this hall in a large band, armed with care. Methinks the tale hath not been told you rightly."

"What else should I believe? Hildebrand told me, that when my knights from the Amelung land asked that ye should give up Rudeger's corse from out the hall, ye did naught but mock the valiant heroes from above the steps."

Then spake the king from the Rhine: "They said, that they would fain bear Rudeger hence, and I bade this be denied them to vex King Etzel, and not thy men, until then Wolfhart began to rail about it."

207

Then the hero of Berne made answer: "Fate would have it so. Gunther, most noble king, now through thy courtesie requite me of the wrongs, that have happed to me from thee, and make such amends, brave knight, that I may give thee credit for the deed. Give thyself and thy men to me as hostages, and I will guard you, as best I may, that none here do thee aught among the Huns. Thou shalt find me naught but good and true."

"Now God forbid," quoth Hagen, "that two knights give themselves up to thee, that still do stand opposed to thee so doughtily and walk so unfettered before their foes."

"Gunther and Hagen, ye should not deny me this," spake Dietrich. "Ye have grieved my heart and mind so sore, that it were but right, and ye would requite me. I give you my hand and troth as pledge, that I will ride with you, home to your land. I'll lead you in all honor, or else lie dead, and for your sakes I will forget my grievous wrongs."

"Crave this no longer," answered Hagen. "'Twere fitting, that the tale be told of us, that two men so brave had given themselves up to you. We see none standing by you, save Hildebrand alone."

Then up spake Master Hildebrand: "God wot, Sir Hagen, the hour will come, when ye will gladly take the peace, if so be any offer to keep it with you. Ye might well content you with the truce my lord doth offer."

"Forsooth I'd take the truce," quoth Hagen, "or ever I'd flee from out a hall so shamefully as ye did, Master Hildebrand. I weened, ye could stand better against a foe."

To this Hildebrand made answer: "Why twit ye me with that? Who was it sate upon a shield hard by the Waskstone, (1) when Walter of Spain slew so many of his kin? Ye, too, have faults enow of your own to show."

Then spake Sir Dietrich: "Ill doth it beseem heroes, that they should scold like aged beldams. I forbid you, Hildebrand, to speak aught more. Grievous wrongs constrain me, homeless warrior. Let's hear, Knight Hagen, what ye twain did speak, ye doughty men, when ye saw me coming toward you armed? Ye said, that ye alone would fain encounter me in strife."

"Certes, none doth deny," Knight Hagen spake, "that I will essay it here with mighty blows, unless be, that the sword of Nibelung break in my hand. Wroth am I, that we twain have here been craved as hostages."

When Dietrich noted Hagen's raging mood, quickly the doughty knight and good snatched up his shield. How swiftly Hagen sprang toward him from the

208

steps! Loudly the good sword of Nibelung rang on Dietrich's head. Then wist Dietrich well, that the bold knight was grim of mood. The lord of Berne gan guard him against the fearful blows, for well he knew Hagen, the stately knight. Balmung he also feared, a weapon stout enow. Dietrich returned the blows at times in cunning wise, until at last he conquered Hagen in the strife. A wound he dealt him, the which was deep and long. Then Lord Dietrich thought him: "Thou art worn out with strife; little honor shall I have, and thou liest dead before me. I will try, if perchance I can force thee to be my hostage."

This he wrought with danger. His shield he let fall, great was his strength, and clasped Hagen of Troneg in his arms. Thus the brave knight was overcome by Dietrich. Noble Gunther gan wail thereat. Dietrich now bound Hagen and led him to where he found the highborn queen; into her hand he gave the bravest warrior that ever bare a sword. Then merry enow she grew after her great dole. For very joy King Etzel's wife bowed low before the knight. "May thy heart and body be ever blest. Thou hast well requited me of all my woes. For this will I ever serve thee, unless be, that death doth hinder me therefrom."

Then spake Lord Dietrich: "Pray let him live, most noble queen. And if this still may be, how well will I requite you of that which he hath done you! Let him not suffer, because ye see him stand here bound."

She bade Hagen then be led away to duress, where he lay locked in and where none did see him. Gunther, the high-born king, began to call: "Whither went the knight of Berne? He hath done me wrong."

At this Lord Dietrich went to meet him. Gunther's might was worthy of praise; no more he bided, but ran outside the hall, and from the clashing of the swords of the twain a mighty din arose. However much and long Lord Dietrich's prowess had been praised, yet Gunther was so sorely angered and enraged, for because of the grievous dole, he was his deadly foe, that men still tell it as a wonder, that Sir Dietrich did not fall. Great were both their prowess and their strength. The palace and the towers resounded with the blows, when with the swords they hewed at the sturdy helmets. King Gunther was of lordly mood, but the knight of Berne overcame him, as happed to Hagen afore. The hero's blood was seen to ooze through the armor rings, drawn forth by a keen-edged sword, the which Sir Dietrich bare. Though weary, Sir Gunther had guarded him most valiantly. The lord was now bound by Dietrich's hands. Though kings should not endure such bonds, yet Dietrich thought, if he set free the king and his liegeman, that all they met must needs fall dead at their hands.

Dietrich of Berne now took him by the hand and led him bound to where he found Kriemhild. At sight of his sorrow much of her fear took flight. She spake: "Welcome, Gunther, from the Burgundian land."

Quoth he: "I would bow before you, dear sister mine, if your greetings were but kinder. I know you, queen, to be so wroth of mood that ye do give me and Hagen meagre greetings."

Up spake the knight of Berne: "Most noble queen, never were such good knights made hostages, as I have given you in them, exalted lady. For my sake, I pray you, spare these homeless men."

She vowed she'd do it gladly. Then Sir Dietrich left the worshipful knights with weeping eyes. Later Etzel's wife avenged her grimly; she took the life of both the chosen heroes. To make their duress worse she let them lie apart, so that neither saw the other, till she bare her brother's head to Hagen. Kriemhild's vengeance on both was great enow.

Then the queen went to Hagen. In what right hostile wise she spake to the knight: "If ye will give me back what ye have taken from me, then ye may still go home alive to Burgundy."

Grim Hagen answered: "Thou dost waste thy words, most noble queen. Forsooth I have sworn an oath, that I would not show the hoard, the while and any of my lords still live; so I shall give it to none."

"I'll make an end of this," quoth the high-born wife. Then she bade her brother's life be taken. His head they struck off, and by the hair she bare it to the knight of Troneg. Loth enow it was to him. When sad of mind the warrior gazed upon his master's head, he spake to Kriemhild: "Thou hast brought it to an end after thy will, and it hath happed, as I had thought me. The noble king of Burgundy now lieth dead, and Giselher, the youth, and Sir Gernot, too. None knoweth of the treasure now save God and me, and it shall ever be hid from thee, thou fiend."

Quoth she: "Ye have requited me full ill, so I will keep the sword of Siegfried, the which my sweetheart bare, when last I saw him, in whom dole of heart hath happed to me through you."

From the sheath she drew it, nor could he hinder her a whit. She planned to rob the knight of life. With her hands she raised it and struck off his head. This King Etzel saw, and sore enow it rued him. "Alack!" cried the lording, "how lieth now dead at a woman's hands the very best of knights, that ever came to battle or bare a shield! However much I was his foe, yet it doth grieve me sorely."

Then spake old Hildebrand: "Forsooth it shall not boot her aught, that she durst slay him. Whatso hap to me, and however much it may bring me to a dangerous pass, yet will I avenge bold Troneg's death."

Hildebrand sprang in wrath towards Kriemhild. For fear of him she suffered pain; but what might it avail her, that she shrieked so frightfully? He dealt the queen a grievous sword-blow, the which did cut the high-born dame in twain. Now all lay low in death whom fate had doomed. Dietrich and Etzel then began to weep; sorely they mourned both kin and liegemen. Their mickle honors lay there low in death; the courtiers all had grief and drearihead. The king's high feast had ended now in woe, as joy doth ever end in sorrow at the last. I cannot tell you, that which happed thereafter, save that knights and ladies and noble squires were seen to weep for the death of loving kinsmen. The tale hath here an end. This is the Nibelungs' fall. (2) (3)

ENDNOTES:
(1) "Waskstone", see Adventure XXXV, note 2.
(2) "Fall". The word "not", translated here "fall", means
    really 'disaster', but as this word is not in keeping with
    the style, "fall" has been chosen as preferable to 'need',
    used by some translators. The MS. C has here "liet" instead
    of "not" of A and B.
(3) The "Nibelungenlied" is continued by the so-called "Klage",
    a poem written in short rhyming couplets. As the name
    indicates, it describes the lamentations of the survivors
    over the dead. The praises of each warrior are sung and a
    messenger dispatched to acquaint Gorelind, Uta, and Brunhild
    with the sad end of their kinsmen. It closes with
    Dietrich's departure from Etzel's court and his return home.
    Although in one sense a continuation of our poem, the
    "Klage" is an independent work of no great merit, being excessively
tedious with its constant repetitions. A reprint and a full account of it will be
found in Piper's edition of our poem, vol. I.

www.ingramcontent.com/pod-product-compliance
Lightning Source LLC
Chambersburg PA
CBHW011342090426
42741CB00017B/3432